Market Aesthetics

NEW WORLD STUDIES

J. Michael Dash, *Editor*

Frank Moya Pons and
Sandra Pouchet Paquet,
Associate Editors

Market Aesthetics

THE PURCHASE OF THE PAST IN CARIBBEAN DIASPORIC FICTION

Elena Machado Sáez

University of Virginia Press

Charlottesville and London

THIS BOOK IS MADE POSSIBLE BY A COLLABORATIVE GRANT
FROM THE ANDREW W. MELLON FOUNDATION.

University of Virginia Press
© 2015 by the Rector and Visitors of the University of Virginia
All rights reserved
Printed in the United States of America on acid-free paper
First published 2015

9 8 7 6 5 4 3 2 1

Library of Congress Cataloging-in-Publication Data

Machado Sáez, Elena.
    Market aesthetics : the purchase of the past in Caribbean diasporic fiction /
Elena Machado Sáez.
        pages   cm. — (New World Studies)
    Includes bibliographical references and index.
    ISBN 978-0-8139-3704-5 (cloth : acid-free paper)
    ISBN 978-0-8139-3705-2 (pbk. : acid-free paper)
    ISBN 978-0-8139-3706-9 (e-book)
    1. Caribbean literature (English)—History and criticism. 2. Historical fiction—
History and criticism. 3. Multiculturalism in literature. 4. Caribbean Area—
Influence. I. Title.
PR9205.4.M33 2015
813.009'9729—dc23

                                                                2014035706

To my models of hope and generosity:
my parents, Ricardo and Teresa,
and my padrinos, Manolo and Carmencita

Contents

Acknowledgments

I AM SO FORTUNATE TO MAKE a living reading, writing, and teaching. Credit goes to Mary Erler, who put me on this path when she told me to apply to PhD programs while I was an undergraduate at Fordham. The W. Burghardt Turner Fellowship Program at SUNY Stony Brook made this dream a reality, providing me with the financial and social support necessary to complete my doctorate. Thanks to my thesis committee for their feedback on the earliest version of the Andrea Levy section: Helen Cooper, Román de la Campa, Gillian Johns, Kelly Oliver, and David Sheehan. My gratitude goes to UVA Press staff for their expertise and professionalism, especially to Cathie Brettschneider for shepherding me through the manuscript process and to Elisabeth Magnus and Tim Roberts for their expert copyediting. I want to recognize the wonderful contribution of my anonymous readers, whose insightful feedback made the manuscript into a much better book. Thank you to the staffs of *Anthurium* and *Contemporary Literature* for the permission to include in the book the revised versions of my articles on Andrea Levy and Junot Díaz: "Bittersweet (Be)Longing: Filling the Void of History in Andrea Levy's *Fruit of the Lemon*," in *Arthurium: A Caribbean Studies Journal* 4.1 (2006), and "Dictating Desire, Dictating Diaspora: Junot Díaz's *Oscar Wao* as Foundational Romance," in *Contemporary Literature* 52.3 (2011): 522–55.

I also want to thank the conference attendees who commented on drafts presented at the West Indian Literature, Caribbean Studies Association, Modern Language Association, National Association for Chicana and Chicano Studies, Northeast Modern Language Association, American Studies Association, American Comparative Literature Association, University of Miami Global Caribbean, Women's Studies at Southern Connecticut State, Caribbean Philosophical Association,

British Commonwealth and Postcolonial Studies, Latin American Studies Association, and Southwest Council of Latin American Studies conferences. Gracias to Marta Caminero-Santangelo and Julie Minich for their feedback on my first drafts of chapter 1, and to Eric Berlatsky, Jane Caputi, Jonathan Goldman, Ylce Irizarry, Sobeira Latorre, Nicolas Mansito III, and Dixa Ramirez for their comments on the Díaz section of chapter 5. I'm grateful to Andrea Shaw for her reassurances that my project was worthwhile and to Pat Saunders for all the intellectual extracurricular fun.

Florida Atlantic University has nurtured my scholarly development with course releases, conference funding, and a full-year sabbatical. I'm grateful to my FAU colleagues, especially those in the English Department, for being a joy to work with (seriously). Thank you to Eric Berlatsky, Andy Furman, and Wenying Xu for their support as department chairs. My gratitude goes to Kristen Block for coordinating productive meet.write sessions during my sabbatical. I'm lucky to have the indispensable friendship of Eric Berlatsky, Kristen Block, Papatya Bucak, Sika Dagbovie-Mullins, Renee Gross, Wendy Hinshaw, Regis Mann, Becka McKay, and Kate Schmitt. Finishing this book required a great deal of child care support, for which I'm indebted to Rafe, Mama, Marina, Bruce, Peter, Fran, and Mike.

I'm especially grateful to Rafe for being such a determined defender of my academic potential, against my (not) better judgment, and for reading everything I write. The index was expertly compiled by Rafe, making it an excellent guide to this book. Lalo, tu sonrisa siempre alegra el corazón. Te hecho de menos, Papá—gracias for teaching me that love equals acts of kindness. Y gracias Mamá, for taking me to la biblioteca pública and teaching me to love reading.

Market Aesthetics

Introduction

Marketing Multicultural Ethnics, Promoting Postcolonial Ethics

AN ETHICAL IMPERATIVE TO WRITE historical counternarratives informs the contemporary phenomenon of a boom in historical fiction by multicultural authors in Britain, Canada, and the United States. The critical reception often discounts the literariness of such writing because of its popularity, but the market success of ethnic historical fiction offers unique insight into the pressures that the genre encounters, particularly in relation to the book market and public discourses of multiculturalism.[1] I anchor my analysis in the cultural specificity and rhetorical locality of the Caribbean diaspora, while also outlining the contributions such authors make to the broader field of multicultural historical fiction. The popularity of historical fiction is certainly a credit to ethnic authors and the works of art that they produce, but that marketability also challenges the writers' goals in shaping the textual encounter with the reader. The market welcomes the consumption of "ethnic spice" associated with Other voices and offers an opportune space for articulating the authors' ethical imperative of historical revisionism. At the same time, the global English book market and its commodification of ethnicity produce writerly anxieties about reader reception, and these concerns are encoded in the novels' form and content. Caribbean diasporic writers translate the challenges of the market and readerships into creative inspiration, into market aesthetics.

I use the term *market aesthetics* to describe the ways that the style and content of the historical fiction articulate a conflict between the pedagogical ethical imperative and the market lens of the reader. Market aesthetics are emblematic of the ways that the fiction understands its materiality as a commodity or form of capital circulating in a global market, where the goals of the writers are both facilitated by and in tension with the market demands placed upon diasporic fiction. Caribbean diasporic authors engage their readership's expectations in the historical novels, with the market aesthetics processing the text's circulation by symbolically encoding the interpretive dialogue between text and reader in terms of an (im)possible intimacy. The critical reception appraises Caribbean diasporic historical fiction in terms of the perceived sentimentality, sensuality, exoticism, and cultural authenticity of the texts. The code of intimacy in the novels contests the rhetorical frameworks used to assess the fiction, including that of multiculturalist discourse. In chapter 1, I discuss how the depiction of sexuality and gender allegorizes the ethical limits of the pedagogical imperative of historical revisionism. I reference book reviews in the remaining chapters to contextualize the allegory of sexuality in relation to the authors' horizon of experience.

Caribbean diasporic writing facilitates a comparative framework for historical fiction because it is an extension of Caribbean nation-state literatures as well as part of ethnic minority literary traditions in Britain, Canada, and the United States. By reading Caribbean diasporic literature as a tradition in and of itself, we examine historical novels that are located at the intersection of the nation and the transnational, the ethnic and the postcolonial. The pan-Caribbean construct of the diaspora allows for a comparative discussion of writing across linguistic boundaries, such as anglophone and francophone literature, and between nation-based frameworks, such as that of African American and Black British studies. Additionally, the comparative literary focus enables a nuanced discussion of the English-language book market as a historical context and of the impact of globalization on literary aesthetics.

Since Caribbean diasporic writers are positioned at the intersection of ethnic and world literatures, local and global histories, multicultural and postcolonial discourses, I argue that these authors have more in common with each other than with isolated ethnic or island literary traditions: first, their work expresses a postcolonial ethics of historical revision, and second, it struggles with the marketability of ethnicity. The novels strive to educate the mainstream readership about marginalized histories and avoid reifying any stereotypes their readers might bring to the text, chiefly the perception that ethnic writers should translate their cultures for effortless and uncomplicated market consumption. Within Caribbean diasporic historical fiction, the pedagogical impulse promotes a postcolonial vision of the past, positing the Caribbean as central to the historical development of Europe and the Americas. This historical counternarrative is nevertheless shaped by a concern about the text's market positioning as "selling" multicultural ethnics as well as by academic and mainstream market expectations for cultural authenticity. The market reception of historical fiction by Caribbean diasporic authors tends to see the pedagogical imperative as running counter to the literary aesthetic and its appeal. Reviewers of Caribbean diasporic fiction will label such writing as "didactic" (Eder 14) or see it as advocating radical politics, for example, promoting a "lesbian propaganda" (Carter 24). Characterizing diasporic fiction as preaching a particular doctrine often goes hand in hand with a critique of the writing's literariness or quality. For instance, one reviewer argues that "several publishers are bending over backward to appear 'culturally sensitive' even if the work is second rate" (Vincent). The belief that minority fiction forgoes the traditional task of "tell[ing] an engrossing yarn" in order to advocate for a progressive politics of recovering marginal voices is not an unusual one (Corrigan). While a writer might be asked by the market to perform the role of native informant, of translating an ethnic population for majority consumption, a concurrent danger lies in being perceived as telling these stories in an overtly political fashion.

Caribbean diasporic writers are conscious of the delicate balance they must strike between popular market demands and their ethical imperatives about how to narrate these histories. As a result of their peculiar positioning, writers such as Julia Alvarez, Robert Antoni, Dionne Brand, David Chariandy, Michelle Cliff, Edwidge Danticat, Junot Díaz, Marlon James, Andrea Levy, Ana Menéndez, and Monique Roffey identify the marketplace as a necessary mediator of artistic production, with globalization opening and closing avenues for circulating a postcolonial politics of narrating history. I offer the developments of globalization and multiculturalism as contexts for this contemporary trend of historical fiction. By outlining the parallels between academic discourses on globalization within postcolonial and ethnic studies, I define this intersection conceptually, centering on the way these fields identify decontextualization as a dilemma specific to the contemporary public sphere and the workings of the publishing industry. Caribbean diasporic authors tailor their historical novels so that they are responsive to their present, either identifying decontextualization as a historical context or "filling in" that gap by highlighting pasts that are relevant for understanding the development of this contemporary problematic. After outlining the historical contexts for the authors' cultural production, I discuss the rhetorical contexts for this book, citing my academic precursors and distinguishing my reading of Caribbean diasporic writing from other approaches.

Decontextualization and the Global
Routes of Multiculturalism

Contemporary globalization as an organizing economic network is an important historical context for understanding the emergence of historical fiction as a genre within Caribbean diasporic writing. In academic formulations of globalization, one finds the repeated claim that decontextualization is a central tenet of this system's functioning, identifying book publishing as an exemplary process. A similar approach is found in the disconnected analyses that have emerged from the academic fields of postcolonialism, which focuses on literatures (usually in English) outside Global North nations, and multiculturalism, which addresses the ethnic literatures of a particular Global North nation (for instance, Britain, Canada, or the United States). The ways that postcolonial and ethnic studies analyze globalization and the ways they understand difference to be commodified and processed are helpful for contextualizing Caribbean diasporic writing.

While decontextualization is understood as a product of globalization, there is also a critical trend that analyzes how academic theories and their valorization of resistance are commodified. In other words, academic discourse has market currency in the publishing field of literary fiction. Academia shapes the literary market because of the centrality of the classroom to the publishing economy. As most faculty recognize, we are a market of consumers who are targeted with promotional materials and who receive certain purchasing privileges in the form of desk or exam copies because we are gatekeepers to a student body of consumers. Academic discourses have a concrete effect on curricular practices, with the introduction of new courses like "Postcolonial Literatures" or "Queer Theory," and such curriculum developments inform publishing practices. For instance, if academics who teach postcolonial or ethnic literature courses display a purchasing preference for texts deemed "resistant," publishers are responsive to these market demands.

The contemporary phenomenon of a creative writing industry in the ivory tower contributes to the interconnectedness of academic and literary spheres. In *The Program Era* (2009), Mark McGurl credits the institutionalization of MFA programs with "the increasingly intimate relation between literary production and the practices of higher education" (ix). Teaching the craft of creative writing is a lucrative business for institutions of higher education, producing a "vast range of writers who have also been students and teachers" (ix). The creative writing curriculum deploys a rhetoric that "issues an invitation to student-consumers to *develop an intensely personal relation* to literary value" (15–16; emphasis added). The student's initiation into literary community constructs intimacy as a central tenet of the classroom marketplace. Intimacy figures as an accessible commodity that is part and parcel of the reading experience as well as the consumer subject's development as a creative writer. I detail in chapters 1 and 3 how this classroom context of intimacy shapes the market aesthetics of Caribbean diasporic writing. "The intimate commerce between reader and book" is not merely something that MFA programs "sell," but this localized niche market of the classroom expresses the constitutive facets of consumerism in a global marketplace (ix). The apparently contradictory twinning of personal and public, local and global, that informs the academic market is the discursive purchase that brings us back to academia's analysis of globalization.

To understand how ideas about globalization's workings circulate in the marketplace, I review here the similarities between various disciplinary understandings of this system, mainly as one with contradictory impulses. Globalization is discussed as a network that expands consumer access and allows for the global interconnectivity of cultures and economies. This globalizing relation is accomplished through delocalization and dehistoricization. The market unmoors commodities from material histories and locales in order to facilitate global circulation. In *Modernity at Large* (1996), Arjun Appadurai identifies decontextualization as a product of the "new media order," which he describes as the increased expansiveness of media circulation. This media order has a democratizing impulse, expanding global media access as well as the consumer base. On the other hand, the globalization of media networks leads to the delocalization of media content. Community becomes conceptualized differently within such media content, rooted less by geographic locale than by global consumption practices. In a 2006 interview published in *Postcolonial Text*, Simon Gikandi alludes to the "mixed blessing" of globalization, which has "created a space where the postcolonial experience can circulate and move in interesting ways" while also foreclosing "a kind of specific historical engagement with culture" (par. 7). While Gikandi does not use the term *decontextualization*, he does describe globalization as a "form of allegorization" (par. 8), implying that cultural products undergo a process of delocalization that renders them mere symbols, floating signifiers emptied of any referent to material conditions or historical contexts. Historical fiction presents a unique conceptual problem to this discussion and the way it theorizes commodification. As a cultural product, historical fiction is full of historical referents and seeks to contextualize particular figures and events. Nevertheless, such fiction is circulated by the same global mechanisms that Appadurai and Gikandi describe, raising the question: Is it possible for a product whose content is about context to be decontextualized?

Like theorists of globalization, academics working in multicultural studies have called attention to decontextualization, mainly with regard to the place of ethnic literatures within the publishing industry.[2] In *The Ethnic Canon* (1995), David Palumbo-Liu frames the commodification of ethnic narratives as part of a process of domestication that seeks to contain the imaginative threat that marginal populations pose to the nation-state. In coining the term *pluralist multiculturalism*, Palumbo-Liu addresses the co-optation of a progressive formulation of the concept, accomplished via decontextualization. By absenting the histories of inequality and oppression that inform these texts, or representing those histories as marginal influences, pluralistic multiculturalism suppresses the elements of critique within ethnic literature that question simplistic notions of national identity. Reading practices also reinforce the dehistoricization initiated by the market circulation of products. Ethnic studies as a field provides us with approaches that explain how a cultural product *about* history could be interpreted in a way that mollifies or suppresses the historicizing impulses of the text.

The discourse of multiculturalism is often critiqued within British, Canadian, and American ethnic studies, and I provide a comparative discussion of this assessment later on in this introduction. For an example of multiculturalism as a rhetoric within US ethnic studies, I turn to George Yúdice's definition of co-opted multiculturalism in "Rethinking Area and Ethnic Studies in the Context of Economic and Political Restructuring" (2003): "Initially a means to 'empower' excluded or marginalized minorities, multiculturalism soon became a quick rhetorical fix of symbolic inclusion and very little material gain. By lumping together Latin Americans and Latinos of all classes and ethnoracial backgrounds, multiculturalism homogenized them as part of the U.S. tendency to panethnicization" (79). Multiculturalism as a political project for racial equality and social justice is translated into a purely symbolic form of representation. I extend Yúdice's use of the term *rhetoric* to emphasize how pan-ethnic categories are relevant discursive contexts for Caribbean diasporic writing. The ethical imperative of historical revision references and honors the political projects of the civil rights and anticolonial movements. Yet the work of creative writing is rhetorical and symbolic rather than material activism. The postcolonial imperative mourns the ways in which it cannot live up to the promise of that earlier political project, while the market aesthetics of the text speak to the challenges of engaging multiculturalism as a system of categorization. A rhetorical approach explores the intersection of the ethical imperative and market aesthetics, highlighting how the contexts of decontextualization and multiculturalism are inscribed literarily, in terms of interpretation and reading practices.

Caribbean diasporic historical fiction encourages us to see a correlation between how pluralist multiculturalism co-opts difference and how globalization decontextualizes difference; although Appadurai, Gikandi, Palumbo-Liu, and Yúdice are participating in disconnected disciplinary conversations, they are describing interrelated systems. Caribbean diasporic historical fiction draws conceptual parallels between postcolonial and multicultural discourses that are currently undertheorized, while also pushing us to consider multiculturalism as a global rhetoric mobilized in Britain, Canada, and the United States. Multiculturalism is one of the historical contexts that differentiates contemporary diasporic writing from that of earlier generations of Caribbean authors. While the trajectory of the diaspora's migration from the Caribbean to the metropole might overlap in some ways with prior generations of exiled Caribbean writers, there are significant shifts in the public discourses of Britain, Canada, and the United States from the 1960s to the present. One significant change is the institutionalization of a discourse about diversity, that of multiculturalism. The canonical writers of Caribbean exile, such as George Lamming, Derek Walcott, Sam Selvon, V. S. Naipaul, and Kamau Brathwaite, certainly did not find in exile a public sphere as systemically receptive to difference.[3] That experience made an indelible mark on the form and content of their writing, and the influence of public discourse is no less relevant for contemporary Caribbean diasporic writing, producing a distinct conception of cultural affiliation and audience. As C. L. Innes notes in *A History of Black and Asian Writing in Britain*: "Although black and south Asian authors before the 1950s often spoke on behalf of an alternative group, they spoke as individual representatives and primarily addressed a white British audience. Moreover, the culture and community they represented mostly lived elsewhere—in Africa, the Indian subcontinent, the Caribbean, or the southern states of America. Now authors increasingly spoke of and to a black and south Asian community *within* Britain" (234). Just as Innes calls attention to the development of a diasporic community and readership within Global North nations, I would add that the Caribbean diasporic literary imagination is also shaped by the public discourse of multiculturalism.

Contemporary Caribbean diasporic writers within Britain, Canada, and the United States find themselves in metropoles similar to those of their precursors but face a unique public discourse of multiculturalism that is ready to assimilate, categorize, and potentially ghettoize their literary work. The discourse of multiculturalism offers a transnational and foundational route for locating Caribbean diasporic writing.[4] Britain, Canada, and the United States have divergent histories, especially with regard to their treatment of Caribbean diasporic communities as ethnic minority populations. I do not wish to collapse these histories together for the sake of creating a pan-ethnic history for the Caribbean diaspora.[5] At the same time, I want to emphasize the importance of multiculturalism as a shared discursive context for Caribbean diasporic writing in these Global North nations. The rhetoric of multiculturalism can be traced back to the liberatory energies of the civil rights and anticolonial movements. There are transnational parallels evident in antidiscrimination and antisegregation legislation as well as reactionary immigration and citizenship policies that are dual legacies of the Sixties.[6] The legal battles over civil rights and the integration of Caribbean immigrants into the nation contribute to the formation of a transnational context for the Caribbean diaspora. Less visible diasporic networks of culture and politics also link the geographies of the United States, Canada, and Britain during the late twentieth century.[7] While often silenced from the dominant narrative about civil rights movements, the Caribbean diaspora informed and shaped 1960s social movements in Global North nations and the Caribbean.[8] The transition from 1960s social justice movements to the 1990s emergence of multiculturalism discourse is not a tidy narrative of social evolution, with more progressive policies instituted as the decades passed. The British Nationality Act of 1981, the Canadian government's negotiations with the Japanese redress movement, and the 2010 Arizona immigration law in the United States point to the always tense racial politics that accompany public narratives about minority populations.[9]

There are some dissonances in the case of Canada, whose Quiet Revolution during the Sixties focused on the rights of linguistic minorities and the autonomy of provinces like Quebec. The way indigeneity and linguistic politics shaped racial politics in Canada significantly differentiates Canada's history from the 1960s histories of the United States and Britain. Clear connections remain, however, if one views the indigenous movement of the 1960s in Canada as part of a broader hemispheric movement for native rights in the Americas. Grassroots activism was an important factor in the cross-pollination between the US, British, and Canadian civil rights struggles.[10] Additionally, the Canadian government's multicultural policy can be situated within a Sixties historical framework.[11] Even though the historical developments in Canada occurred a decade or more after those of the sixties social movements in Britain and the United States, a confluence of multicultural discourse emerged within these Global North countries during the Nineties.

The Sixties form an important backdrop for the contemporary institutionalization of multiculturalist rhetoric in Britain, Canada, and the United States. In *Global Matters* (2010), Paul Jay provides one narrative for understanding this process historically, arguing that the Sixties transformed academia as "the development outside the academy of social and political movements, including the anti-Vietnam War movement, the civil rights movement, the feminist movement, and the gay rights movement," inspired "the rise of theoretical and critical practices within the academy dominated by a sustained and critical attention to difference" (17). One distinction from the experience of the Caribbean exile generation is the role that academic and feminist presses of the 1980s played in the incorporation of Caribbean diasporic writing by women into ethnic canons. The genealogy of feminist presses contextualizes how the incorporation of ethnic and postcolonial writing is tied to an academic audience and its theoretical frameworks for analyzing literature.[12] The attention to difference, which we can understand as the defining facet of multiculturalism's institutionalization, is the product of material changes brought about by these Sixties movements for social justice. Jay signals the changes in "the demographic makeup of the student population and then the professoriate" (19) that were accomplished by demands initiated "in the street and end[ing] in the courts" (20). The 1980s constituted an institutional watershed moment for academia in relation to multiculturalism: Jay gives the example of "'American' literary studies," which began "transform[ing] itself into a study of the literatures of the Americas" because of the "productive pressure of Chicana/o, African American, Asian, and Native American critics" (21). Jay wants to counter the perception that transnational approaches to literary studies are the product of globalization by historicizing their emergence in terms of the effect of Sixties activism on academic institutions.

I concur with Jay's assessment that "the replacement of a unitary, ahistorical, and universalizing model for literary studies with one focused on difference and influenced by the rise of minority, multicultural, and postcolonial studies happened well before anyone in the academy started talking much about globalization" (22–23). The rhetorical purchase of difference in the 1980s academy is a crucial context for the broader development of multiculturalist discourse in the Nineties.

While Jay's historiography of this process is predominantly positive, focusing on how the accomplishments of progressive movements led to the study of literature being a "transnational affair" (22), Gayatri Chakravorty Spivak's *A Critique of Postcolonial Reason* (1999) gives a darker picture of multiculturalism's institutionalization. This is partly because she has a different goal, which is to "account for the sudden prominence of the postcolonial informant on the stage of U.S. English studies" (360). Spivak uses *postcolonial informant* to reference a set of elite professionals from the British Commonwealth who usurp the progressive movement's transformation of academia. According to Spivak this "indigenous elite did not have an established new informant position" in the Global North after decolonization and was not able to adopt such a position in the British academy with "the inception of a 'national' cultural studies in Britain in the '60s, [because] that movement was working-class-based and oriented towards migrant culture from the start" (359–60). However, Spivak sees the "area studies disciplines that sprang up during the Cold War years and gave support to the American self-representation as the custodian of decolonization" as allowing for the "absor[ption] [of] some members of this class" (360).

Globalization is ultimately responsible for the authorization of these elites as native informants during the 1970s, with "the computerization of the great stock exchanges and the dismantling of nationally based capital 'permitting' a benevolent third-worldist cultural studies impulse [. . .] to infect the academy" (360). Spivak sees the institutionalization of multiculturalism in the form of "academic assertions of this difference" as allowing for certain subjects and intellectual approaches to masquerade as progressive despite being ultimately regressive (360): in "supporting the simulated specificity of a radical position, [they] often dissimilate the implicit collaboration of the postcolonial in the service of neo-colonialism" (361). The contemporary legacy of this shift in the 1980s academy is the emergence of "hybridist postnational talk, celebrating globalization as Americanization" (361). Spivak gives us a different origin-narrative for the emergence of multiculturalism as a mainstream public discourse that deploys "culture as a nice name for the exoticism of others" (355). By reviewing stories of multiculturalism's institutionalization within academia, I hope to show that such methodologies, while differing in tone, contain certain historiographic parallels. Jay and Spivak both agree that a set of demographic changes within the academy played a role in the rise of multiculturalist discourse during the 1990s.

Narratives like those of Richard Rodriguez's *Hunger of Memory* (1982) and Neil Bissoondath's *Selling Illusions* (1994) and their denunciation of government policies make evident the currency that multiculturalism gained by the 1990s. These texts illuminate the resemblance between Canadian and US debates about multiculturalism, with Rodriguez challenging the logic of US affirmative action policies and Bissoondath making similar critiques of the Canadian government's policy on multiculturalism. Stephen Henighan also sees the 1990s as a decisive moment in Canadian literature, with a new "trend for immigrant writing" (204). Henighan attributes harmful effects to this shift, judging that "the aftermath of the passage of the Free Trade Agreement" sank "the ship of Canadian identity" so that "ethnic belonging bobbed to the surface for many as the most convenient spar to cling to" (144). When taken together, the reactions of Rodriguez, Bissoondath, and Henighan to the civil rights legacies of affirmative action and the diversification of literary canons attest to the institutionalization of multiculturalism as a public discourse.[13]

Changes in academic publishing and curricula serve as additional evidence of the discursive parallels between Britain, Canada, and the United States. In the introduction to *Adjacencies: Minority Writing in Canada* (2004), Sherry Simon recalls the impact of "the publication in 1996 of the anthology *Making a Difference*" as the type of "moment when gradual changes take a decisive turn and suddenly become pieces of reality" (9). For Simon, the anthology revealed "that much of the most innovative and energetic writing in Canada is today by minority writers" (9). C. L. Innes notes a similar curricular transition in Britain in the 1980s, citing how "organizations such as the Inner London Education Authority (ILEA) and the Association for Teaching Caribbean and African Literature (ATCAL) brought together teachers and writers from educational institutions and community organizations throughout the country to discuss texts and the curriculum, and to disseminate information about black and Asian writing" (241–42). Scholars in US Latino/a studies, like Frances Aparicio and Arlene Dávila, largely credit the civil rights movement with the institutionalization of multiculturalism in terms of ethnic studies departments in academia as well as the development of the multicultural marketing business.[14] As Victoria R. Arana points out in her essay "Sea Change: Historicizing the Scholarly Study of Black British Writing" (2004), the contemporary public sphere was shaped by a "cultural and social movement that is *broader than merely academic and broader than specifically literary*: it is the multicultural and multiracial [. . .] mobilization" (21). Activists, government administrators, educators, and publishers all played a role in the development of a multicultural discourse within Global North nations.

Alongside these historical trajectories, multiculturalism emerges as a *shared* context for Caribbean diasporic cultural production. In *An Ethics of Betrayal* (2009), Crystal Parikh defines "panethnic formation" as a facet of US multiculturalism, a conceptual categorization that "provide[s] a technology for a quiescent multiculturalism that anticipates and manages the coming multitudes of 'others' that the nation encounters in its global ventures" (25). This goal of managing a multitude of difference echoes David Palumbo-Liu's description of pluralist multiculturalism. Parikh also points to the dangers of viewing a "panethnic identity as a commitment to a resistant or oppositional politics," since this formulation can "miss the strategies of accommodation that racial categories provide subjects" (25). If pan-ethnicity is a rhetorical mechanism of control that manages globalization's displacement of Others into the metropole, then its deployment cannot be inherently progressive. Like Parikh, Ashley Dawson calls attention to the way multiculturalist academic theories have decontextualized the formation of Caribbean diaspora in Britain, absenting the material histories of racism and discrimination. In *Mongrel Nation* (2007), Dawson addresses multiculturalism as an empty public narrative by citing the pan-ethnic category of blackness in Britain, arguing that "the label black thus came to operate primarily as a political signifier, denoting experiences of racialization and resistance shared by African, Asian, and Caribbean settlers of the postwar period" (19). Blackness is a form of rhetorical regulation that demarcates Otherness within the British nation, a pan-ethnic label that designates certain populations as second-class citizens. Critics in ethnic studies consistently identify decontextualization as a distinguishing feature of multiculturalist rhetoric, revealing that, like globalization, multiculturalism is a context that erases or absents historical context.

My Rhetorical Contexts: (Dis)Locating
Diaspora in Caribbean Studies

The incorporation of Caribbean diasporic fiction within specific literary canons influences the historical contexts we identify as relevant to diasporic writing. Caribbean diasporic writers contribute to academic and public discourses by reimagining and rearticulating the central "problem" of cultural production within the contemporary public sphere. David Scott describes a problem-space in *Conscripts of Modernity* (2004) as "demarcat[ing] a discursive context, a context of language," as well as "a context of dispute," "rival views," and "intervention" (4). Having mapped out globalization and multiculturalism as contexts for historical fiction, I discuss trends within Caribbean studies and how they have shaped the analysis of Caribbean diasporic writing. The field of Caribbean studies provides a useful set of discursive frameworks for locating market aesthetics. Since "a problem-space necessarily has a *temporal* dimension" (4), the generation of Caribbean diasporic writers that I discuss have a unique rhetorical context that will continue to evolve and change. The next generation may imagine a different, however related, problem-space. As Édouard Glissant notes in *Caribbean Discourse* (1989), "Each conception of the historic [is] accompanied by a particular form of rhetoric" (69). Caribbean diasporic historical fiction references the concept of diaspora as contested rhetoric within Caribbean studies.

Mobility is a localizing factor for Caribbean diasporic writing. Caribbean diasporic writers carry the baggage of marginalized Caribbean history and are attuned to the contemporary effects of globalization, having in some way witnessed the migration of their families as well as the development of informal networks of exchange alongside more formal global systems. As Michelle Stephens notes in *Black Empire* (2005), this diaspora has experienced "two acts of displacement" (2), that of slavery's forcible movement of people from Africa to the Caribbean and the journey from the islands to the diasporic territories of the United States, Britain, and Canada. This dual dislocation parallels the diaspora's relationship to decontextualization: the diaspora is at once removed from the locale of the island homeland and from the history of the nation to which it immigrated. The writers that I analyze reference both layers of dehistoricization by calling attention to the way migration provides the diaspora with a particular vantage point from which to view the Caribbean histories of colonialism, anticolonialism, and postcolonialism as part of a more global context. Diasporic writers see their double inheritance of Caribbean and diasporic contexts as enabling a fuller vision for understanding the effects of multiculturalism and globalization. At the same time, the novels acknowledge that migration is a privilege that is not open to all Caribbean or diasporic subjects. These authors use the locality of Caribbean history as the space from which to understand the workings of globalization, addressing the fragmentation of identity, the decentering of nationalist discourses, the hybridization of culture, and the interconnectedness of global economies.

In recognizing the literary and academic currency of migration, I distinguish my interpretive approach from the dominant critical trends within Caribbean studies that locate diasporic identity solely through mobility. Critics describe mobility as giving rise to a diasporic consciousness that defies national boundaries, specifically those of Global North nations. Emphasizing mobility also figures migration as the diaspora's authenticating link to Caribbean culture. Because Caribbean academic discourse frames mobility as a defining aspect of Caribbean identity and cultural hybridity, the diaspora's migration and cultural production are seen as a logical outgrowth of a Caribbean cultural tradition.[15] Nevertheless, the focus on mobility and hybridity as endemic aspects of Caribbeanness often leads to the conflation of the diaspora with the Caribbean island nation. The localities and contexts differentiating writing from the diaspora versus writing from the islands are suppressed, ignored, or elided. The result is that academic discourse makes diasporic writing *stand in for* local island writing. The problematics associated with this kind of substitution are often analyzed from the perspective of the Caribbean island nation, with diasporic production as a type of "popular" writing threatening local literary traditions.[16] I am more interested in exploring the challenges such a positioning presents to diasporic writers, and for this reason I argue that location is equally relevant to the formation of diasporic aesthetics. Diaspora produces a literary culture whose locale shapes and produces specific types of aesthetics and metaphors. The positioning of diasporic writing as exemplifying Caribbeanness brings with it certain challenges for these authors, as Silvio Torres-Saillant notes: "In the extent to which the international success of Western-based writers and thinkers might have the effect of supplanting their homeland-based counterparts in the ability to speak influentially about the human experience of the Antillean person, the present development could usher in a mixed blessing" (251). Delving into how that mixed blessing is articulated in the stylistic form and content of the historical novels of Caribbean diasporic authors is central to my project. Localizing the diaspora, geographically within Global North nations and discursively at the intersection of multiculturalism and postcolonialism, opens up a nuanced discussion of diasporic production as a global phenomenon. By tying migration and location together, we can examine how the market shapes Caribbean diasporic production and how the genre of historical fiction responds to a specific set of market contexts and public discourses.

The introduction has outlined the contexts that I use to historically situate the market aesthetics of Caribbean diasporic historical fiction, including the discursive locations of multicultural, postcolonial, globalization, and Caribbean studies. Chapter 1, "Mixed Blessings: Readerships, Postcolonial Ethics, and the Problem of Intimacy," specifies how Caribbean diasporic writers inscribe market aesthetics into the form, structure, and content of their contemporary historical novels. To understand how such fiction circulates in the marketplace, I discuss niche marketing as an important context that shapes the process by which a Caribbean diasporic text finds its audience. In turn, I situate academia as an example of one niche market for Caribbean diasporic historical fiction and reference the contexts of globalization, ethnic, and postcolonial studies as sharing a similar set of values. The demand for the representation of resistance is one of the pressures exerted by the academic market upon Caribbean diasporic authors. The market aesthetics of the novels I discuss reference various market forces and audiences and find expression in the ways the novels imagine their readers, develop an ethical vision, and wrestle with the problematic of intimacy in constructing an ethical relationship to their readers. The relationships between author- and reader-doubles within the novels speak to the postcolonial ethics informing Caribbean diasporic historical writing. Sexuality and gender become the dominant themes the writers employ to allegorize the relationship between the text and reader as an intimate encounter. Localizing this queer metaphor within a Caribbean context, I outline the unique market aesthetics of Caribbean diasporic writing.

In chapter 2, "Kinship Routes: Contextualizing Diaspora via the Market in Andrea Levy and David Chariandy," I analyze novels that depict market multiculturalism as an erasing and enabling historical context for diasporic identity. The main characters find themselves unmoored within Canada and Britain as nations superficially valuing multiculturalism and enforcing a regime of color blindness that violently dislodges the contexts of colonialism and racism. The first-person narrators of *Fruit of the Lemon* (1999) and *Soucouyant* (2007) trace a path from rootlessness to belonging that is facilitated by a combination of historical contextualization and consumer citizenship, with a physical or psychological return to island origins in Jamaica and Trinidad. Both Faith and *Soucouyant*'s nameless narrator base their routes of consumerism on familial models, Constance/Afria and the narrator's brother, respectively. These blood relations are foils for the protagonists, tempering their hopeful conclusions of community belonging and historical recovery. Sexual intimacy haunts the margins of the narratives, with prostitution as a troublesome metaphor for the novel's relationship with its readers.

In chapter 3, "Writing the Reader: Literacy and Contradictory Pedagogies in Julia Alvarez, Michelle Cliff, and Marlon James," I concentrate on writers who foreground the pedagogical impulse of Caribbean diasporic writing. The novels teach their audiences about the interconnectedness of US and Caribbean histories while framing women as active participants in liberation struggles, from slave revolts to civil rights movements in Jamaica, the Dominican Republic, Cuba, and the United States.[17] *In the Name of Salomé* (2000), *Free Enterprise* (1993), and *The Book of Night Women* (2009) depict main characters engaged in the act of teaching, with the pedagogical relationship to the reader becoming self-consciously expressed via the novels' structure. While Alvarez, Cliff, and James use different stylistic tactics, the authors all maintain a tension between their depictions of teaching and the novels' structural pedagogy. The intimacy of teacher-student relationships in the historical fiction allows the writers to imagine the various obstacles to the pedagogical project of postcolonial ethics.

In chapter 4, "Messy Intimacies: Postcolonial Romance in Ana Menéndez, Dionne Brand, and Monique Roffey," I focus on historical novels that wrestle with the legitimacy of romance as an anticolonial narrative for writing history, critiquing the masculinist and heterosexist definitions of revolutionary politics. *Loving Che* (2003), *In Another Place, Not Here* (1997), and *The White Woman on the Green Bicycle* (2009) use the genre of romance to reframe public figures such as Che Guevara and Eric Williams within intimate, sexual spheres and to explore the blind spots of anticolonial movements. The investigative journeys of the characters are central to the excavation of marginal histories in Cuba, Grenada, Trinidad, Canada, and the United States. By depicting the archival process as an investigative journey, incorporating public and personal records of history, Menéndez, Brand and Roffey critique the reader's relationship to historical fiction.

In chapter 5, "Dictating Diaspora: Gendering Postcolonial Violence in Junot Díaz and Edwidge Danticat," I turn to novels about the postcolonial legacies of dictatorship. In the historical fiction of Junot Díaz and Edwidge Danticat, the diasporic communities and their locales in the United States continue to be shaped by the histories of the police state from the Dominican Republic and Haiti. The market aesthetics of *The Brief Wondrous Life of Oscar Wao* (2007) and *The Dew Breaker* (2004) teach the reader about the context of dictatorship while deploying dictation as a metaphor for understanding the power dynamics between author and reader. Díaz and Danticat gender the postcolonial experience through the intersection of intimacy and art, exposing the differential relationships that women and men have to authorship.

In my conclusion, "Electronic Archives and the Digital Futures of Caribbean Diasporic Writing," I address how the shift from print to digital publishing is informing Caribbean diasporic historical fiction. By outlining the way readerships contribute to the production of online marginalia for *Oscar Wao* and Robert Antoni's *As Flies to Whatless Boys* (2013), I show how the market aesthetics of Caribbean diasporic writing is responsive to and wary of these new forms of communication and dialogue. The digital divide translates into a different set of challenges in imagining and engaging readerships.

1 Mixed Blessings

Readerships, Postcolonial Ethics, and the Problem of Intimacy

As MY INTRODUCTION DISCUSSED, the genre of historical fiction poses challenges to the dominant understandings of globalization in the humanities. Caribbean diasporic fiction is especially attuned to the contradictions accompanying a contextually minded product entering a decontextualizing marketplace. In *Voicing Memory* (2003), Nick Nesbitt reminds us that in the contemporary public sphere, "once repressed" historical contexts are "no longer absent" but have become "commodit[ies] offered up in newspapers; on local television; in annual commemorations" (6). While Nesbitt is specifically referring to the way cultural institutions deploy the history of slavery as an empty commodity, he also accepts the broader implications of this phenomenon, that "memory itself has become a commodity, circulating throughout society as mnemonic spectacle" (6). I see historical fiction as an ideal cultural product for discussing how the market mediates the consumption of once marginalized histories. This chapter sets the stage for my later readings of the novels by theorizing how Caribbean diasporic historical fiction is responsive to its circulation as commodified memory. Caribbean diasporic fiction self-consciously frames itself as a commodity in order to propose a postcolonial ethics of reading history. The form and content of this genre seek to embody and reconcile some of the contradictory pressures imposed by the way it imagines its readerships. The concept of niche marketing proves useful for understanding the diverse range of audiences that such texts encounter and how the readerships' patronage of certain genres and styles shapes Caribbean diasporic writing. The authors rhetorically position their historical novels at the intersection of multiple readerships in order to comment on the challenges of narrating counterhistories in a mainstream public. Within their historical narratives, the writers often offer models of what can go right or wrong in cross-cultural interactions, seeking to flesh out the ethical (im) possibilities of intimacy.

Imagining Readers and Market Niches

Caribbean diasporic writers face unique problems of audience and authority. Hans Robert Jauss's formulation of horizons in "The Identity of the Poetic Text in the Changing Horizon of Understanding" (1985) helps clarify the relationship between market processes and audience reception. Jauss sees the "'dialogicity' of literary communication," or the conversation initiated by a text's circulation, as inevitably entailing a "problem of otherness: between producer and recipient, between the past of the text and the present of the recipient, between different cultures" (9). For Caribbean diasporic writers, this problem of otherness is heightened by the commodification of ethnicity, which complicates the objectives of the text's ethical imperative of historical revision. Jauss's use of horizon acknowledges how the imaginaries of *both* the writer and the reader inform the interpretation of a text. The writers' horizons of expectation (en)gender a market aesthetics. The creative reimagining of the past is shaped by how the writers envision their contemporary and future audiences. The structure and content of market aesthetics anticipate the reaction(s) of an audience on the basis of the reader reception that Caribbean diasporic writers experienced with their prior works. I engage a paratextual archive of book reviews to supplement the way in which the novels "infer the horizon of expectation of the contemporary public" (20).

Caribbean diasporic writers are aware of how the market positions them as the English-language representatives of their islands of origin and critically engage the market label of the author as authentic spokesperson. Taking advantage of the market's framing as well as the global circulation of their fiction, Caribbean diasporic writers see the dehistoricized condition of the contemporary public sphere as providing a gap of context that they are positioned to fill in. The authors recognize this dehistoricized condition as an opportunity to reach an audience unarmed with competing historical sensibilities. The pedagogical tool of historical fiction aims to teach readers to see evidence of the Caribbean's centrality to the formation of American, Canadian, and European politics and culture. Each historical novel reflects the writer's unique implementation of pedagogy in terms of how the structure and form convey historical context to the reader. Caribbean diasporic authors employ a variety of pedagogical approaches: realist and postmodernist narratives, chronological and antichronological plots, didactic and Socratic forms. In chapters 2 and 3, I describe two approaches to the teacherly imperative: how writers either seek to historicize the decontextualization of the diaspora, as in the case of Andrea Levy and David Chariandy, or offer historical narratives of the Caribbean past to fill in the present gap of context, as in the case of Julia Alvarez, Michelle Cliff, and Marlon James.

While pedagogical strategies are expressed using a variety of modalities, Caribbean diasporic writers imagine the *content* of their historical vision in similar ways. The authors adopt a postcolonial approach to analyze historical progress, framing the Caribbean as a locale for the development of global capitalism and as a space whose consistent marginalization maintains empire's illusion of economic independence, moral superiority, and impermeable national borders.[1] Caribbean diasporic historical fiction is also fraught with ambivalence about its ability to transform readership sensibilities within a book market that packages ethnicity as a commodity and domesticates multicultural voices. The ethical imperative to inculcate a specifically postcolonial historical vision in its readers is fractured by writerly anxieties about the market packaging of the novels and whether such packaging will instead produce unengaged and uncritical readers of these counterhistories. The struggle to imagine an ethical pedagogical relationship between reader and author is encoded in the depictions of student-teacher encounters. For instance, Elizette's relationship with Verlia and Verlia's with Abena in Dionne Brand's *In Another Place, Not Here* are of mentee and mentor as well as of lovers. Verlia's and Elizette's acquisition of a political education within the context of romantic intimacy emerges as a troubled allegory for the text's relationship to its audience.

The work of diasporic writers circulates back to book markets in their Caribbean islands of origin, leading to criticisms about these authors' inability to authentically depict the nation-state's history. The fallout in the Dominican Republic over how Julia Alvarez's *In the Time of the Butterflies* (1994) depicted the Mirabal sisters or in both the DR and Haiti regarding Edwidge Danticat's portrayal of the 1937 massacre in *The Farming of Bones* (1998) come to mind. Many Caribbean diasporic writers, including Alvarez and Danticat, have voiced their discomfort about how their work is received by both island and diaspora readerships. David Chariandy, for instance, explains in a 2007 interview published in *Callaloo* that he was "deeply concerned about titling my novel *Soucouyant*" and how it "would be received by those I imagined to be *intimately* familiar with the word—namely, residents and first-generation immigrants from specific Caribbean islands like Trinidad" ("'Fiction of Belonging'" 810; emphasis added). Chariandy did not want his novel's title "to suggest that the novel was going to offer authoritative insights on a legend that, I fully know, has been discussed and interpreted in many exciting ways, particularly by those with extensive 'first hand' experience with the cultures of Trinidad" (811). Chariandy imagines that his readerships' authority on the Caribbean culture and "intimate and lifelong knowledge of Canada" could call attention to his inadequacies as a representative voice for the Caribbean and its Canadian diaspora (810–11). His self-consciousness about his position as a writer is particularly evident when he declares that he is "not a sociologist" and is "usually quite wary of attempts to typify the attitudes of entire 'peoples' or 'generations'" (811).

Caribbean diasporic writers see the multiple readerships, regardless of training or cultural origin, as motivated by a similar desire to access a level of intimacy that facilitates authoritative knowledge of multicultural and postcolonial experiences. As Doris Sommer notes in *Proceed with Caution* (1999), many readers "feel entitled to know everything as they approach a text, practically any text, with the conspiratorial intimacy of a potential partner" (ix). The sense of entitlement is concomitant with the reader's desire to have intimate access to anOther knowledge. Intimacy is a defining facet of the relationship between reader and text, and readers who are outsiders or insiders to Caribbean culture seek to determine and measure the authenticity of the writer and his or her ability to speak with cultural authority. It makes sense that authors like David Chariandy are described as being "afflicted with imposter syndrome," "consumed with self-doubt," and "struggl[ing] with the potential impact of [public] recognition" (Lederman R1). The pedagogical project addresses this problematic by confronting readers with the unreliability of historical truth while at the same time remarking on the audience's complicity with processes of decontextualization. The conceptual bond between the Caribbean diasporic texts that I discuss is a writerly angst about producing comfortable observers despite or because of a postcolonial rendering of history: the writers claim a certain cultural authority in order to narrate these histories, yet they fear that exoticizing lenses will transform their authority into stereotype. Caribbean diasporic historical novels reference the challenges to their pedagogical project by depicting author-doubles in the form of narrators or historical figures who wrestle with their roles as authentic spokespersons.

Caribbean diasporic writers understand their work to be circulating within the publishing niches of postcolonial and multicultural literatures, and as a result they foresee encounters with different audiences: for example, the book club reader, the academic reader, and the classroom reader—in a variety of localities, including the Caribbean nation-state and diaspora. Additionally, the authors acknowledge the readers that they may never reach, the readerships they aspire to but cannot access (for instance, the conundrum of the illiterate reader depicted by Julia Alvarez in *In the Name of Salomé*, David Chariandy in *Soucouyant*, and Marlon James in *The Book of Night Women*). While addressing multiple audiences, Caribbean diasporic writers encode specific readers into their texts. The pedagogical project of historical fiction imagines a global reader (book club or classroom reader) who, if not ignorant of history, at least needs to be taught or trained to envision history in a different way. At the same time, the postcolonial vision of history has market currency with the academic reader and his or her expectations for a "resistant" text. Caribbean diasporic writers also imagine speaking back to Caribbean populations and nations; as Monique Roffey explains, "Trinidadians are my closest readers, the readers I care most about" ("For Books' Sake," par. 21). I would therefore amend Robert Fraser's claim in *Book History through Postcolonial Eyes* (2008) that "the crisis of the postcolonial author . . . is one not so much of commodification as of audience" (185). I see commodification and reception as interrelated challenges, such that Caribbean diasporic historical fiction ambivalently engages with these nuanced contemporary contexts.

Mapping out the readerships for Caribbean diasporic writing is complicated by the fragmentation of the publishing industry. In *Postcolonial Writers in the Global Literary Marketplace* (2007), Sarah Brouillette makes the case that critics often ignore the fact that the corporatization and globalization of the publishing industry entail "the twinned processes of niche fragmentation and market expansion" (56). One niche market is that of "serious" literary fiction, and within that are numerous submarkets as well (including multicultural and postcolonial, which are of primary interest to me here). Brouillette argues that within this "fragmented market defined by a proliferation of choices, selling specific identities to distinct consumers facilitates the process of consumption" (66). Brouillette's analysis of the book market calls into question any mythic formulation of the global reader or claim that the book market produces one type of reading gaze. Rather, niche marketing circulates cultural production to very specific audiences, and as a result one of the main concerns of Caribbean diasporic writers is how their work is funneled into the categories of ethnic and postcolonial literatures and how those categories can shape the audience-text encounter. For example, Belinda Edmondson discusses the niche of African American literature in *Caribbean Middlebrow: Leisure Culture and the Middle Class* (2009). She describes the conflicted emotions of Caribbean authors regarding their marketing: "For some Caribbean writers, the lure of the American market evokes contradictory desires: they wish *not* to be pigeonholed as black writers, yet they crave access to the lucrative African American reading market, which buys primarily black-authored books" (148–49). Silvio Torres-Saillant reiterates Edmondson's point in *An Intellectual History of the Caribbean* (2006) by remarking on the incorporation of Edwidge Danticat, Eric Walrond, and Paule Marshall into African American literature anthologies and noting how "the designation African American is not devoid of its measure of elasticity" (95). Perhaps this niche explains why some Caribbean diasporic writers make African American historical figures central in their novels: for instance, Caryl Phillips's *Dancing in the Dark* (2005) depicts Bahamian Bert Williams's success as a blackface minstrel celebrity in the United States.[2]

The incorporation of Caribbean diasporic writing into the niche market of African American writing is also indicative of how the literature is concerned with tracing the origins and migrations of its diasporas from a comparative ethnic perspective, drawing parallels between Caribbean and other immigrant diasporas. One of the best-known examples, Zadie Smith's *White Teeth* (2000), narrates Irie's Black British experience within the context of her Jamaican family and alongside that of East Indian and African immigrant communities.[3] In addition to depicting the contemporary multicultural societies where the Caribbean diaspora finds itself, Caribbean diasporic writing is invested in illuminating historically marginalized ethnicities within the Caribbean. For instance, Cristina García's *Monkey Hunting* (2003) and Angie Cruz's *Let It Rain Coffee* (2005) focus on the Asian experience within the Cuban and Dominican diasporas. Perhaps unsurprisingly, diaspora and interethnic relationships are dominant themes within the creative work of Caribbean diasporic writers. This comparative ethnic focus forms part of a broader ethical project of intercultural understanding by means of the global book market.

While the market distribution of US, Canadian, and British Caribbean diasporic writing can intersect with the African American literary category, other types of publishing channels can produce a different set of classifications. In *Caribbean Middlebrow*, Belinda Edmondson distinguishes between the marketing approaches to anglophone Caribbean writing taken by mainstream versus independent publishers. While metropolitan publishers like Warner Aspect and Ballantine "are not shy about their commercial interest in subsuming Caribbean fiction into one of the prescribed categories," Edmondson notes that independent presses often take a different approach, since they "can afford to be more eclectic" and to "concentrate their marketing efforts on a smaller demographic of readers" (157). Mainstream publishers seldom market Caribbean literature "outside the African American genre" because of a belief that "the Caribbean still has no firm place in the American imagination" (158) and that the Caribbean readership is "too small to have its own marketing niche" (156). By contrast, independent publishers see the "unplace-ability" of Caribbean writing as a marketable element that appeals to "readers looking for the 'unusual' or exotic" (158). Edmondson gives the example of "Brooklyn-based independent publisher Akashic Books" as one small press that includes Caribbean fiction within its catalog, marketing it in "much the same way as its other popular fiction, aimed more or less exclusively at young white American college students with a taste for 'underground' themes" (158). Distinguishing between the marketing tactics of major versus minor publishers provides a different perspective on niche market processes as a context for market aesthetics. To clarify the marketing priorities of small presses, Edmondson discusses Marlon James as a writer whose first novel was published by Akashic Books "to critical acclaim" (159). James can be read as a writer who has experienced the marketing transition from an independent to a mainstream press since his second novel, which I discuss in chapter 3, was published by Riverhead, a division of Penguin. Edmondson cites James's assertion that "Akashic's primary readership of white college students worked in his favor" (159), and it's clear that Riverhead marketed his second novel to an African American readership, since it was a finalist for the NAACP Image Award and led James to be named the *Go On Girl!* Book Club's 2012 Author of the Year. The fragmentation of the publishing economy in terms of niche marketing acts as a *shared* historical context shaping the market aesthetics and postcolonial ethics of Caribbean diasporic authors.

Aspirational Ethics of Market Aesthetics

The criticism concerning Caribbean diasporic literature often focuses on how an *ethical* relationship with the reader is facilitated and/or delimited by the market. In *Exhibiting Slavery* (2009), Vivian Nun Halloran argues that historical novels must meet the demands of an "audience willing to spend a defined period of time learning about the past and being entertained in the process" (13). For Halloran, the consumer demand for entertainment means that these postmodern historical novels lack an "ethical perspective" (15). Whereas Halloran positions consumption and ethics as incompatible, I depart from this analysis by situating market demands as an important context for the pedagogical ethics driving these Caribbean diasporic historical novels. Entertainment is one facet of market demands, but there are also academic markets for contextualization. Historical fiction is the product of a complex negotiation between the demands to entertain and to teach, to simplify and to complicate, to make history both palatable and challenging. While teaching the reader about certain historical events and figures, the form that relays historical content plays a key role in shaping reader engagement. The literary "lesson plan" is a combination of seducing the reader and undermining audience expectations.

The literary critics who review Caribbean diasporic fiction often echo the words of Édouard Glissant, who in *Caribbean Discourse* (1989) calls for the Caribbean writer to "dig deep" into the "collective memory" in order to create a "prophetic vision of the past" that avoids the pitfalls of "a schematic chronology" or "nostalgic lament" (64). Academic readers privilege texts that they see uncovering lost and/or marginal cultural histories, while also expecting that this act of recovery is political, that it is prophetic about changing the contemporary perception of Caribbean society, culture, and history. Conversely, this literary mission is viewed as suspect if it falls into the trap of nostalgic sentimentality or of being too prescriptive and dogmatic about "what happened" in the newly recovered past. Santiago Juan-Navarro's concept of the "activist reader" from *Archival Reflections* (2000) is productive for fleshing out the pedagogical impulse of diasporic historical fiction as well as the academic market pressures encountered by Caribbean diasporic writers. Juan-Navarro sees this genre positioning the reader in a way that "oblige[s] him or her to adopt a critical attitude toward the narrated events and to seek a political alternative to them" (265). Inspiring critical thinking and political action, it converts the "active reader" into "an 'activist reader,' implicated not only in the creative process of the work, but also in the process of the transformation of the reality to which the work belongs" (265). Historical novels train the reader through their structural and stylistic composition, some even encouraging the reader to participate in the narrative's construction of meaning. For Juan-Navarro, this training encourages or provokes the reader into a progressive political commitment with the ethical imperative of the historical novel, so that the reader is moved to address the fiction's social critique by taking responsibility for transforming the reality it depicts.

In *Proceed with Caution*, Doris Sommer also describes how a literature of the Americas seeks to construct an ethical and pedagogical relationship with the reader, but she describes this interaction as antagonistic or confrontational. Sommer notes that "readers bent on understanding" are forced by the form and content of the texts—which Sommer describes as particularist—to change their reading practices (ix). Like Juan-Navarro, Sommer describes textual "absences [that] can incite the fill-in work" of the reader, while also interfer[ing] with comprehension" (x). The writing is disrupted by "truncated allusions and purposeful incomprehensibility" that evoke a "refus[al] to flow" (15). Rather than focusing on the reader's interpretive work in decoding a fragmented text, however, Sommer values the gaps of knowledge that the fiction compels the reader to acknowledge, arguing that "worry should be part of the work, if we learn to read the distance written into some ethnically marked literature" (xi). I would add that this literature seeks to impart to the reader a lesson about the impossibility of intimacy. Indeed, Sommer uses metaphors of intimacy to explain the tense relationship between text and reader. The fiction deploys a "slap of refused intimacy" (ix) or a "cold shoulder effect" (31); it "holds readers at arm's length" (xi), while readers display "a possessive intimacy that wants to pass for love" (20). The ethical imperative of "marking off an impassable distance between reader and text" (8) aims to disrupt "facile intimacies" desired by the reader (xiii). However, such creative writing must first "engage readers through seductive education" (31) in order to "produce the desire that will then be frustrated" (15). The audience's seduction is consequently paired with a process of "erect[ing] ethical constraints" (24). The goal is not only to teach the general reader to "draw the limits of sharing" (25) but also to retrain the *academic* reader. Sommer believes that these texts promote "responsible reading" (27) by undermining the "underexamined hermeneutical habits" (25) of literary critics, teaching them "a self-doubting step too lame for conquest" (15). These fictions ask academics to give up their privilege of meaning making or at least to slow down and think through the problematic aspects of such privilege.

I also see the postcolonial ethical imperative as encouraging the reader to think critically about the intersections of empire, migration, and globalization, as well as the ethical limits of understanding and knowledge. I would argue that the market aesthetics of Caribbean diasporic historical fiction is *aspirational* rather than transformational. On the one hand, there are limitations on what types of readers have access to the diasporic text. As Brinda Mehta notes, "Free access in a supposedly global economy is not a democratic ideal but a selected function of race, class, gender, and skin color" (16). By extension, the market broadens consumer access, but that does not mean that the writers can reach all the readers they aspire to transform. As Sommer implies, even transforming the audience who reads the historical fiction is questionable. The texts reference their market access readers by either encoding them as characters or referencing audience expectations. The novels seek to teach such readers a postcolonial reading of the relationship between the Global North nations and the Caribbean, while referencing the obstacles that impede the formation of an activist audience or their access to the "aspirational" reader. The novels reference academic market pressures by complicating and questioning the academic equation of writing with political activism, which often conflates the depiction of resistance with material action. Just as Sommer identifies intimacy as a contested territory in her description of aesthetic distancing tactics, Caribbean diasporic fictions allegorize the encounters of writers and readers in terms of sexual intimacy.

The Academic Market for Literary Resistance

I appreciate Belinda Edmondson's view that it should be unsurprising to us that "marketing and sales play so prominent a role in determining what constitutes Caribbean fiction" because "fiction is, in its broadest sense, part of the entertainment industry, not the academy" (161). But as Mark McGurl's *The Program Era* points out, the proliferation of MFA programs in creative writing exposes the stake that higher education has in the entertainment industry of high (or even low) culture. Any discussion of the market aesthetics of Caribbean diasporic writing must take into account how academia is a market shaping the historical vision of these authors. Just as studies of globalization emphasize the market's decontextualizing function, the academic fields of postcolonial and multicultural studies display similar market values. In particular, the commodification of resistance within academic analyses shapes the formation of literary histories and canons. As Shalini Puri notes in "Beyond Resistance: Notes toward a New Caribbean Cultural Studies," the valorization of "revolutionary consciousness as a precondition for gaining entry into the canon silences" certain literary voices (38). This cult of resistance glosses over the nuances of politics and agency within literature, creating "monotony from subtle" subtexts and simplifying the "tonal contrast" within canonical works (38). If canonization and interpretation are shaped by the values of certain academic readers, then it is equally plausible that diasporic cultural production is informed by academia as an influential market within the publishing field. Graham Huggan's *The Postcolonial Exotic* (2001) addresses postcolonialism as a "critical industry" (4) whose "rhetoric of resistance" (6) "emerges as a commodified vehicle of symbolic power" (29). Huggan ties globalization to the disciplinary formation of postcolonial studies in order to argue that the key link between these two is the decontextualization and domestication of difference, or what he calls "commodity fetishism." In other words, academic fields analyzing globalization as a system echo the conceptual problematics that they define as endemic to globalization. According to Huggan, "Three aspects of commodity fetishism—mythification (or levelling-out) of historical experience; imagined access to the cultural other through the process of consumption; reification of people and places into exchangeable aesthetic objects—help [postcolonial] books and their authors acquire an almost talismanic status" (19). As I discussed in my introduction, critics often presuppose that market popularity must entail the decontextualization of history. The genre of historical fiction by its very nature complicates such an equation. Historicization has a market too, and the context that historical fiction carries is appealing to various readership sectors, especially academics. Reviews comment on the pedagogical value of Caribbean diasporic writing, for example, noting that "student interest in this collection will be negligible" (Birkett 83) or that a text is found to be "very readable, teachable" (Dobson 165).

Huggan's description of the market for postcolonial literatures and discourses resonates with the discussion of Palumbo-Liu's pluralist multiculturalism from my introduction. The keywords vary, with *domestication* supplanted by *cultural translation*, but the process remains that of "channelling difference into areas where it can be attractively packaged, and [. . .] safely contained" (Huggan 24). Timothy Brennan echoes these critiques of academic scholarship in "Postcolonial Studies and Globalization Theory" (2008) by pointing to decontextualization within globalization studies:

> The tendency of intellectual trends to supplant predecessors by erasing the
> history of their own making is not a chance occurrence, nor is it simply the

work of uncharitable scholars. It is rather a characteristic feature of contemporary capitalist societies, which are at once *presentist*—that is, viewing
each moment as the only reality while expunging the past in a gesture of
calculated *anti*historicism—and *modernist* in the technical sense of needing
to judge every current discovery as an utterly new departure, an absolute
rupture with all that went before. This intellectual reflex is, in fact, a central
feature both of what globalization theory argues the world has become, as
well as what that theory unwittingly demonstrates about itself. (38)

Huggan, Palumbo Liu, and Brennan point to how academic discourse,
which assumes independence from market pressures and an objective
interrogation of globalization's workings, can be shown to operate on
the market impulses of decontextualization and exoticism. Perhaps it
is not all that unusual that critics in the distinct fields of multicultural,
postcolonial, and globalization studies similarly describe academia as
implicated in or compromised by the workings of the economic sphere.
What is intriguing is that these critics reveal the hegemonic values of
scholarship by emphasizing parallelism, how academic discourses mirror the systems being analyzed. This conceptual tool of parallelism
proves useful for showing the trends linking these various fields, and
in so doing, pointing to the broader rhetorical field on globalization
engaged by Caribbean diasporic production.

I do not take issue with whether, in the words of Judie Newman, the
historical novels "become fictions in the service of a fiction, since the
existence of globalisation as a new and real phenomenon is both contested and open to multiple definitions" (*Fictions of America* 2). Instead,
my approach toward analyzing Caribbean diasporic historical fiction
frames the market pressures on such literature as both commercial *and*
academic. Carine Mardorossian references the academic appeal of diasporic Caribbeanness in *Reclaiming Difference: Caribbean Women
Rewrite Postcolonialism* (2005) by stating, "That the region [of the
Caribbean] functions as the exemplar of the new global order explains
why its literature is seen as especially representative in postcolonial studies today" (4). The academic market is oriented toward the commodification of literary representations of resistance, equating resistance with
a progressive ideology of contextualization.

In light of the critical appeal of resistance, there is a pressing need
to theorize the values and influence of academic audiences. As Huggan
and Palumbo-Liu note, one challenge is how the ethnic and postcolonial
literary markets commodify difference and produce a specific type of

reader. Sarah Brouillette challenges this accepted truism by pointing out that "critiquing an unnamed cosmopolitan consumer who seeks mythic access to exotic experience is premised upon the notion that there exists a group of educated, elite, distinguished consumers who actually have access to the reality that the other consumer can only wish to possess" (19). The distinction of readerships according to varying levels of privilege informs how Caribbean diasporic authors envision their readers and their own roles as intellectuals. The writers depict and speak to academic readers within their fiction because they have encountered the prescriptive definitions of writerly responsibility (for instance, of authentic advocate for progressivism) circulated by theories of literary studies and education. When asked in an interview about the reception of *The White Woman on the Green Bicycle*, Monique Roffey explains that the novel has "generally been well-received both commercially and critically" and directly acknowledges her academic readers by noting that "it has been studied by academics at the University of the West Indies and here in the UK too" ("For Books' Sake," par. 20). Caribbean diasporic authors are so aware of the academic reception of their novels in part because many of them have taught in university settings: Alvarez at Middlebury College, Brand at the University of Guelph, Chariandy at Simon Fraser University, Cliff at Trinity College, Danticat at the University of Miami, Díaz at the Massachusetts Institute of Technology, James at Macalester College, Menéndez at SUNY Albany, Levy at City Lit (a center for adult education), and Roffey at Goldsmiths/University of London. Of course, this list is by no means exhaustive of the different academic locations where these particular Caribbean diasporic writers have given workshops or lectures. While it might seem obvious to note the close relationship between creative writers and the academy, especially in light of Mark McGurl's work on the proliferation of MFA programs, this is a historical context and readership that critics seldom identify when analyzing Caribbean diasporic writing.

Promoting Postcolonial Ethics

Having mapped out the multiple readerships invoked by the market aesthetics of Caribbean diasporic writing, I define in greater detail the ethical imperative inspiring the historical fiction, which is distinctly postcolonial in context and construct. The ethical framework of the novels is evident in their structure as pedagogical projects seeking to teach the reader. The pedagogical impulse has two facets, teaching historical facts alongside a historical vision. The factual drive of diasporic

historical fiction addresses two problematics: the Caribbean trauma of
a shift from colonialism to postcoloniality and the diasporic reality of
a decontextualization brought about by globalization. By linking these
two contexts of globalization and postcoloniality within their historical
narratives, Caribbean diasporic writers aim to counter the erasure that
is both local and global. Additionally, the writers seek to instill in their
readers a postcolonial interpretive perspective, with the hope that such
a vision will allow their audience to read the history of the Caribbean in
an ethical manner.

The pedagogical task of historical fiction is responsive to the decontextualization of the Caribbean and offers counternarratives that educate the amnesiac reader. The historical novels affirm the relevance of
the Caribbean to European and American histories, particularly as a
space where the seeds of globalization were planted during New World
imperialist enterprises. For example, the triangular slave trade and the
practices of colonization (law, religion, education, etc.) marked the
Caribbean as a space of violent creolization and capitalist profit logic.
The Caribbean's pivotal role in shaping the projects of enlightenment
and modernity has consistently been erased from Western civilization's
narratives of historical progress.[4] Even though the success of the Haitian Revolution reverberated throughout the Caribbean, North America, and Europe, its political and economic significance was disregarded
outside Haiti until Trinidadian C. L. R. James wrote *The Black Jacobins* in 1938.[5] Bringing this erasure into a modern context, the diasporic
migrations that led to the presence of the Black British community in
England and the Puerto Rican population in the United States are rarely
contextualized in terms of the mother country's call for volunteers and
conscription of labor from the colonies during and after World War II.
The Caribbean has inspired European and American art and thought,
from abolitionist to surrealist movements, yet has always been reduced
to a passive embodiment of their philosophies rather than an active cre-
ator.[6] The writers I examine situate the Caribbean as a locale for understanding the hidden costs of modernity and globalization. In essence, by
privileging those very voices and stories that have been thus far excluded
from the historical record, the writers want to inform the reader about
the ways that European and American histories depend upon decontextualization. For instance, Kerry Young explicitly frames her goals in
writing a historical novel about the Jamaican-Chinese community, *Pao*
(2011), in terms of teaching the reader: "I'd like them to learn a bit about
Jamaica and understand [. . .] where we've come from, where we're

going, where we're up to . . . and what a wonderful, beautiful country it is" ("Interview" [*Book Diva*]). The transparency of this pedagogical objective is evident when BBC interviewer Harriett Gilbert tells Young that "you're always very careful to put the undoubted violence of Kingston within an historical context. I mean it seems to me that's almost part of the mission of the novel to say, 'I'd like you to understand why there is this violence in Jamaica'" (Young, "Kerry Young").

Yet the ethical imperative of historical fiction moves beyond a simple strategy of historical recovery, bringing silenced contexts to light. Academics often assume that the recovery of such histories follows a progressive politics, but Caribbean historical fiction troubles this accepted equation. In *Friends and Enemies* (2008), Chris Bongie notes that the "duty to remember" is complicated by the "frustrating entanglement of memory and nostalgia, of agency and governmentality" (151). Caribbean diasporic authors reference the institutional realities of the publishing market as another historical context, one that facilitates and regulates the dissemination of historical fiction. Publishing industry pressures for minority cultures to "explain" themselves to mainstream readers shape the fictional representation of historical facts and position the writer as cultural informant and cultural object. The teaching of a postcolonial historical vision runs against the grain of the project's liberatory energies, positioning the author as a teacher educating the reader on how to interpret a set of facts about a specific historical moment. An ethic of self-consciousness questions the ability of any reader or writer to objectively know what are the "true" historical facts, incorporating self-referential points of anxiety regarding the efficacy of any historical vision (anticolonial or postcolonial). By challenging the idea of historical truth, Caribbean diasporic writers contradict the reader's search for factuality and undermine their project of uncovering "authentic" silenced histories. Returning to the example of *Pao*, Young explains that in addition to teaching the reader about Jamaican history she wanted to encourage her readers to adopt an ethical lens when reading this history. Young explains that the novel asks the reader to see how "good intentions sometimes leads to bad deeds, and bad deeds sometimes leads to good consequences. And [. . .] that we come to our circumstances, um, that are not of our making. We enter into [. . .] something that history has created for us and given to us and we try to do our best" ("Interview" [*Book Diva*]). The ethical vision that accompanies the factual drive of Caribbean diasporic historical fiction is one that highlights the challenges facing the "good intentions" of the narrative's pedagogical project as well as the reader's desire to classify and/or pigeonhole the Other cultures depicted within these historical novels.

Diasporic historical fiction's ethical imperative intersects with the rhetorical trends linking multicultural, postcolonial, and Caribbean studies. The ethical project is directed at transforming a mainstream, metropolitan readership, echoing Silvio Torres-Saillant's hopeful prediction that by "carving their niche in the capitals of the intellectual production of the core countries—England, France, Spain, Holland, and the United States—diaspora voices have begun to creolize the imagination of the metropolitan centers" (250). I would temper the prediction that "the foreseeable result [is] that the West may rehabilitate its conventionally inimical portrayal of the Antillian world" (250) by arguing that the texts display a *desire* to transform the readership's vision. Whether that desire will become a reality is more difficult to evaluate, and these diasporic writers ultimately depict the transformation of the reader as hopeful speculation. It is of greater importance to me to analyze the *terms* of a Caribbean diasporic ethical vision than to judge the degree of success with which they impart that vision to their readers. Kerry Young describes the central challenge to being a writer in terms of "want[ing] to write a book of fiction that could be published by a mainstream publisher" ("Interview" [*Words of Colour*], par. 6).[7] The novels therefore reflect their writers' horizon of market expectations for publishable historical fiction by "ethnic" authors, often in terms of cultural translation. Framing the historical fiction as a lesson plan speaks to the mainstream market's demands for the genre and the ethical imperatives of Caribbean diasporic writers. In teaching the reader about Caribbean history, Caribbean diasporic historical novels depict relationships between characters that are models for the reader-text relationship. These author-and/or reader-doubles espouse a postcolonial vision of history that the novel aims to teach to the reader. However, the authorial double's struggle to fulfill his or her obligations as a representative voice of Caribbean culture reveals the limits of the novel's pedagogical agenda. The ethical vision becomes fractured by the irreconcilability of sexuality, which challenges the formulation of an ideal Caribbean diasporic identity, and by extension an ethical vision of Caribbean diasporic history.

Ethical Readings of the Past

To define the postcoloniality of the historical vision within Caribbean diasporic novels, I turn to David Scott's *Conscripts of Modernity* (2004). Scott distinguishes between the anticolonial and postcolonial eras by arguing that each entails a different temporal understanding of the relationship between the past, present, and future. To acknowledge "what present it is that the past [is] being reimagined for" (2), I outlined in the Introduction some of the contemporary discursive contexts relevant to Caribbean diasporic writing. The presentness of postcoloniality and its unique conceptualization of time shape the historical vision that diasporic writers want to impart to their readers. Scott defines the "postcolonial present" as "our present after the collapse of the social and political hopes that went into the anticolonial imaginings and postcolonial making of national sovereignties" (1). The collapse of anticolonialism is evident not just in the political realities of dictatorships and corruption that plague the postcolonial state but also in the lost currency or co-opting of anticolonial rhetoric. For instance, Scott explains that "today nation and socialism do not name visionary horizons of new beginnings any of us can look forward to as though they were fresh thresholds of aspiration and achievement to be fought for and progressively arrived at; to the contrary, they name forms of existing social and political reality whose normative limits we now live as the tangible ruins of our present, the congealing context of our postcolonial time" (29). A profound sense of loss marks the postcolonial vision of the anticolonial past, where the future is no longer imagined as full of utopian possibility. Scott is specifically interested in understanding the shift from anticolonial to postcolonial by analyzing the work of C. L. R. James and the revisions that were added to the 1938 edition of *Black Jacobins* during the 1963 reissue: "More than teaching us about historical facts or about revolutionary theory [. . .] [it] teaches us about fidelity to a distinctive mode of historical criticism, one in which the nature of the question the past is called upon to answer is self-consciously shaped by the discontent in the present it seeks to change in order to fashion a future without those sources of dissatisfaction" (22). I am interested in applying the lesson that Scott ascribes to those revisions by arguing that Caribbean diasporic historical fiction employs a postcolonial vision similar to the one that Scott describes James using to teach his readers. Caribbean diasporic texts offer a historical vision that makes the past relevant to the present by teaching a specific mode of reading rather than solely historical facts. This vision is not utopic regarding resistance and revolution—an element that academic criticism often glosses over in order to assert a set of reifying values and unequivocally portray the writer as a model political activist.

Diasporic historical fiction incorporates romance and tragedy as modes of reading and historicizing. Scott defines these genres in the process of summarizing disciplinary forms of historical narration and roots his theorization in Hayden White's concept of "emplotment," which refers to how "a number of temporally connected events are constituted into a narrative such that readers recognize it to be a particular kind of story" (46). Scott associates romance with the emplotment of an anticolonial vision of history, and tragedy as the postcolonial mode of narrating historical events. As Donette Francis in *Fictions of Feminine Citizenship* (2010) points out, Scott's strict demarcation between these genres and his privileging of tragedy over romance as a mode of contemporary historiography are encoded by gender. Francis notes that such historiographies "occlude women and others not invested in a story that charts a linear anticolonial progression culminating in disappointment with the failed promises of romance" (144). While implicitly dismissing the contemporary relevance of romance as a feminine genre, Scott constructs a teleology of anticolonial romance giving way to a more rational or realistic postcolonial tragedy. Keeping this critique of Scott in mind, I explore in this book how the Caribbean diasporic texts that I analyze operate with a postcolonial vision of history but also alternate between these two genres to address different aspects of the past that are relevant to the present, the romantic anticolonial hope for a utopian future and the tragic postcolonial nightmare of the present. As a result, multiple tensions remain at the heart of the historical vision that Caribbean diasporic writers seek to impart to their audience. The historical fiction adopts a tragic perspective on the present's fulfillment of those anticolonial goals (for example, the exoticizing multicultural market co-optation of the civil rights movement's discourse on diversity and equality) and wants to emphasize the reader's complicity with those co-opting forces. However, a profound nostalgia for anticolonial narratives of possibility, which prescribe a romantic overcoming of oppression, also drives the historical vision of the novels. Each Caribbean diasporic writer navigates this tension in different ways, but the aesthetic and ethical project of teaching the reader consistently contains elements of both the romantic and the tragic. Additionally, the historical fiction tackles the gendered associations of these historical periods with the genres of romance and tragedy, recognizing how nationalist discourses about history and progress exclude and marginalize certain knowledges and bodies. The second half of this book will address how writers employ the genres of romance and tragedy in historical fiction, with authors such as Dionne Brand, Ana Menéndez, and Monique Roffey deconstructing the sexual and gendered parameters of the anticolonial revolutionary in the Caribbean while Junot Díaz and Edwidge Danticat tackle the (hetero)sexist legacies of dictatorship in the Dominican Republic and Haiti.

Self-Conscious Ethical Strategies

The ethical tension between romantic and tragic modes of narrating and reading history is a product of a writerly strategy of self-consciousness. Scott suggests that the ethical mode of postcolonial historical criticism is informed by the present failure to fulfill the promise of anticolonial projects, and critics must address how that discontent with the postcolonial present guides them to evaluate specific historical events in the past. Understanding the ends to which the past is deployed depends upon a self-consciousness about the present condition and how it informs the gaze into the past: "The question the past is called upon to answer is self-consciously shaped by the discontent in the present it seeks to change" (22). This implied ethic of self-consciousness for scholars can also be found in multicultural studies; Jeff Karem's *The Romance of Authenticity* (2004) sets up a specific conceptual solution to the valorization of authenticity in US ethnic literature. Karem quotes Stuart Hall regarding the impossibility of escaping representational demands and argues that even if those demands cannot be dissolved or avoided, it is "possible to be more self-conscious about representation and our use of that term, to recognize what kind of representative work is being asked of authors and their texts" (207). Karem's tactic of self-consciousness, like Scott's, is intended to address a disciplinary problem, this time found in literary studies rather than history. Karem localizes disciplinary work at the intersection of the classroom and the book market, and the strategy of self-consciousness addresses problematic reading practices and offers a more ethical vision of ethnic literature. In the classroom it is "especially important for teachers to be self-conscious about representation because their students are often quite eager to join in this economy of authenticity, seeking marginal texts (sometimes with the best intentions, sometimes not) as a way to gain authoritative knowledge of an 'other' group" (208). Karem distances student practices from intent, so that the implied ethical approach to such decontextualized reading lenses is to respond with a hyperawareness of the teacher's role in shaping representational values. The strategy of self-consciousness is framed as an oppositional engagement with the market: "If scholars and teachers refuse to be self-conscious about cultural representation and the marketplace, we will have to concede to publishers the powerful role of shaping what multiculturalism means to this country and what will be taken as 'authentic' representatives of our nation's cultural margins" (209). The danger of complicity with the market is the flip side of the self-conscious academic ethic.[8] Gayatri Chakravorty Spivak makes a similar call for "vigilance" in *A Critique of Postcolonial Reason*, asking scholars to perform a "persistent taking of distance" that is "out of step with total involvement," since making "any bigger claim" (like that of activism, perhaps) "within the academic enclosure is a trick" (363). Spivak argues that the academic must recognize that he or she is positioned within "'cultural work' niches" that delimit the potential for changing global inequalities but that also permit scholars to "supplement the globe-girdling movements with 'mainstreaming,' somewhere between moonlighting and educating public opinion" (379). A crisis of authority in the humanities informs academic work, with scholars anxiously self-aware of their liberatory potential as educators as well as the disciplinary boundaries that restrict their ability to shape public discourse.

The disciplinary articulation of the scholarly role is akin to how Caribbean diasporic writers inscribe an ethical historical vision in their novels. An aesthetic of self-consciousness permeates the structure and emplotment of these Caribbean diasporic fictions that is articulated in terms of a narrative self-referentiality. In depictions of author- and/or reader-doubles, central characters engage in the practices of reading, writing, and teaching in ways that mirror the novels' imagined relationship with their readers. For instance, Julia Alvarez's *In the Name of Salomé* opens by depicting its classroom reader in the figure of a college student organizing Camila's family papers. In some ways this self-referentiality is used to offer models of ethical reading practices; in other instances the self-consciousness expresses concerns about potential obstacles to those ethical relationships. Regardless of which aspect the narrative highlights, Caribbean diasporic historical fiction consistently exhibits a self-awareness about its ethical project, displayed via its structure, narration, and/or symbolic content. The struggle of narrating an ethical historical vision and transmitting it to the reader is self-consciously embedded in the Caribbean diasporic historical novel through the depiction of author- and reader-doubles.

The self-consciousness of the historical fiction and its author/reader-doubles translates into an evolution or a fragmentation of voice in the novels. In Marlon James's *The Book of Night Women* and Junot Díaz's *Oscar Wao*, the narrator's identity is not immediately revealed: in James's novel a first-person voice opens and closes the novel while the body of the narrative is in the third person, and in *Oscar Wao* the narrative voice is nameless until halfway through the novel when Yunior is revealed as the narrator. These delays can lead the reader to doubt the trustworthiness of the narrator, in this case Lovey or Yunior, who is mediating our encounter with the story of another character, Lilith or Oscar. Structurally, the novels often alternate between different voices. The dialogue between various viewpoints fosters a comparative analysis, evaluating whether these historical perspectives are compatible or irreconcilable. This stylistic tactic encourages the reader to compare and contrast the postcolonial present to an anticolonial past; for instance, Monique Roffey's *The White Woman on the Green Bicycle* shifts between an omniscient third-person perspective on contemporary Trinidad and Sabine's first-person voice in letters written to Eric Williams during his rise to power, while the first-person voice in Ana Menéndez's *Loving Che* moves between Teresa's memories of the Cuban Revolution and her nameless daughter's journey to Special Period Cuba. The encoding of voice facilitates the novels' intersection of public history with private intimacies and symbolically references how the reader's market context informs his or her encounter with Caribbean histories and identities.

Impossible Intimacies, (En)Gendering Ethical Utopias

Caribbean diasporic writing articulates the challenge to its ethical and pedagogical imperative in terms of the irreconcilability of gender and sexuality. When I began analyzing the historical novels in a comparative manner, in particular pairing Julia Alvarez and Michelle Cliff together, I kept wondering how and why sexuality fit into the question of diasporic market aesthetics and its pedagogical, ethical impulse. Why were Alvarez and Cliff writing about these women? What did I make of the odd symbolic coincidences between the novels (cemeteries and gravestones, teachers and classrooms)? Did it matter that these historical figures were being framed as closeted lesbians? How so? While researching pedagogical practices, I was struck by a quote from Spivak's *Outside the Teaching Machine* (1993): "For Irigaray, sexual *difference* is the limit to ethics" (165). The significance of this sentence for me had less to do with Spivak's assessment of Irigaray than with understanding what challenge gender and sexuality pose for the diasporic project of historical fiction. Spivak frames the ethical challenge in terms of a teachable moment: "The hardest lesson is the impossible intimacy of the ethical" (171). The ethical relationship that Caribbean diasporic writers strive to build with imagined readerships is one that requires a certain intimacy that is impossible. The ethical project is challenged by the impossibility of understanding the reader, the impossibility of closeness to the reader, so that an ethical relationship is being pursued and foreclosed by the impossibility of knowing this Other, the reader. It is a necessary ethical impossibility that the narratives accept; after all, that type of invasive understanding is what the novels see as a dangerous by-product of multiculturalist market demands. Yet intimacy seems necessary for building a genuine ethical relationship between text and reader, in order to avoid stereotypes and simplistic cultural translation.

The novels rely on a symbolic rhetoric that addresses this problematic of intimacy and ethics by focusing on how gender and sexuality represent sites of contestation in the formulation of a Caribbean diasporic identity and history. This symbolism explains, for example, why Junot Díaz's narrator in *Oscar Wao* frames the reader as toto or "pussy." Meanwhile, Ana Menéndez's *Loving Che* and Dionne Brand's *In Another Place, Not Here* imagine sexual intimacy as central to anticolonial rhetoric. Gender and sexuality are the dominant metaphors for the conflict of intimacy and ethics within Caribbean diasporic writing. Locating the allegory of sexuality within Caribbean studies helps explain why diasporic writers use it to articulate the threat posed by globalization and market pressures. Caribbean studies approaches to gender and sexuality provide a model for interpreting the centrality of these tropes within the market aesthetics of historical novels by Caribbean diasporic writers. The queer equation of sexual desire with the threat of readerly intimacy within Caribbean diasporic historical fiction is specific to a Caribbean imaginary. Rosamond King and Vanessa Agard-Jones offer a set of conceptual approaches that contextualize the imaginative processing of globalization's mixed blessing in relation to Caribbean queer embodiment. The writers depict and deploy sexuality as the site of (in)visibility, the open secret of Caribbean history.

In *Island Bodies* (2014), Rosamond King localizes el secreto abierto or the open secret of sexuality within a Caribbean context. She explains el secreto abierto as a "situation in which many people 'know' someone is a homosexual though the fact is not openly acknowledged" and in which this shared information is such that "people 'know' the 'secret' without being told, through any combination of factors such as behaviors, speech, or dress" (64). The rhetoric of sexuality within the market aesthetics follows this logic of el secreto abierto, asserting the vulnerability of the Caribbean subject within the marketplace by following the circumscribed mandate for queer sexualities within the Caribbean. King notes that, "instead of a mandate of constant revelation, in Cariglobal communities there is a mandate of discretion, which is not (always) the same as hiding" (64). Rather, "the 'secret' is not fully hidden, and thus explicit revelation is not necessary and could, in fact, be redundant" (64). The mechanism of el secreto abierto delimits the metaphor of intimacy within Caribbean diasporic market aesthetics, the queer implications of which are both evident and obscure. A Caribbean cultural context generates the imagining of an encounter between reader and text in terms of sexuality and accentuates key vulnerabilities of market circulation. The mandate of el secreto abierto entails a tension between knowing and not knowing that speaks to the delicate balance that the historical novel strives to maintain with its ethical imperative: educating the audience about Caribbean history but resisting the readerly impulses to access and categorize Caribbean interiority. The market aesthetics of Caribbean diasporic historical fiction translates the paradox of globalization and market access into the "seeming paradox of unofficial-official policies towards sexuality [that] exists throughout the Caribbean" that allow one "to 'know without knowing,' without acknowledging knowledge of another's sexuality" (72). The contradiction of el secreto abierto with regard to knowledge evokes the market conditions of positionality, the emotional stakes behind intimacy with the reader and the potential for both betrayal and transformation.

Sexuality is consistently deployed in imagining the impossible intimacy with the reader, in part because the logic of el secreto abierto references a danger or threat to the ethical integrity of the pedagogical project. As King notes, "Another component of el secreto abierto is that it requires the community's complicity" in the sense that "the 'secret' is both known and (relatively) tolerated by those around the individual" (64). The provisional tolerance of el secreto abierto indicates the tenuous public acceptance of sexual minorities and the potential danger behind a more visible expression of queer identity. The market aesthetics of Caribbean diasporic historical fiction facilitate the complicity necessary for el secreto abierto, depicting its readership via the tense negotiation of intimacy while limiting the visibility of the sexual metaphor's deployment. The writerly anxiety over collusion with dominant structures of oppression versus a responsibility to ethically depicting a marginalized population finds its expression via the sexual metaphor. Here, "exploring el secreto abierto's mechanisms and structure" might not provide "insight into how sexual minorities [. . .] live and love in Caribbean communities," but instead Caribbean diasporic market aesthetics might display layers of rhetorical engagement with a local historical context of sexuality (64).

The question remains whether the way that market aesthetics engages sexuality as a metaphor forms part of an ethical approach to depicting the contemporary historical context of queer identity in Caribbean and diasporic communities. For King, the market aesthetics of Caribbean diasporic historical fiction would probably remind her of the way that "Caribbean literature usually treats trans characters as not fully human (or as somewhat more than human) tools in service of 'normal' men and women who *are* fully human, complete with limits *and* flaws" (25). The visibility of queer sexualities within the historical novels I discuss varies, from Junot Díaz's depiction of Oscar's violent silencing to Julia Alvarez's treatment of Camila as a closeted woman-desiring woman to Dionne Brand's imagining of Elizete as a sexual queer woman. However, the deployment of sexuality as *metaphor* within the market aesthetics of the historical fiction is a strategy that does appear, to borrow King's terminology, "backhanded" (25). King argues that, "on the surface, portraying trans people as having special insight and abilities to help others may seem positive—because it places them in a position of power and shows them using that power to benefit others" (25). However, as she convincingly shows, "The deliverance is backhanded because Caribbean trans characters are also consistently kept on the margins of the texts and are deprived of their own individuality" (25). The historical fiction does depict queer characters as flawed subjects, as evidenced by Levy's Faith, *Soucouyant*'s brother, Alvarez's Camila, Cliff's Annie, James's Lovey, Brand's Verlia, and Díaz's Oscar. By distinguishing the representation of queer subjectivities from the rhetorical deployment of queer metaphors, sexuality and queer intimacy operate as floating signifiers within Caribbean diasporic market aesthetics, as "devices used to flesh out" and articulate the market-based threats posed to the novels' pedagogical imperative (39). The articulation of intimacy with market aesthetics can be seen as accepting queer sexualities "as part of Caribbean culture but [doing] so in a backhanded maneuver" (25). However, queerness remains central to the imagination of the historical novels rather than "marginal" (25). The market aesthetics of Caribbean diasporic historical fiction is fundamentally compromised at the inception of its imaginary, fractured by its dependence upon sexuality as the rhetorical expression of the conditions by which it enters a commodifying marketplace as a product of historical memory.

A more generous reading of market aesthetics might imagine how the metaphor of sexuality, despite or because of its deployment, could be reinvested with some productive meaning. Vanessa Agard-Jones examines the metaphor of sand as an alternative to the trope of water within academic discourse about Caribbean identity. She makes the case that the image of sand as sediment can facilitate another way of seeing "the repository of memory," one that can allow for an engagement "with more fine-grained and ephemeral presences than our usual archives would allow" (340). This rhetorical shift is especially important for locating "an unstable, atomized archive of queer relation" (331). Using the example of how Martinican public discourse employed the metaphor of Sodom following the 1902 explosion of Mount Pelée, Agard-Jones asks, "How might the image of Sodom have stood in for a range of things that could not be said or that could not have been spoken directly into the archive? Looked at differently, what traces might this image help us reveal?" (33). Because the historical record will not address el secreto abierto of queer sexuality in the Caribbean, the recuperative move to reread the archive must look at how marginalized sexualities are rhetorically encoded or indirectly articulated. Agard-Jones reads the invocation of Sodom as "a nod toward a mountain of things that could not be referenced directly," particularly to el secreto abierto of "same-sex desire [and] other modes of nonnormative relation and gender transgression" (330). In the market aesthetics of Caribbean diasporic historical fiction, the invocation of sexuality is a defining element that references the fiction's locality and contemporary context. The genre of historical fiction takes the archive to task for what it says and does not say about Caribbean populations. As Agard-Jones notes, "Fiction captures something that social science often cannot. It moves beyond what can be readily observed, measured, and tabulated to more ephemeral phenomena that empirical methods often fail to capture" (331). Is it possible to see how the metaphor of sexual intimacy productively contains "trace[s] of queer relationality" (332) that are part and parcel of the historical novels' ethical imperative? Perhaps, but it is also possible that decoding the ephemeral traces of resistance runs against the grain of cultural texts that are emphatic about their compromised ethical mission. The rhetorical project that articulates the fragility of the ethical imperative and the rhetorical project at least can be said to concur that "sexual *difference* is the limit to ethics" (Spivak, *Outside the Teaching Machine* 165).

The ethical project of diasporic historical fiction may be best summed up as depicting the discursive problem-space that its ethical project of historical revision encounters. In the essay "Global Minoritarian Culture" (2007), Homi Bhabha discusses the work of W. E. B. Du Bois in order to argue that the "burden of minoritarian 'message' is not merely the demand for respect or recognition of cultural or political differences"; rather, "this very aesthetic act of communication or narration is also an ethical practice" (191). An ethical practice of historiography may be judged an impossible task by Caribbean diasporic writers, but by combining the strategies of a postcolonial vision and a self-conscious ethics the project of narration becomes conceived solely as one of representation. Transformation or resistance is not an achievable goal, but the aesthetic work of representation provides an entry into *imagining* what a debate about the merit of such tactics might look like. While I will not go as far as Bhabha to declare that "the responsibility of the minoritarian agent lies in creating a world-open forum of communication" (191), I would argue that these Caribbean diasporic writers are using historical fiction as a genre and engaging the market as global public sphere to lay bare the contemporary problematics of enunciation for minority, Caribbean, and postcolonial writers. Those writers wrestle with the ethical responsibilities that are placed upon them and that they assume *in order to* narrate counterhistories within a global market. Caribbean diasporic fiction seeks to promote an ethical reading of the past, self-consciously setting up its historical lens as exemplary, but then uses narrative conflicts over gender and sexuality as the representational means by which to also admit the impossibility of transforming the reader into the ideal ethical subject.

The remaining chapters 2 through 5 are organized according to a comparative approach to the Caribbean diaspora. The comparative scope of this book reveals how the genre of Caribbean diasporic historical fiction encompasses writers located in the Global North nations of the United States, Canada, and Britain who are of anglophone, francophone, and hispanophone Caribbean backgrounds. By employing an approach of "transcolonial comparativism," I aim to tease out the implications of historical fiction as an emerging trend within Caribbean diasporic writing.[9] Chapters 2 and 3 draw attention to the two modes of historical revision that Caribbean diasporic writers use to respond to the contemporary problematic of decontextualization. I identify Andrea Levy and David Chariandy as writers in the first mode who depict decontextualization as constitutive of the diasporic identity, historicizing history's absence by revealing it to be a product of market multiculturalism. Alternately, I situate Julia Alvarez, Michelle Cliff, and Marlon James as part of the second approach to decontextualization that instead focuses its energies on "filling in" the gap of history by depicting specific pasts and historical figures as relevant to understanding the present condition of the diaspora. The second half of the book continues to address historical novels that employ both approaches, historicizing the diaspora in the Global North and the Caribbean nation-past, but narrows down to two historical contexts inspiring the work of Caribbean diasporic writers. While I give Dionne Brand, Ana Menéndez, and Michelle Roffey as examples of writers who focus on the anticolonial period and Junot Díaz and Edwidge Danticat as authors who highlight the nationalist legacy of dictatorship, these writers employ similar codes of ethics and intimacy to depict the effects of these historical contexts on the diaspora. The book's conclusion expands the discussion of market aesthetics to reflect on how the digital revolution is shaping Caribbean diasporic writing with the development of online communities, paratexts, and archives, particularly in relation to the work of Junot Díaz and Robert Antoni.

2 Kinship Routes

Contextualizing Diaspora via the Market in Andrea Levy and David Chariandy

THE MAINSTREAMING OF MULTICULTURALISM is an important context for understanding the market aesthetics of Caribbean diasporic historical fiction, particularly in terms of public policies intended to contain the perceived threats of ethnic communities (for example, the 1981 British Nationality Act or the 1988 Canadian Multiculturalism Act). Caribbean diasporic historical novels often contextualize the diasporic community as an ethnic minority within Britain, Canada, or the United States by depicting the effects of multiculturalism's co-optation. In chapter 1, I referred to this pedagogical approach as historicizing the ahistorical, where the novels depict how the discourse of multiculturalism erases the histories of colonialism and empire that have prompted the immigration of Caribbean populations to the Global North. One trend within this approach is exemplified by novels that structurally mimic the amnesiac condition of the public sphere while identifying key historical moments in the diasporas' decontextualization as ethnic minorities. Some of the most critically popular historical novels in this regard are Zadie Smith's *White Teeth* (2000) and Junot Díaz's *Oscar Wao* (2007). I discuss Díaz's novel and its reception in chapter 5 and the Conclusion, but I offer here my reading of historical fiction that has received less critical attention. Andrea Levy's *Fruit of the Lemon* (1999) and David Chariandy's *Soucouyant* (2007) articulate a Caribbean diasporic market aesthetics by encoding the silences of decontextualization within their stylistic structure. The novels encourage the reader to adopt the perspective of the first-person narrator and to embark on a search for silenced histories about the character's family and diasporic community. The protagonist's journey from reader-double to author-double marks the aspirations of the novel's postcolonial imperative to transform the reader into an ethical subject as he or she engages with Caribbean histories.

Set in the 1980s, *Fruit of the Lemon* and *Soucouyant* identify market multiculturalism as a productive and destructive historical context informing diasporic identity in Canada and Britain. The identity crises of the diasporic narrators are credited to their alienation from Caribbean and Global North histories. At first, Levy's Faith and Chariandy's unnamed narrator stand in for the reader's ignorance of historical contexts, and the audience is invited to experience the disorientation of the narrator, encountering a story that at first refuses any historical referent. The narrators transform into author-doubles, acting as first-person storytellers as they collect the fragments of history in an effort to reroot themselves into a specific Caribbean diasporic identity and history. The narrators' evolution from decontextualization to cultural belonging is patterned after familial models for acculturation, Faith's cousin Constance/Afria and the unnamed narrator's brother, respectively. These family members exercise strategies of consumer citizenship, performing as foils that teach the narrators how to navigate diasporic existence. The narrators acquire a set of historical contexts by consuming commodities and reimagining belonging through consumer citizenship. Bookstores and street graffiti are central images of the novels' market aesthetics that symbolize the benefits and pitfalls of entering the literary marketplace.

The difficulty of imagining ethical interactions within the context of market multiculturalism challenges interfamily dynamics. Faith's cousin and the *Soucouyant* narrator's brother are templates for ambivalent intimate encounters with consumerism. Constance/Afria and the brother turn to the market for an alternate definition of diasporic belonging, developing a new political consciousness. However, the commodification of civil rights discourses that valorize ethnic beauty and community solidarity, like that of Black Power movements, does not ultimately resolve the marginalization of these characters. The reader/author-doubles are haunted by the figures of Constance/Afria and the brother, who were either left out or awkwardly integrated into the market as a space of belonging. Family relations become emblematic of the vulnerabilities produced when one is constructing an identity via consumerism. Blood ties expose Faith and *Soucouyant*'s narrator to the dangers their family members encounter: of being "known" and stereotyped. The specter of sexual intimacy as a symbol of market perils haunts the margins of these relationships, as Faith and the narrator attempt to ethically interact with their peers while disidentifying with the conclusions that their cautionary lessons teach about market-based identities. Intimate knowledge and sexuality are more explicitly aligned with the effects of globalization and market multiculturalism in chapter 2's discussion of Julia Alvarez, Michelle Cliff, and Marlon James.

A Diasporic Tourist's Recovery of Roots: Andrea Levy's *Fruit of the Lemon*

Andrea Levy's *Fruit of the Lemon* is an unusual historical novel in terms of its relationship to the emplotment of history. Levy's novel takes as its subject the historically specific dilemma of belonging faced by the Afro-Caribbean diaspora in Britain during the 1980s but opens with no explicit sense of this historical time frame. The nuclear family tree image at the start of the 1999 British edition of the novel contains no birth date information, and the Jackson family is not overtly associated with the Windrush generation of immigrants to Britain.[1] This lack of explicit historical contextualization leads a critic to remark that "the novel is primarily concerned with coming to terms with [Faith's] individual sense of identity rather than the wider social and political contexts of racism and gender discrimination."[2] Such a reading speaks to how effectively the novel's market aesthetics simulates the decontextualization of ethnic minority populations within the British public sphere. I connect the novel's social commentary to the ways in which the fragmentation of the narrative's structure and descriptive gaps in the plot reference decontextualization as a historical context. My approach resembles that of Michael Perfect, who adopts Said's theory of the contrapuntal to analyze *Fruit of the Lemon*. He explains that "to read a text contrapuntally is to pay attention to its silences, with an exploration of what is *not* said allowing us to uncover histories and experiences that are concealed by (and yet in an interdependent relationship with) its dominant voices(s)" (32). Moving beyond encoding silences, the market aesthetics of *Fruit of the Lemon* provides the reader with a mode of contextualizing what is not said or is erased from dominant narratives of European and Caribbean history. After commenting on the reception of the novel, I analyze Part I and its depiction of British society, primarily the structures that lead to Faith's nervous breakdown. I then read how Part II signifies Faith's recuperation in Jamaica in terms of contextualization and nostalgia. I offer the character of Constance/Afria as a paradigm for Faith's formulation of her Afro-Caribbean identity, which is informed by a market-driven context.

The novel connects the development of its main character, Faith, to an identifiable historical context via markers of popular culture, such as the movies and TV shows that the characters watch or the music that they listen to. Blaxploitation movies such as *Shaft* (1971) or *Superfly* (1972), comments made regarding Margaret Thatcher (1979–90), and Faith's mention of Lady Di as part of the royal family (1981) give the reader the sense that the novel is set sometime during the 1980s. By engaging and disengaging from British culture during Part I, *Fruit of the Lemon* references the contemporary decontextualization of the public sphere while locating commodities as an alternate source of identification. The reader must engage in the same process of contextualization via popular culture and commodities that Faith eventually embraces. The second half of the novel is set in Jamaica, where Faith goes to recuperate a historically specific nostalgia, to "hear her family history, a saga inseparable from colonialism, stretching back to Cuba, Panama, Harlem and Scotland" (Prasad T4). Faith is transformed from reader-double to author-double, with nostalgia facilitating the acquisition of an intimate and relationary historical context via commodities.

Fruit of the Lemon links the identity crisis of the main character, Faith, to globalization's workings and the co-optation of multiculturalism. The novel portrays a British society where consumer multiculturalism does not translate into racial tolerance but rather creates a regime of color blindness that disguises the contexts of colonialism and racism. As Weihsin Gui points out, Levy's novel forms part of "a literary response by postcolonial and Black British writers" to the "Thatcher government's increased attention to national heritage" and the "1980 and 1983 Heritage Acts" (74). I position *Fruit of the Lemon* as Caribbean diasporic historical fiction in order to argue that Levy is responsive to more than the context of British racial politics: the historical fiction of Levy and Chariandy depicts transatlantic parallels that locate the 1980s as a pivotal historical moment for diasporic identity. The public discourse about multiculturalism in Britain and Canada is shown to rely upon institutional racism and violence—not just the physical violence of hate crimes but also the psychic violence of decontextualization. For instance, Gui analyzes the attack on the black bookstore owner Yemi in *Fruit of the Lemon* as an allusion to the "infamous 1968 'rivers of blood' speech by Enoch Powell and the 1993 death of Stephen Lawrence" (82).

In an essay published in the *Guardian* a year after *Fruit of the Lemon*, Levy declares, "I hate being English when I hear what happened to Stephen Lawrence" because "every day seems like a battle against racism, and hatred, and the quiet, polite hostility that holds many black and Asian people back from fulfilling their potential" ("This Is My England," par. 30). Levy's concern for the more muted but no less damaging effects of racism is evident in the way that her historical novel ties racist attacks like the one on Yemi to a systemic decontextualization of British culture and society. Levy notes in her essay that people "blame the multi-cultural nature of England for the country's plight" (par. 28), often ignoring that this diversity was a product of "old Empire coming home to Mother Country" (par. 17). The character of Faith begins as a double for this readership ignorant of the historical legacy of empire. Faith reaches her full potential when she shifts from understanding herself as an isolated ethnic minority to understanding herself as a historicized Caribbean diasporic subject. This self-conscious journey toward accumulating context is symbolic of Levy's hope that "the vitality of multi-culturalism is the catalyst that is speeding up a necessary period of soul searching" following the realization that "Empire is over" (par. 28). Faith's soul-searching is posited as an aspirational model for the reader's ethical transformation. The structure of the novel, with Part I set in Britain and Part II set in Jamaica, proposes historical contextualization and consumer citizenship as ways of mitigating destructive sociopolitical forces. Faith's travel to Jamaica is a traversal of geographic space that enables a shift from rootlessness to belonging through the accumulation of a combined context of history and commodities. Faith constructs a Caribbean diasporic identity via the nostalgic acquisition of a historical context that is maintained by commodities. The novel ambivalently figures the global market as a space that opens and closes avenues for cultural and political consciousness. The workings of market multiculturalism lead to Faith's emotional breakdown, but it is through a combination of consumer citizenship and family history that Faith is able to formulate an Afro-Caribbean and Black British subjectivity.

Faith Jackson, the novel's protagonist, is born and raised in a London filled with rhetorical silences. These silences are both gaps in Faith's family history and violent abjections of colonial history in the public sphere. The novel represents the gaps of familial and public contexts as refusals of social recognition that have destructive effects on social interactions in the novel, contributing to Faith's identity crisis. The novel's preface opens with a first-person narration of a childhood memory, which recalls a racist playground taunt: "Faith is a darkie and her mum and dad came on a banana boat" (3). Faith's voice, by contrast, avoids racial markers while recounting the incident. The perpetrators of this harassment are described in detail with only oblique references to race: they were "boys with unruly hair, short trousers and dimpled knees that went bright red in the cold" (3). Since Faith is unable to respond verbally to these taunts, her friends fill in Faith's silence by rejecting outright the narrative of her parents' banana boat passage: "Oh no they never. Leave her alone" (3). This childhood memory signals the decontextualization of the Black British community; the children in the playground access the image of the banana boat as symbol of Caribbean migration but have no sense of the socioeconomic forces motivating such migrations. The banana boat is appropriated and resignified as a derogatory insult, one that highlights Faith's racial difference in order to tell her that she does not belong.

Following her decontextualization in the schoolyard, it is disconcerting for Faith when her mother does not dispute the accuracy of the banana boat as symbol for her Caribbean origins: "It was a bit of a shock when Mum told me, 'We came on a banana boat to England, your dad and me'" (3). Upon hearing this, Faith remarks, "The little white boys were right," for the first time defining them by their race (3). Faith connects the authority of the boys to their racial identity and accepts their stereotypy. Although her mother explains that it was a "proper boat with cabins and everything," Faith pictures her parents "curled up on the floor of a ship, [. . .] trying to find a comfortable spot amongst the spiky prongs of unripe bananas" (4). Faith's banana boat image of her parents is derived from the "illustrations of slave ships from my history lessons" (4). The school assignments coldly calculate the system's workings without any sense of human suffering: "We had to write essays telling the facts—how the slaves were captured then transported from Africa to the New World" and "draw diagrams of how the triangular trade in slaves worked, like we drew diagrams of sheep farming in Australia" (4). In narrating the history of slavery, the educational system erases the enslaved person's humanity and reinscribes the system's violence by equating the slaves with livestock. Without any mention of subjectivity and emotion, the lessons reduce the experience of slavery to "the facts" of geography and movement. The historiographic tone, particularly on the grounds of sentiment, references market reception and readership. The positive reception of Levy's previous novels emphasizes the "assured economy" (Foster 38) and "unsentimental" (Blake 37; Reid 17) "restraint" of her writing (Foster 38; Crampton WE/13). The market aesthetics of *Fruit of the Lemon* criticizes objectivity and restraint as modes for narrating history. The novel signals such language as code for a cultural nationalism that defines Britishness as ethnically homogeneous. Faith interprets the lack of sentiment in her history lessons as another layer of racist invective: "Although there were no small boys laughing and pointing, I felt them. 'Your mum and dad came on a slave ship,' they would say. 'They were slaves'" (4). The context of enslavement invalidates Faith's claims to Britishness, just as the emphasis on Levy's unsentimental economy of earlier writings reassures readers of her Britishness, her ability to depict British society without being excessively influenced by her otherness.

Faith connects the boys' racist taunts to her school history lessons but does not contest her contextualization as a Black British child; she is ashamed to be associated with slavery's victimization and cannot formulate an oppositional narrative of community. In Chariandy's novel, education is also a repressive institution that decontextualizes Caribbean diasporic identity, situating ethnic minorities as a threat to the Global North nation-state. Such depictions of the classroom play a role in the market aesthetics of the historical fiction, referencing a student reader. In *Fruit of the Lemon*, the violence of historical erasure in the public spaces of the schoolyard and classroom is compounded by the absence of an intimate, personal context that can offer a different foundation for identity construction. Faith remarks that "there was no 'oral tradition' in our family" (4). Since "mum and dad never talked about their lives before my brother Carl and I were born" (4), the reasons for the parents' migration to Britain from the Caribbean are inaccessible to Faith. Even Faith's desire to know about her parents' past is actively discouraged: "Most of my childhood questions to them were answered with 'That was a long time ago,' or 'What you want to know about that for?'" (4). Such stonewalling is not ultimately sustainable, and when small admissions of the past are made, they are treated as private secrets that cannot enter the public realm: "If Mum ever let something slip— 'You know your dad lived in a big house,'—then I was told with a wagging finger not to go blabbing it about to my friends, not to repeat it to anyone" (4). Faith's mother hints that any public revelation of a family past is dangerous, highlighting the Jackson family's vulnerability within British society. For Faith's mother, familial historical narratives must remain in the personal realm because their circulation into the public could imperil Faith and her family. It remains unclear, however, what are the risks or sources of danger. Her truncated explanation about the consequences of letting a family story circulate in the British public sphere is an example of the novel's market aesthetics and the logic of el secreto abierto, which I discussed in chapter 1. The historical fiction enacts the revelation that Faith's mother warns against, narrating an intimate picture of a Caribbean diasporic woman's struggle to belong in British society. The unspeakable danger that her mother refers to becomes more fully articulated later on in the novel, when it depicts the marketplace as consuming ethnicity.

While her mother's secretive strategy aims to protect the family, one unintended result is that Faith sees herself as unmoored from any Caribbean past and increasingly anxious regarding her place within contemporary British society. To make sense of the "little scraps of [her mother's] past," Faith must fill in the gaps with her own fictions, "like a game of Consequences I used to play as a child—fold the paper and pass it on—until I had a story that seemed to make sense" (4–5). In comparison to the public narratives of history, this family story is tenuously positioned not only because of its dependence on orality rather than documentation but also because of the serious gaps of relation within that family story. Faith must imagine how the information obtained through the revelation of these small intimacies can create a web of meaning, but she can only reach a point where the story *seems* to make sense. Her parents' unexpected announcement about their plans to leave England and retire in Jamaica calls into question Faith's confidence regarding her basic understanding of her family. Even though she realizes that "my parents had come from there" and "we had relations there," Faith believes that "what Mum and Dad really loved was snow and cold evenings" (45). Faith's parents try to allay her fears of being abandoned by giving her a new car and buying "their way out of bad feeling" (47). This effort to reroot Faith through consumerism fails because Faith cannot imagine a future of belonging outside her nuclear family. The parents' potential return to Jamaica disputes Faith's knowledge of her parents, challenging the intimacy of their bond, and she is unable to imagine an alternate source of relation by which to connect herself to a diasporic community.

The gaps in her family history mirror silences in the public sphere regarding British colonial legacies. As Michael Perfect points out, *Fruit of the Lemon* "highlights the importance of recognizing the complexities of imperial history in combating racism and prejudice in the contemporary postcolonial moment" (36). I would add that the novel reveals how colonialism is silenced as a context for understanding the contemporary structures of globalization and consumption. Separating the past from the present makes it possible for Faith's friend Simon to remark on how "they used to use ivory for these sort of portraits but you can't nowadays" (121). Although these colonial traces are evident, the novel sustains Simon's silence. No explanation is given for why ivory was used in "those days," or why that system of production is no longer possible. Faith's narrative in *Fruit of the Lemon* reproduces decontextualization to make it a visible silence. The lack of historical context connects the public realm to the personal sphere of the family. The novel represents these gaps as systemic, hinting that the unanswered question of how British society has been shaped by its colonial legacies is linked to the question of Faith's presence in that society—why and how did Faith's own Jamaican family arrive there?

Without an awareness of how public and personal histories are interconnected, the novel shows that Faith lacks the confidence to handle major challenges to her identity. The dearth of contextual knowledge prevents Faith from being able to counter the racism within the British public sphere, and her rootlessness produces a lack of self-consciousness. For example, when her father asks, "Your friends, any of them your own kind?" Faith is not "sure what he mean[s]" (28). Her father draws attention to Faith's lack of intimate ties with ethnic minorities in Britain and the importance of belonging to a diasporic community. Meanwhile, Faith displays an inability to imagine herself as a diasporic subject. Her rejection of racial stereotypes leads Faith to disassociate herself from all ethnic and cultural markers. Faith's confusion in response to her father's question reveals that she cannot read social interactions through any of these lenses. When her father clarifies his question, his tone alludes to his own discomfort with mentioning racial markers in public: "'I mean any of them . . . any of them . . . ' He looked around himself to see if anyone was listening and then whispered, 'Coloured?'" (29). Faith shares her father's feeling that an explicit discussion of racial and ethnic identity is dangerous. The father's transgression, of entering into such a vulnerable territory of discussion, pushes Faith to divulge how strongly she represses any sense of racial identity. Rather than engaging her father in conversation, Faith explains that "I didn't ask him to explain. I didn't ask him to finish what he was saying. I didn't want him to" (29). The public systems of erasure are so ingrained within Faith that she refuses to pursue a line of inquiry that would permit a new level of intimacy with her father, permitting her to relate to him as a member of the African diaspora. In doing so, she shuts down avenues for alternative modes of self-consciousness, racial awareness, and diasporic community.

Faith is not the only color-blind character in the novel. *Fruit of the Lemon* represents a British society that is predicated on the consumption of the Other, through the commodification of culture and ethnicity. Market multiculturalism does not engender racial tolerance and equality but instead establishes a regime of color blindness that conceals the racist logic organizing the public sphere. Color blindness and its insidious effects are evident during two pivotal moments in the novel. The first involves Faith's job market experiences and the second is a racist attack on Yemi, a Black British bookstore owner. When Faith obtains her first job, she is told that she is one of the "lucky ones," but this career achievement is explained in terms of her race: "My tutor decided that it was something to do with my being black and everyone else on the course being white" (31). While it may appear that this rationale is "color-conscious" rather than color-blind, it does not imply awareness regarding the function or context of race but reduces race to a market(able) category. Indeed, it is the market appeal of Faith's difference that the tutor interprets as the reason for Faith's success. She tells Faith that her "work has an ethnicity which shines through" and is "simply exciting" (31). Rather than considering the possibility that Faith "was just better than everyone else," the tutor persuades Faith to view the job offer as inspired by "some sort of collective unconscious that was coming through my slave ancestry" (31). The logic of "eating the other" erases Faith's creative authorship to highlight the market value of difference, vaguely formulated as having an "African or South American feel" (31).[3]

The tutor's explanation of the job offer from Olivia does not acknowledge Faith's agency or creative ability, but it does foreshadow the logic underlying Olivia's work practices. Olivia is depicted as a consumer of Other cultures; for instance, she wears an "upturned-multicoloured raffia bin on her head" (31). This appreciation for non-European fashion might be taken as an example of progressive open-mindedness and nonconformity; nevertheless, Olivia turns out to be a dishonest and manipulative employer. Faith finds out that Olivia intends to exploit her creative talents in a sweatshop-like environment. While Faith sits "on a stool in front of an old table loom" weaving new patterns for sample fabrics, Olivia "waft[s] about the room, chat[s] to her international clientele on the telephone," and claims Faith's hard work on the patterns by "stick[ing] them on little bits of card and call[ing] them her own" (32). The global nature of Olivia's business enables her to distribute her goods widely while never having to recognize Faith's creativity and labor. By having Faith produce her work at Olivia's home, Olivia owns the means of production and negates Faith's presence within that home space. Faith's isolation as a worker is evident when she comments that she has "no one else to talk to" and that Olivia never invites her on what could be egalitarian "tea breaks" (32). In the end, Faith is fired because she accidentally trespasses into Olivia's intimate space, an intrusion that forces Olivia to acknowledge the too-visible presence of her worker and decide that Faith is expendable: "I got to work early and caught Olivia standing by the door wearing a silk kimono, kissing a man. [. . .] As she turned around startled, her breast slipped out. I stared momentarily at her porcelain-white tit with its tiny pert pink nipple. [. . .] She, after suffering my mute sullenness for a week, packed a week's wages in a window envelope and sacked me" (32–33). Faith unwittingly oversteps the bounds of her role as worker inside this home-factory. She witnesses the unveiling of Olivia—this is the first and only moment in which Faith explicitly identifies Olivia's whiteness for the reader, via her exposed breast. Whiteness is the flip side to the color-blindness regime, the whiteness that defines otherness and difference, underlying the kimono, normally hidden from view. Faith's sullenness reveals her discomfort with recognizing the invisible privilege of whiteness; she remains mute, unable to articulate the power dynamics of race, cultural production, and the market. The specter of same-sex desire also looms at the edges of this momentary exposure, with Faith's detailed attention to Olivia's breast.[4] However, sexuality, like race, is another forbidden subject in Faith's world.

The color-blindness regime underscores difference while rendering whiteness invisible. Since linguistic markers of difference are limited to "black" or "coloured," Faith has no access to an alternate vocabulary by which to describe the privilege of whiteness. As Andrea Medovarski notes, "Faith is unable to fit herself into this racialization of nationality" (38). The problem of language is particularly evident when Faith decides to apply for a promotion at the BBC television center where she works. Recognizing that she is "wasted sticking labels into costumes," Faith wants to apply for a dresser position and "be on the studio floor— with the lights, the camera, the actors" (70). When Faith inquires about the procedures for such a promotion, her coworker Lorraine encourages her to apply with the caveat, "They don't have black dressers" (70). Lorraine's warning emphasizes the absence of Others in dressing positions, framing the presence of an Afro-Caribbean woman like Faith as an exception to the rule without actually voicing "the rule" in terms of whiteness. She comforts Faith by explaining that while the managers "didn't think the actors would like a coloured person putting their clothes on them," Faith's boss Henry pointed out a gap in their analysis: after all, "What if the actor was coloured?" (71). As Lorraine explains that "some of them are now on television," implying the exceptional presence of Black British actors, Faith's "hands beg[in] to shake" (71).

Despite the narrative's first-person format, Faith's interiority is not transparent to the reader. For example, the source of Faith's anger is never explicitly named, since she responds to the question "You're not upset are you, Faith?" by shrugging (71). Faith's inability to voice her indignation is a product of the color-blindness regime—to whom should she direct this anger, and what exactly is she angry about? The reader can only make an interpretive leap and guess. The reader's access to Faith's public behavior and speech does not translate into intimacy with Faith's inner thoughts—creating a parallel between Faith's difficulties reading the world around her and the reader's ability to interpret Faith. The managers and her coworkers make Faith aware of the racist rules of the workplace only to "put her in her place" and marginalize her. While Faith is encouraged to apply for the position anyway "because everybody likes" her, she is shocked into silence (71). Faith's narrative consistently avoids racial markers, and this conversation obliges her to face the way that they shape and limit her experience. Faith's self-censorship and color blindness are vulnerabilities because she cannot accurately read the power dynamics of such situations to navigate her way through or around them. Faith's denial of racist realities is so pervasive that the narrative consciousness only hints at her emotional condition by noting her physical gestures. The narrative aligns the reader with Faith, since we are also given only the surface level of social interactions, without entry to the depths of Faith's own self-consciousness.

The attack on Yemi, the bookstore owner, forces Faith and the reader to connect the rhetorical erasure of her racial identity to social violence, but the event is so traumatic that it leads to Faith's nervous breakdown. After attempting to help the bleeding woman back into her bookstore, Faith sees that the assault marks the woman's body and her lifework as well: "The shop had been sprayed with angry red paint. And all over it said NF, NF, NF. The red paint was over the walls—over the spines of books—arcing down the shelves and along faces on posters. [. . .] A swirling hate of NF NF NF Fuck Off" (151–52). At first Faith perceives the violence to be aimed at an individual, but the condition of the bookstore evokes a larger scope of racist hate: "A half-full bag of shit was splatted on the table—while the other half of its contents slid down the bookcase of gay and lesbian books. And the black and Third World fiction was spray-painted with 'Wog'" (152). The market aesthetics reference the threat that such texts pose to mainstream notions of British identity. This scene evokes the contemporaneous context of the violent reaction to Salman Rushdie's *The Satanic Verses* (1988), which

Paul Gilroy analyzes in *The Black Atlantic* (1993) as "the outcome of a
distinct historical period in which a new, ethnically absolute and cultur-
alist racism was produced" (10). Gilroy describes *cultural insiderism* as
the redefinition of racism by culture rather than biology. The new historical context of cultural insiderism "explain[s] the burning of books
on English streets as manifestations of irreducible cultural differences
that signposted the path to domestic racial catastrophe" (10). It is worth
noting that Muslim ethnic minorities composed the population burning
Rushdie's books and that the media's framing of them as undisciplined
and uncivilized outsiders to British society contributed to their othering
as well as that of Rushdie.

Rather than a book burning, Levy depicts the destruction of a bookstore as a market for selling multiethnic writing. The attack speaks to
the anxieties regarding the reception and readership of Caribbean diasporic fiction, particularly in terms of the ethical imperative. The racist
violence makes the pedagogical goal of reeducating a public seem dubious at best, considering that a group like the neo-Nazi National Front
is threatened by a mere visual incorporation of minority voices into the
British literary marketplace. The graffiti superimposes the National
Front's definition of what belongs in the space of the bookstore, the
bloody red paint symbolizing the violence of this corrective gesture.
The signature of "Fuck off" adopts the aggressive intimacy of sexual
profanity (152), emphasizing how this readerly vision dismisses literature that is deemed Other. The bookstore's market logic appears to
facilitate the homophobic and racist attack. The store's space is organized into discrete sections, with the "bookcase of gay and lesbian
books" alongside "the black and Third World" (152). The incorporation of ethnic and sexual minority voices into the marketplace seg-
regates them into essentialized categories, making it easy for the NF
gang to impose their destructive labels on the texts. The market aesthetics highlights the ghettoization of diasporic writing, offering the
disturbing translation of "the black and Third World" book category
into the racist invective of "Wog" (152). With a black woman as both
the bookstore owner and the victim of this attack, the novel alludes to
the positioning of Caribbean diasporic writers: engaging with the necessary evil of book market categories in order to ambivalently circulate
counternarratives of American, Canadian, Caribbean, and European
histories. The attack on the bookstore owner conflates the public men-
ace of literary representation with her individuality, marking Yemi as a
spokesperson of difference because of her black female body.

The bookstore's destruction initiates both Faith's depression and her transformation—indicating the ambivalent potential of the literary marketplace. Faith's previous coping mode of denial cannot function in this space of blatant racist and heterosexist violence. Her state of mind is signaled by the marking of her body. In picking up the phone to call emergency services, Faith notes that the phone "had a shaft of paint across it on its way to finishing the F" and as she places the receiver back down after making the phone call, her hand gets stuck (152). In order to remove herself, Faith has "to hold [the receiver] down with my other hand and pull it away with a force that left some of my skin behind" (152). The violence of Faith's physical movement signals the extent to which she wishes to separate herself, to not identify with this black woman, even as the horror of social violence is inscribed onto Faith's body.

The racist attack is not simply an accident, the work of some extremists. The violence mirrors a more subtle institutional racism, which quickly begins to marginalize the bookstore owner and mark the racist context as irrelevant. The police who arrive at the scene offer interpretations of the violence that either downplay the racist overtones of the attack by calling the assailants "just a bunch of thugs" or blaming the victim: "We've told them not to have people in the shop on their own. One woman like that on her own. I mean, they were just asking for trouble" (154). While these processes of erasure are occurring, Faith's identification with the woman moves her in the opposite direction, formulating the bookstore owner as an individual: "My head was hurting like it had come out in sympathy with Yemi. That was the woman's name, which I learnt from the ambulanceman shouting" (154). Faith rejects the dehumanization of the bookstore owner, reinforcing her named subjectivity as Yemi, while also finding that such a contextualizing move comes with its own consequences: identifying with Yemi as a fellow human being means Faith also feels her pain. Here the potential of empathy as a form of solidarity appears to be offset by the danger of intimacy, of being exposed to the same racist violence.

Faith finds herself alone in her empathy for Yemi when she returns to her house and hears her friend Simon retelling the story of the incident. Simon's interpretation excises the identity of Yemi and the racist motives for the attack. Faith tries to counter Simon's color blindness, repeatedly filling in his silences: "I interrupted the story twice. 'She was a black woman,' I said. Simon had just called her the woman who worked there. Twice I had to tell them that the woman that was struck on the head was black like me" (156). Faith receives only silent nods in response to her corrections to Simon's narrative, and eventually her comments and presence are completely ignored. Her friends crowd around Simon, comforting him regarding the traumatic experience he has witnessed, but none reference Faith's trauma, having seen a woman much like herself become the target of vicious racists. Faith is rendered invisible as a witness and as another casualty. The comfort that is provided to Simon and from which Faith is excluded comes in the form of sexual intimacy, with Marion's consolation of Simon ultimately involving sex. The scene therefore highlights the two missed opportunities for relation, the first being that of Faith's heterosexual desire for Simon. While both are witnesses to the attack on Yemi, their bond does not translate into Simon and Faith's consoling each other through physical intimacy. The second missed occasion for intimacy is that between Marion and Faith; Faith is marginalized from Marion's comforting attention, and the reader might wonder to what extent Faith's jealousy is derived from same-sex desire for Marion. However, Faith is not framed as sexual subject by the novel, leaving sexuality as the ultimate abject symbol of difference.

Faith's identification with Yemi's doubled victimization through violence and erasure leads her finally contextualize her roommates in terms of race, watching "three white hands and one black stretch forward" to pick up coffee mugs on the table (157). The privilege of whiteness is no longer invisible to Faith. The trauma of the violent attack and this sudden self-contextualization disturb Faith's consciousness to the extent that she cannot maintain an engagement with her reality any further. Faith endeavors to divorce herself from reality by disappearing into her room and rejecting all social intimacy and relation. Remarking that "I didn't want anyone to see me," Faith retreats to her bedroom to close the window shades that "let in too much life" so that "I could not see where I was stepping" (160). Faith creates this state of darkness in her room, accepting the conditions of her social erasure by attempting to occupy invisibility. Faith adopts the logic of the color-blindness regime that has so dominated her life: "But as my eyes adjusted to the dark I could see my reflection in the wardrobe mirror. A black girl lying in a bed. I covered the mirror with a bath towel. I didn't want to be black any more. I just wanted to live. The other mirror in the room I covered with a tee-shirt. Voilà! I was no longer black" (160). Faith aspires to universal identity, but such a move is implicitly self-destructive because it entails translation into being "not-black" so as to acquire the privileged invisibility of whiteness. Faith escapes into the darkness of her bedroom, where she is "safe," and rejects all attempts for communication with her housemates (161). Faith also refuses to get out of bed for her job because "they didn't want me at the television centre. And I wanted to be wanted" (161).

Faith's parents offer a way out of this escapism by recognizing Faith's need for an alternative social and historical context. When told that her parents have planned a trip for her to Jamaica, Faith responds, "I don't want to go to Jamaica. It's too far. What's wrong with Spain or somewhere" (162). Her mother insists on the specificity of Jamaica as a location for Faith's recovery from her nervous breakdown. Explaining that the trip "might help you," Faith's mother tells her that "everyone should know where they come from" (162). Having seen the covered mirrors in Faith's bedroom, her mother understands that Faith's inability to accept her identity can be addressed only by the acquisition of a cultural and historical foundation within the geographic space of the Caribbean, through her extended family and a broader web of intimate relations.

The void of history prompts Faith to embark on a journey to the Caribbean, where she negotiates her position as both a diasporic returnee and a tourist. By means of her travel to Jamaica, Faith acquires an oral family history that expands her formulation of the Jackson family tree, providing her with an Afro-Caribbean cultural and historical context. The narrative situates the recovery of Faith's Caribbean roots within a tourist economy, refusing to represent the trope of diasporic return in solely utopian terms. The ambivalence of Faith's position as somewhere between authenticity and imitation, belonging and outsiderness, is foregrounded much earlier in the narrative. The novel's concerns regarding the possibility of locating an authentic Caribbean culture are referenced by the title of the novel, *Fruit of the Lemon*. The lemon that inspires the narrative is a story about a family member in Jamaica and her mistaken assumption that eating lemons with sugar is a well-established British tradition. This practice is imposed on Faith's relative, Constance, as a way to emulate high British culture, and it contributes to her adult crisis of identity. The sugared lemon symbolizes an object of consumption that is both sweet (desirable) and sour (unpleasant). The centrality of the lemon story intimates the importance of consumption and commodification within Faith's journey of identity, positioning Constance as a family model informing Faith's development. The novel presents itself as the fruit of a fiction about cultural tradition and production, contextualized by a history of colonialism and reappropriation. Cultural authenticity is turned on its head: *Fruit of the Lemon* ironically valorizes this lemon, investing it with meaning due to its relevance within the family memory and despite its misguided cultural origins.

The second half of the novel plots Faith's return to Jamaica in terms of expanding her schema of family relations. By meeting her extended family in Jamaica, Faith gains entrance to a broader community, connecting her Afro-Caribbean background to her Black British subjectivity. The accumulation of individual intimacies and life stories expands the nuclear family tree diagram that opened the novel, although the stories do not follow any particular genealogical order. Rather, they are organized by Faith's errantry, her journey on the island and the family members she speaks to.[5] The novel incorporates new first-person narratives that interrupt Faith's first-person voice and contest her narrative authority while also contradicting each other, emphasizing no single truth or origin. Faith's familial context redefines intimacy beyond the individual or the nuclear family to a broader network of communal shared experiences.

The family histories encourage Faith to claim Jamaica as a space of belonging via a new web of relations. Included in this web is the story of Constance, whom Faith meets during her travels. At a family wedding, Faith comes into contact with her narrative double, a member of the family who has also undergone a crisis of identity and community. Faith is introduced to a woman with the "face of my mother—but my mother with a white skin" (301). The woman, Constance, is the cousin of Faith's mother, Mildred; however, she insists on being called Afria instead. Faith is overwhelmed by the physical similarities between her mother and Constance as well as the differences: Constance's "skin was white and her eyes were the palest blue," and she wore "African queen" clothing (302). The incompatibility of Constance's white body with her African pride clothing begs for explanation, so Faith and the reader come to learn Constance/Afria's personal history within the context of diasporic immigration.

After Constance creates a scene, having spit rum onto the bride "for good luck [so that] they will fear no white man," Faith's aunt Coral narrates her family context (304). To explain Constance's strange behavior, Coral tells the story of Faith's maternal grandaunt, Matilda. Matilda, who was very light-skinned, married an Englishman and was obsessed with teaching her daughter Constance the "ways of the English," such as eating lemons with sugar and using knives and forks to eat mangoes (312). As with Faith, education delimited Constance's self, and her migration led to a crisis of identity that opened up other modes of ethnic identification. During World War II, Constance was sent to a boarding school in England and upon her return she found a changed Jamaican society. Whereas before the war, people admired Constance for her pale skin, she found that whiteness was no longer valued. Constance became good friends with Mildred, Faith's mother, and while Mildred copied Constance to sound more British, Constance tried "to lose her rounded vowels and speak once more like a Jamaican" (316). Constance embarked on a journey like Faith's, researching the family history, attempting to find her grandmother Amy's grave so that she could be reburied in the family plot. Constance also traveled to Sierra Leone in hopes of tracing her ancestry to Africa but did not expand her network of relations, since she was not accepted because of her phenotypical whiteness. Constance turned to the market in order to formulate an African diasporic identity because the option of developing intimate relationships with an African community was foreclosed.

The crisis in identity and community led Constance to change her name to Afria and to adopt a more "African" style of dress. Constance's search for belonging in the Afro-Caribbean community is the flip side of Faith's experience assimilating into white British society. Afria's current occupation within the tourist industry indicates how tenuous Faith's reconnection with Caribbean culture and identity is, especially since Afria employs the same tools of acquiring familial historical context and "authentic" commodities. Tourism provides a place where Afria finds some solace selling "raffia baskets with 'Jamaica' woven on the side" to tourists (318). These raffia baskets recall Faith's employer, Olivia, and her "upturned-multicoloured raffia bin" (31). The consumption of ethnicity that Olivia exploits for profit is equally at work within the tourist economy where Afria is able to ambivalently occupy the space of authenticity despite her skin color. The tourist industry, often figured as the quintessential site of globalization, provides Constance with a new cultural identity, Afria, otherwise not available to an individual on the margins of an Afro-Caribbean community. Afria is a mirror image of Faith, foreshadowing Faith's own complex and ambivalent negotiation of her Caribbean diasporic identity. Through the figure of Afria—almost an anagram of Faith—the novel tempers what could be a utopic reading of Faith's recovery of roots. The translation of Constance into Afria references the market's co-optation of Black Power discourses, so that Afria is a parody of Faith's more earnest model of recovering a Caribbean diasporic identity.

Faith's acquisition of an Afro-Caribbean historical context and identity is quite similar to that of the market-enabled Afria. As Faith prepares to return to England, her suitcase is packed to the brim with T-shirts she has bought from a tourist shop on the beach, saying, "Jamaica," "Irie," "No problem," and "Don't worry, be happy" (322). Along with the shirts, Faith packs a clunky chopping board that her aunt assures her is an "all-Jamaican product" (322). Faith also takes with her a stone that she picks up at Fort Charles, which she imagines "could have been lying on that ground for several hundred years" and "that could have been kicked by the young Horatio Nelson" (323). Faith even packs a bag of red coffee berries that she intends to roast when she gets to London, "as my grandfather used to do" (323). The mix of commodities, imagination-history, and a tradition of consumption come together to form an incomplete but sufficient foundation from which Faith will rebuild her "authentic" cultural self. As products of consumption, they provide Faith with reminders of the oral history she accesses in Jamaica. Just as narrator and audience together shape the stories, these objects contain value despite their mass production because Faith invests cultural meaning in them. While packing her suitcase, Faith realizes that her Caribbean family has "wrapped me in a family history and swaddled me tight in its stories. And I was taking back that family to England. [. . .] I was smuggling it home" (326). Faith's hopeful return is articulated in terms of acquiring a safe and even secretive context of familial intimacy. Nevertheless, the metaphor of secretly trafficking in history is undercut by the novel's self-referentiality as a fictional text with a public readership.

The novel's last section represents Faith's return to England and her initiation into a historically contextualized nostalgia. Part III is entitled "England" and evokes the origin story of Faith's parents' migration, completing a circle in terms of the narrative structure and family history. Faith notices the fireworks in the sky at her return, thinking, "It may be a welcome for me having traveled so far and England needing me" (339). It is Guy Fawkes Night, the time when "there are always fireworks," but Faith makes no reference to the historical reasons for this celebration, namely a religious minority's failure to overthrow the British government (339). The reader is given only the context that this is the same day Faith's parents were greeted by England with the lights in the sky. Repeating her parents' experience and travel, Faith claims England as her home, and she comes with a mission: "I was coming home to tell everyone . . . My mum and dad came to England on a banana boat" (339). As storyteller and author-double, Faith is inserted into a traveling community, the migrant generation of her parents, via the acquisition of a family history, a web of relationality that redefines the banana boat symbol from the beginning of the novel. The text closes with the family tree Faith constructs and labels "fruit of the lemon," the same title as the published novel. With its question marks and remaining gaps, the family tree stands as the context that Faith is lacking when she leaves England, a context she is bringing back with her from Jamaica and that she plans to narrate to whoever will listen.

Fruit of the Lemon's ending celebrates Faith's initiation into a contextualizing nostalgia. With a suitcase full of commodities, Faith relives her parents' arrival in England with a difference. Faith claims her Afro-Caribbean self through these objects, as well as the inheritance of the Windrush generation and a colonial legacy: "I am the granddaughter of Grace and William Campbell. I am the great-grandchild of Cecelia Hilton. I am descended from Katherine whose mother was a slave. I am the cousin of Afria. I am the niece of Coral Thompson and the daughter of Wade and Mildred Jackson. Let them say what they like. Because I am the bastard child of Empire and I will have my day" (327). Levy's novel delineates nostalgia as a product of globalization that possesses the potential for resisting or transgressing its decontextualizing impulses. Faith maintains nostalgia for Jamaica with the personal and public histories she obtains there and the objects she carries back to England with her. However, there is no question at the end of the novel that Britain is her home.[6] Her identity is presumably strengthened, more whole, because of her contextualization within an Afro-Caribbean and transatlantic family history. In claiming Afria, and not Constance, as her cousin, Faith aligns herself with Afria's model of consumer citizenship.

At the end of the novel, Faith's declaration of a "bastard child of Empire" is possible because of her trip to Jamaica and access to an expanded web of familial relations. The specter of sexuality haunts this assertion of newly whole subjectivity, just as Afria's whiteness alludes to the unequal power relations of colonialism that enforced sexual intimacies. The fractured structure of the family tree that concludes the novel locates the origins of Faith's extensive family in the relationship between "Mr. Livingstone (plantation owner)" and "Katherine's mother (slave)" (340). The offstage encounter of this foundational pairing means that sexuality haunts the margins of the novel and Faith's confident declaration of identity. Faith's self-construction, as a bastard child of empire who "smuggles" the historical context engrained in the commodities she brings home, suggests another set of sexual encounters: the smuggling that tourism enables in terms of trafficking bodies for sex. Pairing the historical context of empire with the contemporary context of market multiculturalism allows the novel to posit a bittersweet relationary nostalgia as a means of allaying the destructive and decontextualizing energies of diaspora. The ghosts of those illegitimate children of empire, of the relationship between tourism and prostitution, are not directly addressed in *Fruit of the Lemon*. For this, I turn to discuss David Chariandy's historical novel *Soucouyant*.

Men on the Margins: David Chariandy's *Soucouyant*

David Chariandy's *Soucouyant* encodes its postcolonial pedagogy within the novel's structure: the reader is disoriented by a fragmented narrative that encourages identification with the dilemma of diasporic belonging. Andrea Levy's metaphor of historical amnesia becomes literalized in Chariandy's historical novel, with Adele, the mother of the narrator, suffering from early-onset dementia.[7] The novel adopts the perspective of the first-person younger son, whose identity crisis leads him to abandon his mother and older brother. The novel opens with the nameless narrator returning to his childhood home and confronting the vestiges of his mother, whose mental deterioration means that she no longer recognizes her child. Chariandy depicts these Caribbean and diasporic characters as unmoored within a Canadian nation that superficially values multiculturalism and enforces a regime of color blindness that violently dislodges the contexts of colonialism and racism. The reader is positioned as a student learning to interpret the narrator's decontextualized world, accumulating snippets of historical context that eventually constitute broader counternarratives of Canadian and Caribbean history.

Alongside this pedagogical project of teaching the reader about Caribbean history, the ethical imperative structuring the novel is in tension with *Soucouyant*'s representation of the marketplace. As with Levy's historical fiction, the market aesthetics of Chariandy's novel trace a path from rootlessness to belonging that relies upon a combination of historical contextualization and consumer citizenship. The fictional narrative of rememory, of reconstructing the past through fragments, is both facilitated and undermined by the market. Excavating cultural memory reveals that globalization and its neocolonial roots shape *both* the Caribbean past and the Canadian present. While the Canadian marketplace facilitates access to and interaction between marginalized cultures (Afro-Canadian with African American, Indo-Caribbean with Afro-Caribbean), the recuperated Caribbean past exposes the violent undercurrents of market multiculturalism, tying it to histories of economic and sexual exploitation.

Soucouyant is subtitled "A Novel of Forgetting," and it defines historical amnesia and decontextualization as a crucial facet of diasporic belonging. Critics of the novel focus on how Adele's dementia is a meta-phor for the diasporic condition.[8] My analysis is shaped by David Chari-andy's distinction of two Caribbean diasporas in Canada; in his 2007 academic essay published in *Callaloo*, Chariandy distinguishes between "the visible-minority immigrant, with her self-evidently foreign ways or customs," and the "discomfortingly intimate stranger born here" (819). I will therefore direct my attention to Adele's sons, the nameless nar-rator who acts as the chronicler of Adele's deterioration and mediator of her memories as well as the absent brother whose visual fragments are the epigraphs for each chapter in the novel. The postcolonial imper-ative of *Soucouyant* is most directly articulated in the representation of the narrator and his brother, since they are second-generation dia-sporic men whom Chariandy describes as the "new subject" of "anxi-eties over Canada's multicultural citizenry" (819). These nameless men are the only characters with first-person voices in the novel. *Soucouy-ant* addresses the perceived threat such "intimate strangers" present to Canadian national identity while also depicting their uniquely second-generation perspectives as Caribbean diasporic men.

The pedagogical drive of the novel places the brothers within two his-torical contexts: Canadian multiculturalism and the mother's memory of Trinidad. In referring to the first context in his *Callaloo* essay, Chari-andy ascribes an ethical imperative to diasporic writers and alludes to the apprehensions that such responsibility might occasion: "Multiculturalism as a social reality is not going to go away, and it remains our responsibil-ity, as cultural workers, to demand that this reality is better recognized and affirmed, even as we need to acknowledge, perhaps far more care-fully, how our demands always threaten to be translated, against our best wishes, into deeply cynical gestures by governments and corporations" (828). The market aesthetics of the novel, the way globalization functions as a context for Adele's immigrant generation and her sons' second-genera-tion diaspora, is symbolic of the anxieties the novel displays as a commod-ity within the book market. The threat of translation, with the potential of being misread, is central to the way the text imagines its readership and structures the voices of the narrator and brother.[9] Even as the novel takes seriously the ethical imperative to reeducate its readers, encourag-ing them to adopt the viewpoints of these Caribbean diasporic charac-ters, it calls into question the truth-value of historical narratives, including those reconstructed in order to resist mainstream discourses about ethnic-ity and race. *Soucouyant* mourns the ways in which the market supports and impedes access to certain readerships.

The novel opens with a "verse fragment" from a Caribbean folktale about the soucouyant, a creature that masquerades as an old woman by day and emerges as a ball of fire by night, traveling from house to house, sucking the blood of children. A Caribbean reader might approach the verse with such a cultural context in mind, understanding that the repetition of "Old skin, 'kin, 'kin, You na know me," refers to the soucouyant's inability to put on her old woman disguise after the skin has been salted by someone intending to halt her future attacks. A reader without this context finds no immediate explanation of the Caribbean verse in the text or even its link to the novel's title. As a result, the verse is predictive of the mainstream reader's relationship to the entire narrative. With the reader positioned *as* a soucouyant, the opening verse indicates that the audience will be faced with "na knowing," with a crisis of self-recognition and the constant challenge to understand the text's surface, to read the narrative's skin. Like the soucouyant traveling from house to house for nourishment, the mainstream reader is forced to collect fragments of knowledge in the novel and piece them together to build symbolic meaning and plot chronology. For instance, the first explanation of the term *soucouyant* does not appear until page 23, when the narrator defines the soucouyant for his mother as an "evil spirit" who "sucks your blood at night" (24). The reader then learns of the mother's encounter with the soucouyant, how she saw the creature "loss she skin at the military base in Chaguaramas" (24). These snippets of information, of a child facing a monster at a military base in Trinidad, are not fleshed out fully in this passage, and their true significance is not understood until the novel's final pages.

Not only does the text begin with dehistoricized Caribbean cultural terminology, but the narrator-son provides little sense of the historical time frame for his family. *Soucouyant*'s reader lacks intimate information about the familial context for the characters. We begin with a "she" who is described as having "become an old woman" and whose aging has not led to any comfort of recognition, since she "looks out from the doorway of her own home but seems puzzled by the scene" (7). By contrast, we have a sense that the narrator has contextual knowledge that the readers *and* woman lack: "avoiding the stool that has always been untrustworthy," the narrator hangs a coat "on the peg tucked invisibly beside the fuse-box" (7). Although the names of the characters, the gender of the narrator, and even the relationship between the narrator and the woman remain unspecified, the narrator gives one hint of the plot's time frame with "the same wildlife calendar with the moose of

September 1987, now two years out of date" (7). This is representative of the narrator's delaying strategy throughout the novel: the reader
must actively construct meaning and recognition by reading past what
is said to what is implied—for example, that the narrator is speaking
from the year 1989. This approach seduces the reader into accepting the
narrator's authority, his ability to translate the foreign into the familiar.
Once the narrator transforms the "old woman" into "my mother" and
describes himself as "a dark young man" that she is "entirely unwilling to admit she has forgotten," the narrator indicates that he shares
more with his mother than mere genetics. Just as Faith is bonded to
her parents by more than blood, eventually recognizing her cultural ties
through a parallel experience of their Guy Fawkes welcome, *Soucouyant*'s narrator reveals that he and his mother share a dehistoricized condition: "both of us free from our past" (8). Of course, the mother, who
we eventually learn is named Adele (49), suffers from dementia and her
forgetfulness is not a choice. In claiming the connection of ahistoricity,
the narrator reveals that his investment in the story he tells is very much
shaped by a desire to move beyond the past, whether through denial or
self-censorship. As in Andrea Levy's *Fruit of the Lemon*, there is a pervasive silence enveloping this nuclear family, an absence of personal history that functions as a historical context for the mother's identity crisis
as well as that of her sons.

The evolution of the older brother's representation follows the over-
all narrative's progression from rootlessness to belonging, from silenced
to recuperated history. In many ways, this progression mimics that of
Faith's trajectory in *Fruit of the Lemon*, and *Soucouyant* at first encourages its audience to accept the storyline of emancipation that the narrator gives us about his brother. However, the absent brother's emplotment
becomes complicated by his embodiment of a suppressed familial history that is similar to his mother Adele's soucouyant encounter and has
broader implications for the market aesthetics of the novel. Beginning
with his brother as a child, with his "real fountain pen and a notebook of
handmade paper" (17), the narrator describes him as an intellectual role
model who transforms the ordinary into poetry and challenges mainstream stereotypes about Afro-Canadian men. Working at the Happy
Chicken restaurant, the brother "memorized the specials of the day"
and translated them into "the poetics of the sale" (27). The fast-food
forum of consumerism and consumption not only allows the brother to
take on "a new role as the working man of the family" after the death
of their father but also politicizes the brother, transforming him into a

public advocate and an activist (27). When a man on the bus "stifles a laugh" after seeing the brother read a book entitled *A Girl's Gay Garland of Verse*, the brother does not simply wonder, as the narrator does, "what exactly was so funny about seeing a young man read a book" but confronts the man with an angry combination of vulgarity and literariness: "Something *funny? Incongruent,* motherfucker?" (28). The acuity of the brother's discursive analysis is implied here, that the man in a business suit is laughing not merely at a young man reading but at a *black* man reading. The brother, as a teenager who successfully breaks free from the confines of his broken family home (a dead father, a senile mother) and defies the racist expectations of the Canadian educational system, embodies for the narrator an ideal, Black Power–like intellectualism and masculinity. Upon becoming "'known' by teachers, neighborhood watch volunteers, and police," the brother does not allow their recognition to define him (28). He escapes what the narrator sees as the "worst of all possible fates, to be known by professional knowers," and becomes a successful bohemian poet (28). Here recognition takes on a darker side: being "known" entails being categorized into stereotypes about black manhood. The specter of the soucouyant reemerges in the Canadian state and its institutions, which use familiarity and comprehension to thwart the intellectual growth of black boys—consigning their imaginations to a fate of poverty and violence.

The narrator recounts his family dynamics because he wants to posit an alternate fate for his older brother, one that white Canadian society cannot conceive of for a Caribbean diasporic man. The detailed narrative about the brother's career as a poet does not appear until one hundred pages later in the novel, and the narrator's use of future tense to imagine their reunion suggests how tentative this picture of success is. The narrator envisions finding his brother by coming across a book of poetry at a bookstore, glancing through the pages to detect its characteristic style and content: "I'd recognize an investment in naming the world properly and a wariness of those moments when language seems to spill and tumble dangerously. But I'd notice other things too, a father's shoulders heaving at a sink, a mother's streaked makeup and her burnt-milk emergencies" (128). With a re-encounter facilitated by the marketplace, these familiar codes of memory and language lead the narrator to discover that the brother is "writing under a new name" (128). The narrator imagines embarking on an investigative journey, locating his brother at his next public reading in a bookstore. As in Levy's novel, the bookstore is a marketplace enabling detection and disidentification. Even though he does not challenge the fiction of his brother's alias, the narrator believes their mutual recognition will lead them to share a meal together. During a conversation at a fast-food location, "an all-night pancake place" (128), the narrator expects to find that the brother's artistic life remains inspired by the intersection between the intimate-personal and the public marketplace. Echoing the implications of Faith's cousin Afria and her career, the narrator pictures his brother working on a "book-length work on either love or global capital" (128). Desiring no explicit recognition from his brother of their blood relation or shared family history, the narrator instead creates a monologue of forgiveness, telling the brother how much he "understood the need for poetry," "understood his use of pseudonym," and, ultimately, "understood it all, even his decision to leave home, to leave me behind" (129). Accepting the dissolution of their relationship as necessary for his brother's economic and artistic upward mobility, the narrator concludes his fantasy by walking away.

The vision of an Afro-Canadian man who rises from poverty into poetry and gains a public through the market by selling his artistic productions is a product of the narrator's disavowal of his own circumstances. The older brother's story is a fiction, and much like the origin family story of Faith's fruit of the lemon, it says more about the narrator's desires than about those of his brother. The conclusion of forgiveness represents the narrator's hope for absolution after abandoning his mother and brother. As the novel continues, we learn that the story that the narrator has fashioned reflects a deep-seated denial about his familial realities and even intimate knowledge of his brother. In the same way that Adele constructs the soucouyant narrative to process and supplant the reality of her and her mother's exploitation by US marines in Trinidad, the narrator has filled in his painful past as a Caribbean diasporic man in Canada with equally monstrous fictions. After his mother dies, the narrator is forced to face his buried memories about his brother as he cleans out the basement with his mother's caregiver, Meera. Meera discloses that the brother visited regularly during the two years the narrator was absent, bringing "crumpled bills of money" even though it was clear that his financial situation was dire: "He was famished. His jeans and sweater had holes, and he smelled" (169). Potentially homeless, the brother's reality counters the narrator's vision of upward mobility and reveals that the brother does not abandon his mother even though he is destitute. Meera's description also challenges the fundamental defining personality trait ascribed to his brother, his poetic sensibilities. Having presumably heard about his literary talent, Meera recounts asking the brother for "something to read the next time he visited. Perhaps some poetry, perhaps some Derek Walcott" (169). On his last visit, the brother brings Meera a "massive box full of books" that contains "no poetry" but a random assortment of dictionaries (54, 169), Greek and German philosophy classics (54, 169), and specialized textbooks such as *XML in Plain English* (119), *Radar Ornithology* (82), and *Molecular Chemistry* (54). The reader thus learns that the odd books the narrator always saw Meera reading around his mother's home were derived from his brother's literary archive. This is certainly not the cultural production that the narrator fantasized his brother engaging or creating.

Meera's suggestion that "all things considered, he really could be someone to look up to," provokes the narrator rather than reassures him of his brother's archetypal status (169). The statement leads the narrator to make an investigative journey into his mother's basement and to tear open the "red metal toolbox" where his brother stored his writing (170). This archival element of market aesthetics, seen in the historical fictions of Dionne Brand, Ana Menéndez, and Michelle Roffey or Yunior's archive of Oscar's writing in Junot Díaz's novel, is discussed further in chapters 4 and 5. *Soucouyant*'s narrator finds only fragments in this second archive, containing "three small wire-bound notebooks": "Two have had all of their pages ripped out so that only the cardboard covers remain" and a third still has "quite a few of its pages intact" (170). After the narrator declares, "Inside is my brother's poetry," the reader is confronted with a visual text whose encoded meanings would have been completely impenetrable if presented at the start of the novel (170). The visual poem alludes to two historical contexts, familial and economic, while also showing how the brother's creativity is undermined by his inability to write. It is clear that the educational system did fail the brother, since his writing is so fragmented that he does not form phrases or sentences but only a set of seemingly disconnected and incoherent words. The writing's visual rendering is marked by struggles of articulation with misspellings, letters written backwards, and repeated crossing out and rewritings. Despite the apparently undisciplined form of the brother's poem, there remain points of recognition for the reader. The plot's accumulated context allows the poem's embedded meanings and symbols to be recognizable and knowable.

There are a network of familial terms: Roger, the narrator's father; dementia, which is Adele's disease; Meera's name; the slurs "packy" and "nigger," which recall the brother's sexual assault against Meera at school and her racist labeling of him in retribution (159). The only name that remains a mystery is that of Josef. Scrawled below the word *me*, the decontextualized name indicates that Josef is either the narrator's or the brother's name. The visual poem is the brother's fragmented version of the narrator's story up to this point and, despite its illegibility, in some ways it gives the reader more information than the narrator has revealed thus far. The brother's first-person narrative is *structurally* contextualized when the narrator turns the page of the notebook and finds "an attempt at a word," the word *soucouyant* (171). This additional visual fragment is recognizable because each chapter in the novel begins with illegible fragments of handwriting, also with letters written backwards or crossed out. As the reader follows the plot of the novel, the epigraphs acquire some limited meaning due to their visual evolution toward totality as well as the fragments of context relayed by the narrator: we understand that these are attempts to spell the word *soucouyant* and that the term refers to a central character in Adele's origin story about her childhood. During the entire novel, the reader has been ignorant of the most important context for these visual fragments: the narrator has been interspersing the voice of the brother throughout his first-person narration. The narrator's tactic of delay reveals that even as he was constructing a narrative that translated his family experience to his audience, the brother's silenced reality haunted that origin story.

The emplotment of the narrator and the delayed revelation of the brother's context are indicative of the market aesthetics of the novel. On the one hand, they show the desire to withhold certain negative stories from an audience of "professional knowers" who might convert those narratives into stereotype. On the other hand, the haunting absence of the brother symbolizes the audience that the novel aspires to reach but cannot, because of the social and economic structures of racism and classism that keep diasporic black men like the brother on the margins of the literary marketplace. By depicting its mainstream readers as well as the audiences but who are inaccessible within the book market, Chariandy's novel shares much with historical fictions by other Caribbean diasporic authors. In chapter 3, I discuss how Julia Alvarez's *In the Name of Salomé* mourns a similar lost readership, that of an illiterate poor boy of color. The alternate public for men on the margins is obliquely referenced in the brother's poem. He appears to be functionally illiterate, with perhaps an undiagnosed learning disability, and the novel encodes in the poem an alternate career for the brother. The phrase *blow job* recalls the graffiti scrawl that the narrator was embarrassed to hear his mother read aloud while on a walk with her and Meera: "Should we call Steven Wright for a . . . a blow job?" (109). This particular graffiti tag might not be the brother's, but it suggests that the brother might have moved his writing from the page, where it would ultimately find no future, to the street. The novel mourns the translation of the brother into street artist. Graffiti tags facilitate authorial anonymity while also necessitating exclusion from the literary marketplace. As such, graffiti do not allow for any future recognition between the narrator and his brother. Conversely, perhaps the medium is too public to operate as a commodity or a profitable career. The content of the graffiti references another possibility, the economy of prostitution. The advertising of a queer contact for a "blow job" carries its own set of implications regarding the brother's sexuality, notwithstanding his public sexual attack on Meera. The potential danger of sexual exploitation on the street means that the brother's fate as a diasporic male in Canada may be comparable to that of his grandmother, Adele's mother, in Trinidad. The market aesthetics of *Soucouyant* acknowledge the limitations of it's postcolonial ethics, since the novel cannot imagine facilitating the reunion, reconciliation, and healing of its diasporic men, the narrator and his brother.

The brother's rootless epigraphs are contextualized by the poem on page 171 as well as the mother's narrative of the soucouyant and the violent context of neocolonialism that produces that fiction. The brother's first-person narrative does not resolve the mystery of the nameless Caribbean diasporic sons. His voice does connect the personal familial narrative to a broader public of the market, much in the way that Adele's soucouyant story references a postcolonial history. The brother's poem cites Happy Chicken, the fast-food restaurant where he got his first job, and links it to a corporate economy of NBC, Shell, and Coca Cola. These companies are global conglomerates, each specializing in a different product for consumption: media, oil, food. The commodities and popular culture that are consumed by the Caribbean diaspora in Canada are contextualized by Adele's memory of the neocolonial past, related by the narrator on the day that he abandoned his mother, two years earlier. By bringing the revelations about the brother and mother together at the conclusion of the novel, the narrator constructs a history of globalization, its own origin story. Like Levy, Chariandy's novel cites empire as a context for understanding Caribbean diasporic belonging *as well as* Canadian mainstream society.

Consumer citizenship is a mode of diasporic belonging throughout the novel, since the marketplace is the backdrop for interethnic collaboration and solidarity. For instance, when the narrator abandons his mother in 1987, he describes his white roommate as having "the insight to prepare [himself] for life as a world-famous rapper by carefully studying the best of the best. Grandmaster Flash and the Furious Five, Run DMC, and most recently, Public Enemy" (30). Similar to the role tourism plays for Afria in *Fruit of the Lemon*, African American popular culture of the 1980s offers the roommate a route of belonging and artistic creativity in Canada. Nevertheless, the novel indicates that this commodification of ethnicity perpetuates racist stereotypes. Through the decontextualization of the urban African American experience, market multiculturalism translates the unique cultural production of African American hip-hop into the standard-bearer of Afro-Canadian identity.[10] Delimiting what kinds of behavior and language can be judged as authentically black, the roommate questions the narrator's allegiances as an Afro-Canadian, asking, "What's your story, homeboy? You're always visiting bookstores and reading poetry and shit. You talk all good. Man, you talk as if you're whiter than me, and my grandfather was in the bloody Asiatic Exclusion League!" (30). The racist legacy of the roommate's white Canadian family is ironically referenced to defamiliarize the narrator as a Canadian subject *and* situate him as an inauthentic black man. A regime of color blindness allows the roommate to invoke his racist ancestors in order to call out the narrator's literariness as a pretense at whiteness, while his authority as consumer of African American culture enables him to decontextualize the narrator's Afro-Caribbean cultural roots and claim that he is insufficiently black. The roommate invokes and revokes the relevance of colonialism and racism as historical contexts in his request to understand the narrator's story.

Just as globalization and market multiculturalism are seen as negative forces, the novel depicts the Canadian marketplace as facilitating interethnic dialogue that otherwise might not take place in the Caribbean. At the Kensington Market, described as "one of the few places where a newcomer might have a chance of getting her hands on breadfruit or fresh coconut or the sunny heft of a mango" (69), the parents of the narrator, Adele and Roger, first fall in love. The narrator's fantasy of the brother's next poetry book on love or global capital could surely be about this space: a market where Canadian ethnic minorities come to sell and buy the goods transported from their homelands. Almost knocked over by Roger making deliveries on his bike, Adele can only address him with a racist slur: "Coolie fool!" (70). The narrator explains that even though "they didn't know each other," "there was a history between them all the same" (70). The intimacy that connects them is not simply their Trinidadian origins but the economic history of empire and its exploitation of labor: "An African and a South Asian, both born in the Caribbean and the descendants of slaves and indentured workers, they had been raised to believe that only the other had ruined the great fortune they had enjoyed in the New World" (70). Despite their training to see each other as enemies and competitors, Adele falls in love with Roger and his narrative of denial after he tumbles from his bike because of a wayward chicken—the other "Happy Chicken" of the novel:

> There's a tussle of feathers and a fall as spectacular as any Charlie Chaplin could ever attempt. The man bounces up to reassure everyone on the street.
> 'Is only a pothole,' he says, 'Is nothing, I alright.'
> There is no pothole. Nobody on the street seems to notice or care. There's a chicken feather plastered upon his wet forehead. She falls in love precisely then. (71–72)

After cursing him, Adele finds herself drawn to Roger because of his quick response to his fall of the bike, partly because he invents the existence of a street pothole to replace the real obstacle of the chicken and partly because of his concern to reassure a public that barely acknowledges his existence, much less expresses concern for his safety. The immigrant strategy of disavowal in order to assimilate, as well as the goal of creating affirmative fictional narratives for surviving trauma, bonds Adele and Roger together.

The parents' consumption of American culture indicates that their survival strategies to abject history are part and parcel of a larger system of decontextualization. Just as Faith's parents in *Fruit of the Lemon* remain silent about their lives prior to the births of Faith and Carl, Adele and Roger "agree never to wax nostalgically," since they "have almost no interest in their respective pasts" (73). The only exception they make to this rule is their movie outings because, "while growing up in the Caribbean, each received their first tastes of escape through these films" of *Casablanca* and *Morocco* (73). The American culture industry has also trained them as children in the Caribbean, so that Canada is merely "a North America they had each inhabited long before arriving" (73). The circulation of the US culture industry and the conglomerates that the older brother mentions in his final poem intersect in the final recounting of Adele's soucouyant trauma at the US Marine base in Trinidad. The novel's conclusion reconstructs the history of globalization and the consumption of American culture, with the market framed as an instrument of neocolonialism as well as racial and sexual oppression.

During the final scenes of the novel, the narrator's voice fractures into different perspectives and memories, alternating between a third-person narration of Adele's memory of her childhood encounter with the soucouyant, a dialogue between the narrator and mother, a third-person historical voice that summarizes the context of the US military base in Trinidad, and a third-person perspective of "Okie," one of the marines on that base. Critics focus on the narrator's role in reminding Adele of her destructive encounter with the US marines but often ignore the context of this conversation—the eve of the narrator's teenage abandonment of Adele for two years—as well as the other narrative perspectives that precede the reconstruction of Adele's soucouyant trauma.[11] By focusing solely on the narration of Adele's past, critics miss out on analyzing how storytelling and the recovery of Adele's memory are traumas for the narrator. The market aesthetics of the novel come to the forefront at the text's conclusion, echoing the warning that Faith's mother gives about repeating family stories in the public realm. The intimate bond of mother and son means that *Soucouyant*'s narrator has access to these private family secrets. The reader learns that on the day the narrator abandoned his mother, he used his storytelling of Adele's soucouyant memory to render her invisible and irrelevant so that he could walk away from her, having finally categorized her as the product of her childhood trauma. The novel is therefore self-reflective about its project as a historical fiction and the vulnerabilities entailed in sharing Caribbean diasporic stories with its reader, namely the dangers of stereotype and marginalization.

Since the narrative reenactment bears traces of the brother's poem, the narrator's memory of recounting the soucouyant origin story historicizes the brother's keywords of Shell and Coca Cola, tracing his brother's fall from grace to its presumed origins: Adele's childhood encounter with the soucouyant. Delving into the archive of Adele's lost memories, the narrator does not re-memory her in order to heal her amnesiac present or psychic childhood wound. Rather, the narrator's conversation takes on an aggressive, almost violent tone. In the dialogue sections, the narrator interrogates his mother, asking her if the educational system taught her "that your birthplace was a major producer of oil for the entire British Empire" (175). As with Levy's Faith, Adele's education is another system of domination that silences the colonial context of the Caribbean's relationship to British imperialism. British colonialism and its oil economy contextualize the US neocolonial influence on the Caribbean region during World War II. Using a third-person historical perspective, the narrator describes how the construction of the US base in Chaguaramas forcibly displaced Trinidadian populations from their land, undermining their livelihoods as fishermen and farmers and forcing them to become dependent on the US military economy. Providing this historical context, the narrator desires to logically explain the circumstances for Adele's encounter with the soucouyant, while also "solving" the problem of how such a fantastical monster could possibly appear in the "real" world of Trinidad.

The narrator's evolution from reader-double to author-double is made explicit with the final story of the soucouyant. The son's adoption of a storyteller role turns out to have much in common with the professional knowers the narrator describes earlier on in the novel. If the worst fate the narrator could imagine for his older brother was to become "known by professional knowers," then it appears that it is a fate to which he wishes to consign his mother (28). The narrator claims comprehension and ownership of Adele's story in order to stifle her, to contain the threat that she poses to the narrator's identity so that he can abandon her. The narrator links the public history of the US base in Chaguaramas to Adele's cultural memory by following the third-person historical debates about the "American presence" with Adele's singing of the calypso "Rum and Coca Cola," which takes as its subject the sexual exploitation of "mother and daughter, working for the Yankee Dollar" (179). The narrator tells the story of the soucouyant because Adele asks his seventeen-year-old self to explain the song she just heard herself singing, and when he explains that it is by the Lord Invader and that he recognizes it because she has explained its context to him before, Adele asks, "What else I tell you?" (180). The narrator is asked to contextualize her at a moment that he wants "to settle the past" so that he can leave her (180). He reconstructs her memory not out of a desire to heal her but so that he can declare his complete knowledge of Adele, relegate her to his past, and walk away. The narrator tells the soucouyant story because he wants to establish himself as the professional knower of his mother: "I'm leaving you now, but I'm telling you what I know, what you accidentally told me" (184), and "I didn't want to tell a story like this, I just wanted you to realize that I knew" (195). As the narrator tells Adele's story, his narrative priorities are challenged by the very tale he feels compelled to tell. For example, the narrator's investment in the marketplace as a space of escape for the brother is troubled by the mother's experience within the Caribbean economy of neocolonialism.

That economy drives the exploitation of the Caribbean female body and the circulation of US commodities and culture. As a child, Adele "comb[s] the blonde hair of an American doll" as her mother sells her body via prostitution in order to feed herself and her daughter (185). The American marine called "Okie" is the first to offer Adele access to this economy of the body, giving her a dollar after she plays with the lighter he shows her (187). This marine is the one who initiates Adele's love of American cinema, since he gives her pictures of Gary Cooper, Humphrey Bogart, and Marlene Dietrich as gifts. Adele translates the trauma at the US base of her mother's immolation and her own physical scarring by the marine's lighter into a story about encountering the soucouyant, employing a Caribbean folk tale to process a gap in her understanding of how and why this violence happened.[12] At the same time, Adele's cultural tastes and imagination are permanently marked by her childhood encounter with US imperialism, so that she becomes a lifelong consumer of American popular culture.

The narrator's authority is constantly thwarted by his mother's dementia, and Adele's story is fragmented by the dialogues between the seventeen-year-old narrator and his mother. The frustrated narrator asks, "How can I tell the story if you don't listen to me?" (190). The narrator seeks recognition from his mother not simply as her son but also as her audience, as someone who "could hear and understand and take away" (195). When Adele's dementia makes it impossible to obtain her acknowledgment of himself as her reader, translator, and critic, he bursts into tears, confessing, "I don't really understand at all" (195).[13] The novel's conclusion finds the adult narrator admitting to the desires inspiring his creativity and delimiting his depiction of his mother: "I wanted to imagine her growing, not diminishing. I wanted to portray her as awakening to something that we wouldn't have guessed at otherwise" (194). In that "we" the narrator also acknowledges how the idea of his own audience, and by extension, the novel's readership, have informed his longing to depict his mother as a woman who would become rooted through her contextualization within a particular set of histories and memories.

In closing, the narrator recalls that for his mother the most important context for her youngest son was his blessing at the hands of his grandmother in Trinidad—a context that, Meera notes, "she never forgot" (196). The narrator accepts that he does not remember this blessing, "not even a little bit" (196). Recognizing that gap, the narrator provides a new personal memory with an equally meaningful context for his childhood trip to Trinidad: "My grandmother stumbling and reaching, without thinking, for Mother's hand. Each reaching for the other and then holding hands for the rest of the way. I remember being awed by this. It was all so incredibly ordinary. They were just a mother and daughter" (196). The verse from "Rum and Coca Cola" returns, its sexual connotations still part of the historical referent for the narrator's translation of his memory, but he privileges the familial intimacy of the parental relationship *over and above* the violent history that marks these women's bodies and minds, as well as that of their progeny. The novel's postcolonial ethics recontextualize the market and its commodities so that the women are subjects of history rather than objects of consumption. The narrator's choice of phrasing denotes the creative tension informing the market aesthetics of this Caribbean diasporic historical fiction and its anxiety over translating cultural inheritances for a mainstream audience.

The market aesthetics of Andrea Levy's *Fruit of the Lemon* and David Chariandy's *Soucouyant* foreground how consumerism enables and delimits the narration of Caribbean diasporic subjectivity. The job market and the bookstore in Levy's novel are spaces of dangerous exploitation and violent rejection of ethnicity even as tourist culture provides both Faith and her mirror subject, Afria, with tentative ties to cultural authenticity. The marketplace enables productive cross-class and interethnic encounters for the parents of *Soucouyant*'s narrator while also permitting his white college roommate to claim authority in deauthorizing the narrator's claim to belonging. The bookstore and graffiti offer alternative discourses for imagining encounters with unattainable readerships in both Levy's and Chariandy's historical novels. In Levy, the bookstore defaced by graffiti evokes a market reception that will be racist, homophobic, and sexist and that will ghettoize, if not reject the validity of, minority writing as a field of literature. The bookstore reading and the brother's graffiti in *Soucouyant*, on the other hand, are the script of alienated, illiterate diasporic men who form an inaccessible readership as well as a marginalized group of writers. The market aesthetics of these novels identifies graffiti as a mode of writing that engages and yet exists outside the mainstream literary market, and as such symbolizes the threats and obstacles to the ethical project of educating and transforming readerships.

Andrea Levy's and David Chariandy's novels provide us with a useful introduction to the market aesthetics of Caribbean diasporic writing, especially the approach to the decontextualization of the diaspora within Global North metropolitan centers. *Soucouyant* advances a less optimistic negotiation of the diasporic experience than that of *Fruit of the Lemon*, but both novels share an interest in historicizing the ahistorical condition caused by commodification and the regime of color blindness during the 1980s. Levy's and Chariandy's work provides us with a transition into discussing those historical novels whose pedagogical imperative focuses on teaching the reader about specific historical pasts and figures. This trend within Caribbean diasporic historical fiction forms part of a recuperating-silenced-histories approach to the ethical project of historical revisionism, which I discuss in chapter 3.

Andrea Levy's literary trajectory parallels that of Julia Alvarez and Michelle Cliff. These writers began their careers by publishing semiautobiographical fictions, such as *Never Far from Nowhere* (1996), *How The Garcia Girls Lost Their Accents* (1991), and *Abeng* (1985), and later transitioned into historical fiction. Levy's *Small Island* is critically popular and won numerous awards such as the 2004 Orange Prize and 2004 Commonwealth Writer's Prize. The straightforwardly realist and historical tenor of *Small Island* (2004) and *The Long Song* (2010) perhaps explains why academic attention has eluded *Fruit of the Lemon* by comparison. Nevertheless, Levy continues to develop market aesthetics invested in the recuperative approach to the historical fiction genre. The frame of *The Long Song* (2010) opens with a first-person dialogue between Thomas Kinsman, the fictional publisher-editor, and his mother July, competing over how best to address their readership in 1898 as well as who has a better sense of their audience's market demands for storytelling. In the following chapter, I discuss how this recuperative approach imagines the encounter with the readership as one of tense intimacy via its depiction of education and literacy as well as the structural form the novel adopts to teach its reader about historical counternarratives.

3   Writing the Reader

Literacy and Contradictory Pedagogies in Julia Alvarez, Michelle Cliff, and Marlon James

POSTCOLONIAL ETHICS THAT AIM TO TEACH the reader about Caribbean history are key to the aesthetic design of Caribbean diasporic historical novels that exemplify the traditional defining qualities of the genre. The pedagogical imperative is primarily expressed through the genre of realism, illuminating a previously marginalized aspect of Caribbean history or challenging the dominant narrative about a historical period or figure. Junot Díaz's footnotes in *Oscar Wao* are overt examples of this contextualization strategy, an academic mode of providing historical context for the reader who is ignorant of Dominican history. More commonly, writers provide a descriptive gloss to communicate historical information. For example, Esmeralda Santiago's *Conquistadora* (2011) concentrates on (and aims to provide a sympathetic rendering of) the landowning and slaveholding class in Puerto Rico, with detailed descriptions of how the land was colonized, including lists of the herbs and vegetables grown in eighteenth-century Puerto Rico. By educating their readers, diasporic writers highlight the ethical lessons that can be drawn from Caribbean history.

The goal of reeducating the reader-audience is allegorized in the tense negotiations over literacy and the interaction between teacher and student within *In the Name of Salomé* (2000), *Free Enterprise* (1993), and *The Book of Night Women* (2009). The historical novels of Julia Alvarez, Michelle Cliff, and Marlon James are instructive about how the pedagogical imperative comes into conflict with pressures from the multicultural book market. The novels incorporate author-doubles who embody the concerns of the Caribbean diasporic author as ethnic writer. Alvarez's Salomé is a too-popular poet in the Dominican Republic, complaining that people expect her writing to continue in the previous nationalistic, political mode, while she instead longs to write in a minor, personal voice. Cliff's Annie Christmas is a light-skinned Caribbean woman who desires to become one of the masses by rejecting her upper-class upbringing and joining the abolitionist movement in the United States. James's Lovey Quinn is a gender-ambiguous narrator who is inspired to write his/her story but instead becomes compelled to ventriloquize his/her mother Lilith's account about enslavement in Jamaica. These author-doubles provide a metacommentary on the challenges that Alvarez, Cliff, and James encounter in the multicultural book market, particularly how those market pressures shape the aesthetics of their historical fiction.

The depicted teacher-student relationships are a blueprint for the obstacles that stand in the way of the fictions' educational advocacy. With literacy as the site where pedagogical challenges are explored, Alvarez, Cliff, and James identify intimacy as a threat to the ethical integrity of the writerly project. *In the Name of Salomé* and *Free Enterprise* teach the reader about the interconnectedness of Las Américas, drawing parallels between social movements in the Caribbean and the United States while highlighting colonization and imperialism as shared historical contexts. Alvarez and Cliff also situate queer subjects as agents of history and depict the novels' encounters with the market through a queer character's ambivalent relationship to teaching literacy.[1] Intimacy and sexuality trouble the teacher-student relationships, suppressing unspeakable queer desires. Literacy acquisition in James's novel contains comparable allusions to the text's anxious encounter with the audience, although *The Book of Night Women* is concerned with the ethical representation of slavery's violence. James's project of historical revision imparts another version of the postcolonial imperative, one that does not offer a comparative historiography but references market pressures on neo-slave narratives and their depictions of violent historical traumas.

Writerly Authority and Audience Reception

Julia Alvarez, Michelle Cliff, and Marlon James recognize how the market reception of their fiction has placed them in the uncomfortable position of spokesperson for their respective Caribbean cultures. Alvarez, Cliff, and James identify their fiction as a space where they process the influence of market readerships on their writerly authority and creativity. To understand the symbolism of the author-doubles, it is useful to review the personal contexts of each writer, drawing attention to the ways in which their positioning as public intellectuals has been called into question in terms of authenticity and cultural authority. The

Caribbean diasporic writer's contemporary historical context of market reception informs the pedagogical imperative of the historical fiction.

Compared with other diasporic authors, Julia Alvarez has experienced some of the harshest critiques of her public persona in relation to her writing. In *The Latino/a Canon*, Dalleo and I identify Alvarez as part of a generation of Latina writers who "have been criticized for achieving their market success at the expense of the political ideals of the Sixties generation" (133). In her examination of *In the Name of Salomé*, Jessica Magnani reiterates the association of Alvarez's popularity with an apolitical aesthetic by arguing that "much of the appeal of Alvarez's work among US readers comes from its non-threatening consumability" (33). In addition to having her dedication to progressive politics questioned, Alvarez has had her authenticity as a Dominican American woman challenged.[2] The publication of her first historical novel, *In the Time of the Butterflies* (1994), initiated a forceful backlash in the Dominican Republic and the United States regarding Alvarez's depiction of the Mirabal sisters. For instance, Roberto González Echevarría's book review in the *New York Times* denounced her for being too "Americanized" to "really be able to understand" or depict the experiences of her Dominican characters (28). Alvarez's novel *Saving the World* (2006) directly references the critical reception of *Butterflies*. The novel opens with an author-double who is having difficulties writing because of the demands of her agent and publisher as well a negative review written by "Mario González-Echavarriga" (20). However, *Saving the World* is only one example of how Alvarez illustrates the effects of market reception on the creative process. *In the Name of Salomé* is the first text of historical fiction that Alvarez published after *Butterflies*;[3] its project of recovering the pedagogical legacies of Camila Henríquez Ureña and Salomé Ureña de Henríquez engages the questions of authenticity generated by the reader reception to her prior work. Alvarez's market context informs the depiction of author-doubles in her historical novel, specifically that of "Camila Henríquez Ureña [as] a Dominican intellectual whose life in the United States approximates [Alvarez's] own" (Magnani 18).

In *If I Could Write This in Fire*, Michelle Cliff refers to similar accusations of cultural illegitimacy when she states, "I have been accused of wanting to be black" (87). Critics such as Myriam Chancy and Laura Michelle Issen have pointed to the introduction to the Heinemann anthology *Her True-True Name* as an example of how Cliff's cultural and racial allegiances are often called into question. While the anthology's editors, Pamela Mordecai and Betty Wilson, choose to incorporate

Cliff into their collection of Caribbean women writers, their introduction reveals doubts about whether she belongs in the project, going so far as to say that Cliff is the only one of the collection's recently published Caribbean writers who "does not affirm at least aspects of being in the Caribbean place" and "could be regarded as being more in the alienated tradition of a 'francophone' than an anglophone consciousness" (xvii). In an interview with Meryl Schwartz, Cliff labels this a "nasty swipe" and translates the critique as follows: "They say something to the effect that I am light enough that I might as well be white, which is not true. It's one thing to look x and to feel y, rather than to look x and feel x, and that's part of the difficulty being light-skinned: some people assume you have a white outlook just because you look white. You're met immediately on that level. But it varies a great deal. I felt I was included in that anthology because they couldn't exclude me, but to put me in they had to make a crack about me" (607). To explore the implications of this appraisal of her authenticity, Cliff contextualizes her identification with an Afro-Caribbean heritage in *If I Could Write This in Fire* by giving several biographical examples of her difficulties creating and maintaining relationships with white people and discussing her historical novel *Free Enterprise* in relation to the example it gives of a successful interracial friendship. Cliff describes her work as imagining "hard-won" interracial relationships, which she sees "culminating in the truly revolutionary connection between Mary Ann Pleasant and John Brown" (88). Cliff nevertheless feels the need to "assure the reader that I did not make this friendship up" and relays her personal experience of seeing Pleasant's tombstone and its inscription, which was "chosen by her" and described her as a "friend of John Brown" (89). Cliff declares "such friendship is a triumph of the imagination—on every level an act of liberation" (89). *Free Enterprise*'s project of historical revision is inspired by Cliff's interrogation of writerly privilege, of her authority to speak about the African diasporic history and experience.

   Marlon James's online blog, maintained from 2006 until 2009, provides some insight into related questions of cultural authenticity as well as the gendered challenges faced by male Caribbean diasporic writers. In an entry, James references Chris Rock's comedy sketch "The Routine" as a way of discussing how "true blackness was measured by how little you knew and how less you cared" ("Is We Stoopid?," par 5). James gives a personal anecdote regarding the litmus test for cultural authenticity as a black male, recalling how he and his friends were "accused of playing white because we knew the capital of Zaire and that Titus may be the most misunderstood of Shakespeare's plays" (par. 5). In addition to drawing links between African American and Caribbean diasporic experiences, James expresses concern about how black masculinity is defined in the Caribbean public sphere:

> Of all the interviews I've had the most stupid was from a fellow Jamaican who couldn't think of something more profound than "did you write the book to get girls?" I complained and was told that it was all about publicity and fun and sometimes one had to play the game. What game was that actually, pin the tail on the dumb-ass-sex-mad Negro? I was offended by the question. I'm as irreverent as anybody and pride myself on a perverted sense of humour, but I bristle at stupidity and go apeshit at dumbness commoditized and thrust upon me. (par. 4)

For James, the commodification of ignorance is tied to mainstream stereotypes of black masculinity and sexuality. In chapter 2 I discussed how the narrator of David Chariandy's historical novel negotiates the weight of this stereotype. Published only a year after this post, James's *The Book of Night Women* challenges the association of blackness with ignorance through the main character Lilith's acquisition of literacy. James likewise critiques the restrictive code of black authenticity through the depiction of Lilith and the gender-ambiguous author-double of Lilith's child, Lovey, who is the novel's narrator. James's novel is inspired and delimited by the way the book market privileges the female mainstream reader, and his blog posts reference the prior critical reception of his work. The reaction to his first novel, *John Crow's Devil* (2005), contextualizes James's concerns about authenticity and stereotype. One reviewer goes so far as to say that this novel "encourages the foreign view of Jamaica as a place of exotic oblivion, rum-fuelled assaults and vendetta" (Thomson 21). Claims that what the novel depicts is "profoundly Jamaican" (Polk 54) suggest that certain readerships do perceive the violence depicted as endemic to the Caribbean. *The Book of Night Women* is responsive to this interpretation, contextualizing contemporary violence through a history of slavery, while also apprehensive that its depiction of slavery's brutality will reinforce stereotypes of Caribbean culture.

The critical and mainstream reception of their fiction generates a crisis of authority that leaves its imprint on the historical imagination of Caribbean diasporic writers. The depiction of literacy acquisition references anxieties over market discourses of authenticity, with teacher-student relationships as metaphorical encounters between the text's author and its readers. The author-doubles in the historical fiction wrestle with related challenges, alluding to the contemporary contexts of the writers as public figures and the authority of particular individuals to stand in as spokespersons for an oppressed population. Author-doubles struggle to find their own voices as they narrate the experiences of others. Since literacy and learning are central to the emplotment of the novels, the narrative structure and content of the historical fiction also addresses various modes of pedagogy that can be used to transmit a historical education.

Paulo Freire's articulation of progressive teaching practices and Édouard Glissant's ideas about free versus forced poetics are useful contexts for understanding the pedagogical approaches of Caribbean diasporic authors. Freire's essay "The 'Banking' Concept of Education" (1970) provides an essential outline of the way in which liberation struggles of the 1960s envisioned pedagogical practices in binary terms. Freire distinguishes between oppressive and progressive pedagogies by identifying "banking" versus "problem-posing" styles of teaching. For Freire, the banking concept of education sees students as passive learners in the classroom because it cannot envision students as sources of knowledge or dynamic subjects: "The students are not called upon to know, but to memorize the contents narrated by the teacher. Nor do the students practice any act of cognition since the object towards which that act should be directed is the property of the teacher rather than a medium evoking the critical reflection of both the teacher and students" (74). Banking pedagogy's content-driven mode of learning transfers knowledge hierarchically, from teacher to student via lecture and memorization. By contrast, Freire states that the "role of the problem-posing educator is to create, together with the students, the conditions for [. . .] true knowledge" (74). The classroom is a space of collaboration, with the "problem-posing educator constantly reform[ing] his reflections in the reflection of his students" (74). Since the pedagogical mode is one based in intellectual exchange, "the students—no longer docile listeners—are now critical coinvestigators in dialogue with the teacher" (74).

Freire's oppositions—between memorization and participation in knowledge creation, or passive listening and active cognition—shape the form and content of these Caribbean diasporic novels. However, these historical novels do not necessarily value one mode as more politically progressive than the other. The pedagogical imperative of Julia Alvarez's, Michelle Cliff's, and Marlon James's historical fiction becomes evident in the structure of the narratives as well as the depiction of literacy acquisition. Caribbean diasporic fictions often portray banking models of teaching in the educational encounters of the characters and/or adopt a stylistic structure that transparently conveys or packages the significance of historical information and setting for the reader. Unlike Freire, the writers do not describe banking as necessarily an oppressive strategy for inculcating knowledge; rather, they concede the progressive potential of a banking approach when one is rescuing a vulnerable or marginalized source of knowledge for a dehistoricized student-reader. In the novels I discuss here, the problem-posing form of teaching is depicted as either a positive alternative or an equally useful approach to education. Caribbean diasporic historical fiction adopting the problem-posing model illustrates egalitarian student-teacher relationships and/or structurally engages the reader as a "coinvestigator" in the project of historical revisionism.

Glissant's opposition of natural versus forced poetics supplements the context provided by Freire's pedagogical binary. In *Caribbean Discourse* (1989), Glissant distinguishes between a free poetics that develops when a collective is able to adequately express its desires in a specific language without self-doubt. By contrast, a "forced or constrained poetics" occurs when "a need for expression confronts an inability to achieve expression" (120). Counterpoetics are produced when the language that a community has access to stifles the very desires it wishes to express. By depicting the acquisition of language and literacy alongside the suppression of queer desire, Caribbean diasporic writers allude to the problem of articulation that Glissant describes in *Caribbean Discourse*. The historical fiction struggles to imagine educating and transforming its readerships. Representing literacy acquisition as a site of intimacy and vulnerability also speaks to the way that the marketplace delimits the discursive language of imagination. Caribbean diasporic market aesthetics can be then understood as a forced poetics that is informed by both "deformation" and "resistance" (Glissant, *Caribbean Discourse* 121).

A Teacher's Queer Handicap in Julia Alvarez's *In the Name of Salomé*

Caribbean diasporic historical novels often impart to their readers a comparative vision of history, revealing parallels between the Global North and the Caribbean. In Alvarez's *In the Name of Salomé*, these comparative moves counter stereotypes the reader might have about the Caribbean. A passage in Alvarez's novel describes how the dictator Meriño slaughtered a group of positivist intellectuals as a warning to Eugenio María de Hostos and Salomé Ureña de Henríquez. The narrative of Dominican political turmoil is followed by a description of contemporaneous public violence in the United States: "That summer the American president Garfield was shot by a man caught stealing stationery inside the White House. [. . .] Good men were being killed off. Meanwhile the rich and greedy were in control. Our papers reported that the richest man in the world, a Mr. Vanderbilt, had said, 'Everybody but me and mine be damned'" (184). US and DR histories are shown to mirror each other, with *both* governments prone to corruption and *both* nations wrestling with an excessively powerful upper class that lacks a sense of social responsibility. As Dalleo and I note in *The Latino/a Canon*, "Placing U.S. history into this broader history contests the tendency towards American exceptionalism" (136). The reader is confronted with a historical vision that situates political chaos as plaguing the United States and the Caribbean, challenging the labels promoted by First versus Third World hierarchies. Dalleo and I therefore argue that, "in this way, the United States becomes part of New World history, not only as its main protagonist but also as just another player with a history of corruption and turmoil not so different from those of its neighbors" (136).

The comparative approach to historiography is mirrored by a dialogic structure, in which the narrative alternates between Camila's and Salomé's perspectives as well as between the various geographic spaces they occupy. Most critics comment on how the form of Alvarez's historical novels generates this comparative dialogue. Charlotte Rich associates *In the Time of the Butterflies* with a structure of "dialogism" because of its multiple narrating perspectives, arguing that its "decentralized or 'centrifugal' narrative" incorporates viewpoints that "question or challenge authority" (175). The stylistic organization of the novel directly shapes its mission of historical revision, since dialogism "counters the 'official' voices of Trujillo's vast bureaucracy of dictatorship and machine of propaganda throughout the novel" (179). Marion Rohrleitner makes a similar argument about *In the Name of Salomé* in terms of how the structural dialogue between mother and daughter mirrors the novel's comparative approach to history, "illustrating the way the United States, the Dominican Republic, and Haiti have been part of the same geopolitical constellation since the late eighteenth century" (98).[4] Anna Brickhouse uses the term *hemispheric* to describe Alvarez's fiction while also emphasizing the role that readerships play in the novels' historical imagination or the "inextricability of this hemispheric historical legacy from a network of authorial and readerly relations among multiple American literary traditions spanning the course of a century" (254). The academic reception views Alvarez's approach to recuperating silenced histories as offering a distinctly comparative vision of the Americas. Nevertheless, the academic reception of *In the Name of Salomé* does not connect the structural form of the novel to a broader pedagogical imperative, nor does it address the tensions between the mode the novel adopts to teach its readers about marginalized histories and the teaching styles that the novel's characters model for the reader.

A contradictory pedagogy underlies Alvarez's revisionist history of Las Américas. *In the Name of Salomé* showcases one type of pedagogical approach in *how the characters teach*, but the narrative structure employs a contrary mode of *teaching the reader* its comparative vision of history. The imaginative tension over teaching approaches is evident in how the novel closes with a graveyard setting, indicating writerly anxiety about the ethical future of its pedagogical project. A blind Camila Henríquez Ureña teaches a child, Duarte, to read using her own headstone, and the novel emphasizes the collaborative effort with which literacy is being taught: "His smaller hand closes over mine and he leads my fingers over the cut letters. [. . .] The boy has guided my hand, and now I put my hand over his. 'Your turn,' I say to him. Together we trace the grooves in the stone, he repeating the name of each letter after me. 'Very good,' I tell him when we have done this several times. 'Now you do it by yourself.' He tries again and again, until he gets it right" (353). Camila's pedagogical approach generates an egalitarian power relationship; Camila's blindness means that she needs the boy to lead her inasmuch as Duarte needs her literacy. Once Camila lets go, the boy becomes his own teacher, tracing the letters until he produces knowledge. The novel closes with a scene where Camila's problem-posing method of teaching literacy is aligned with her mother Salomé's pedagogical legacy (since her name is included as part of Camila's headstone) and Camila's literacy brigade work for the Cuban Revolution's Ministry of Education.

The novel does not instantiate a comparable relationship between the reader and its historical narrative. While Alvarez's text educates the reader about Dominican historical figures, focusing on the time frame of 1864–1960, it does not encourage the reader to become an active contributor to interpretive meaning. In this sense, Alvarez structures the novel using a banking form of pedagogy that lectures and processes history for the reader. The lecture mode of the narrative prompts one reviewer to remark that "it is as if Alvarez seized on these [historical] details during her research and felt compelled to mention them over and over as a stamp of authenticity" (Acker 168). The banking pedagogy is evident in the historical gloss found in the narrative and in the way the novel is structured. Each chapter opens with explicit references to the character's narrative perspective, the date, and the setting of the story. As the chapters alternate between Camila and her mother Salomé, the chapter titles remind us of whether we're in Santo Domingo, Vermont, or Cuba. The novel's chronology is especially transparent, with Camila and Salomé's narratives following a linear progression: Camila's entries go backwards in time, while Salomé's advance forwards, so that mother and daughter move temporally toward each other. Using a banking model of educating the reader, the novel assumes that the audience has little knowledge of historical contexts and imagines readers as empty vessels that must be filled with comparative analyses of history. In other words, the novel does not structurally engage the reader as "coinvestigator" in the project of historical revisionism.

The pedagogical contradiction between the problem-posing pedagogy employed by Camila and Salomé and the banking model structuring the novel, between how the characters teach and how the novel teaches, arises from the way the novel imagines its reader-students. Some critics have addressed Alvarez's mission of historical revisionism in terms of teaching the reader. For instance, Trenton Hickman argues that her historical novels are "moralizing parables designed to provide examples worthy of readerly emulation" (99) and that the aim of the narratives is to "glorify these women and the progressive, secular ethics that they embody" (101). The historical figures are ethical models for the reader, so that *In the Name of Salomé* "proselytize[s] readers into taking a journey from interest to inheritance, from vicarious individual involvement to a more intimate, personal invocation of the life of Salomé Ureña" (112). I argue that even as Alvarez's historical fiction seeks to engage the reader as a student of history and ethics, the narrative is fundamentally ambivalent about its pedagogical project. Looking more closely at the representation of teaching uncovers the text's contradictory relationship to its readers, revealing the nuances of Caribbean diasporic historical fiction's market aesthetics.

In The Name of Salomé depicts a specific reader at the start of the novel, with a one-page family tree that is constructed by the American college student who helps Camila pack for Cuba. Camila decides to leave her teaching position at Vassar in 1960 to join the Cuban Revolution and finds that her assistant crafts this chart in order to sort through the family archive. The diagram divorces the family members from the historical context informing their relationships. Referring to the family's "historical background," the student writes "tons of revolutions and wars, too numerous to list" (9). The classroom reader is imagined as an audience who will render historical context irrelevant, reducing the Dominican Republic's history to a stereotype of Third World chaos. As Maya Socolovsky notes, this chart "can be read as Álvarez's examples of an American narrativization of a difficult history, and a writing over of events in order to position the U.S. centrally and view the Dominican Republic from a U.S. perspective" ("Patriotism" 15).The novel's ending skips ahead from the 1960 opening frame of the novel to 1973; the years in between are absent. As a result, the teacher-student encounter moves from the American college classroom that opened the novel, with the family tree compiled by Camila's student helper, to a graveyard in the Dominican Republic, where the blind and ailing Camila is trying to figure out if her nieces kept their promise to engrave her full name on her gravestone. Here in this space of death, Camila seeks to recover the pedagogical tradition of literacy from her mother and the Cuban Revolution and pass it on to the illiterate Dominican boy she finds cleaning her gravestone. For María Cristina Hamill, the "handholding shows the power of education to attain unity between the sexes" and allows Camila to realize "an identity without obstruction as her mother's daughter, as a revolutionary and most importantly, as an educator" (55–56). However, the very headstone Camila uses to teach Duarte to read also symbolizes the obstacles to extending the line of that inheritance. Duarte is learning to read, but his knowledge will remain incomplete, since it is necessarily limited to the letters in Camila's name. Alvarez opens the novel with the global market reader she pictures her text encountering (white, female, college educated) and concludes by mourning the reader that she aspires to reach, an illiterate, poor boy of color whom she cannot access because of flawed literary and educational institutions. The forced poetics of the novel express concern as to whether the historical narrative of an icon like Salomé could provide a model for the incorporation of other subjectivities, like that of Duarte, into Caribbean and US histories. The novel's imaginative difficulty in reconciling these different readerships produces the conceptual contradiction between the novel's banking-lecture form and the egalitarian model of Camila's teaching. The pedagogical disjunction echoes that of the novel's forced poetics, which must attempt to articulate a communal identity within a market discourse that negates or restricts such subjectivity. The novel therefore speaks to the mixed blessing that Simon Gikandi ascribes to globalization and that I discuss in my introduction—how the multicultural book market provides the ethnic writer with the possibility of reaching an audience who is ignorant of Caribbean history and its intersections with US history, while also restricting access to a population marginalized from that marketplace of ideas.

The novel's pedagogical contradiction is also informed by Alvarez's choice of a closeted queer subject as a main character. While there is some historical precedent for representing Camila as a woman with queer desires, it is significant that Alvarez has chosen to examine Camila as a model of revolutionary activism and pedagogy. While we do not learn the details of Camila's romantic relationship with Marion until much later in the novel, it is an important context for the banking structure of Alvarez's historical fiction. With Camila as the author-double, Marion stands in for the reader that the novel anxiously imagines encountering. The relationship between the author-double and her student-reader is an allegory for the contemporary historical context of Alvarez as a Caribbean diasporic writer who has been criticized for being too popular or too American to write about the Dominican experience. Camila as author-double references the authorial historical context of Alvarez as public figure and her supposed failure to embody an entire culture, nation, and ethnicity.[5] Camila's relationship with Marion represents the ethical quandary of the Caribbean diasporic writer's relationship to her or his readership. El secreto abierto of their queer relationship allegorizes the challenges of an ethical encounter between reader and text.

As early as page 2 of the Prologue, Marion appears, described simply as Camila's friend who has "flown up to help with the move" to Cuba in 1960 (3).[6] Marion's goal is to drive Camila from Vermont to the ferry in Key West in order to convince Camila that she should not join the Cuban Revolution. Marion's request for an explanation, asking, "What's the story," initiates the novel's move into the past (8). Camila believes that Marion needs historical contextualization to understand Camila's present decision to go to Cuba, so she has to "start with my mother, which means at the birth of la patria, since they were born about the same time" (8). Even though the personal is political for Camila, the authorial "mission to tell the story of the great ones who have passed on" requires her to "eras[e] herself" and turn "herself into the third person, a minor character, the best friend (or daughter!) of the dying first person hero or heroine" (8). The 1960 frame is followed by the college student's family tree document, and the body of the novel alternates between Camila's third-person voice as she travels farther into the past and Salomé's first-person voice, which journeys toward the present.

Just as Camila as a storyteller is positioned as an author-double, Marion is aligned with the novel's readership. For example, the novel emphasizes the parallels between Marion and Camila's college student. Even after more than forty years of friendship, Marion shares the student's ignorance about Caribbean history and applies stereotypes to Camila's story. Like the college student, Marion is "easily impressed by [the] somebodies" of Camila's life, focusing on how "'Camila's mother was a famous poet.' 'Her father was a president.' 'Her brother was the Norton Lecturer at Harvard'" (3). The college student also remarks "Wow!" in response to Pedro's Ivy League credentials and after labeling Salomé "the National Poetess" wonders, "Should I have heard of her?" (9). Marion confesses to Camila on their drive to Key West, "I honestly don't think I would ever have heard of your mother unless I had met you" (7). Camila's indictment of Marion easily applies to the student organizing the family archive: "She's not surprised. Americans don't interest themselves in the heroes or heroines of minor countries until someone makes a movie about them" (7). Camila's critique speaks back to the market success of Alvarez's previous novel, *In the Time of the Butterflies*, and its 2001 television premiere starring Salma Hayek, Edward James Olmos, and Marc Anthony. Camila's depiction as author-double suggests the problematics of writerly success, in turn positioning Marion as the adult version of the classroom reader.

The literary project of rescuing Camila from historical invisibility is tested by the imagined relationship to the reader, in such a way that the pedagogical dynamic becomes predicated upon a mandate of discretion that silences Camila's queerness as a historical subject. I discuss a similar censorship of sexuality in chapter 2 with Andrea Levy's *Fruit of the Lemon*, chapter 4 with Dionne Brand's *Another Place*, and chapter 5 with Junot Díaz's *Oscar Wao*. Camila's sexuality is subsumed so that the pedagogical thrust of the narrative can become primary, emphasizing an *ethical* teacher-student relationship. With Camila as author-double and Marion as the adult version of the classroom reader (who also could be understood as the book club reader), the sexual intimacy and pedagogical context of their relationship symbolize the novel's concerns about the book market. That anxiety centers on how the market decontextualizes cultural products in order to make them more easily consumable. The dangers of market reading practices are evidenced by how the college student and Marion respond to Camila's story, as well as Camila's censorship of her sexuality in order to narrate the historiography of her family and the Dominican nation.

At the novel's opening, Camila's third-person narrative only vaguely alludes to her past romance with Marion, noting "they had lived through so much, some of which is best left buried in the past, especially now that Marion is a respectable married lady" (5). Their queer past is slowly revealed as the novel progresses, most explicitly when Marion announces her new relationship with Leslie in 1950 during Camila's visit to her at Middlebury College. Finding out that Leslie is a man, Camila mentions her assumption that Marion "preferred women," with the third-person perspective explaining that Camila's discomfort comes from a dislike of "labels that pin the self down to only one set of choices" (82). Camila's stated preference for queerness as an open sexual identity does not translate into a willingness to explore that as a reality. Camila rejects Marion's offer to rekindle their romance together because of an obligation to her biographical narrative. Camila's third-person voice opens up the closet of her queer desires only to shut them down for the priorities of emplotment: "Marion already played the best part, glorious first love forever preserved in her memory" (83). The burial of Camila's queer desires is in part a function of historiography, in the sense that this marginalized identity supposedly has no place in a public narrative about a nation's history. The novel notes that her brother, Pedro Henríquez Ureña, also censors Camila's sexuality by using the phrase "personal life" in his letters to "refer to his sister's perverseness" (109). The effect of an imagined public on Pedro's writing is clear, since the novel attributes the euphemism to his "knowledge that in the future his correspondence will be published (he *is* that famous)" (109).

Even as Camila categorizes her sexual desire for Marion as a youthful error that is not relevant to her 1950s present, the novel travels further into Camila's past, unraveling the story of their romance. The novel's travel backwards in time gives the reader the illusion of accessing a Camila who has not yet completely effaced herself in favor of narrating the lives of historical heroes. Camila's first-person letters to Marion punctuate the third-person narration of Camila's 1923 section set in Washington, D.C. Writing is the main method by which Camila purges the ghost of her sexual attraction to Marion. Just as her brother Pedro abides by a mandate of discretion in his letters that censors her sexuality, Camila is "writing these letters that outline a new situation" for herself and Marion in an attempt to "get free of their special connection" (197). Marion and Camila's queer relationship is a historical trauma that Camila processes by narrating it into silence; hence the opening of the novel can declare Marion to be a friend and nothing more. Camila's tactic parallels that of *Soucouyant*'s nameless narrator when he first abandons his mother, as I discussed in chapter 2. Her letters to Marion remain unsent, making clear that silencing this past will require the silencing of Camila's first-person voice. The classroom context of their queer sexualities is an important backstory for understanding why Camila's "voice sounds strangely her own and not her own" (8). The "teacher's handicap" of "vanish[ing] into whatever she's teaching" is the reason Camila's narrative is relayed in the third person (8). As the novel travels further back into Camila's past, we learn that this teaching technique of erasing her self is tied to a romantic encounter with Marion that originated in the classroom.[7] This trauma of intimacy informs Camila's conception of herself as a teacher, and by extension sexuality emerges as a metaphor for the challenges to the pedagogical imperative.

Camila first meets Marion in 1918, when Marion enrolls as a student in the Spanish conversation class that Camila teaches at the University of Minnesota. Camila describes their relationship as beginning "quite innocently, lying back together on the bed—where else in Marion's small boarding-house were they to sit?—reading out loud, first Marion reading a paragraph and then Camila the next, 'So you can practice your English.' Her student had become her teacher. That is how it started" (233–43). This censored personal history is an important context for Camila's 1960 move to Cuba and the final scene of Camila in 1973 using her headstone to teach Duarte to read. The physical intimacy of the child's hand guiding that of the elderly blind woman finds its pedagogical precursor in this sexual encounter, with Camila and Marion alternating between learning Spanish and English. Camila's narration assumes that queer sexuality has no public in 1918; limited to the confines of the bedroom, her queer identity cannot become part of her public history. Her brother Pedro's letters reveal how unspeakable such a subject position is, but his stalking and policing of Camila's movements—to the point that he barges in on a sexual encounter between Camila and Marion (251)—emphasizes why Camila buries this part of her identity in the past. The novel frames the Cuban Revolution as a new opportunity for Camila to engage in a pedagogical relationship, but one that is not complicated by queer sexuality. By adapting the Revolution's legacy of literacy brigades, Camila replaces her relationship to Marion with the supposedly more socially appropriate and ethical relationship to Duarte, the illiterate boy—in other words, an asexual heteronormative pairing.

The project of countering economic inequality by teaching literacy can be articulated as a public project, while that earlier queer relationship could find no public narrative or language of advocacy.

Just as the figure of Duarte allows the novel to imagine another readership, an alternative to the classroom reader, the pedagogical dynamic of Camila's relationship to Marion turns out to have contemporary resonances. In a tender moment with Marion, Camila realizes "how silly love talk would sound to someone who is not a participant" (243). Camila reassures herself, "But who could be listening?" while also noting that her denigration of romantic language is due to her brother's "invasion of privacy," which forces her to see "herself through their eyes" (243). When Camila asks, "Who could be listening?" it is possible to imagine that the readership is also invading Camila's privacy and informing Alvarez's portrayal of this queer relationship. El secreto abierto of Camila's sexuality is delimited by the audience to whom she imagines narrating her life. Marion's interrogation initiates Camila's story, and the muted revelation of their sexual history together means that Camila's self-censorship has its roots in the threat that such intimacy represents to the author-reader relationship. Camila's reference to the "invasion of privacy" acknowledges the effects imagined readerships have on the construction of a cultural product as well as how the encounter with the market audience can also shape the interpretation and meaning of that product. Additionally, Pedro's silencing of Camila's sexuality is symbolic of the novel's anxieties about how its readerships might silence certain elements of its revisionist history.

Camila's queer identity is at the center of the creative tension regarding pedagogy in Alvarez's novel. The college student's entry for Camila on her family tree remarks that the archive contains "tons of love letters she wouldn't let me read to her" (9). Even though Camila refuses to listen to her own first-person voice from the past, these are the letters that the reader eventually accesses to learn of Camila's relationship with Marion. With those private thoughts becoming public in the course of the novel's plot progression, the narrative expresses misgivings about translating Camila's closeted sexuality for a contemporary audience. The silencing of Camila's sexuality is made visible as a problematic outcome of the historical project. *In the Name of Salomé* encodes a tension between the depiction of teaching approaches and the pedagogical structure of the novel. The fracturing of this historical fiction's pedagogical imperative frames the market and historiography as rhetorical spaces that cannot imagine a *sexual* queer woman as an ethical agent of history. The closeting of Camila's queerness, the censoring of sexuality, alludes to how market pressures and dominant modes of narrating national histories privilege the "socially appropriate" role of female teachers even as those narratives remain troubled by queer desires. Michele Cliff's novel *Free Enterprise* illustrates several queer historical subjects while narrating an abolitionist history of Las Américas. Although the novel is stylistically very different from that of Alvarez, it exhibits similar tensions in terms of form, pedagogy, and imagined readership.

Fragile Knowledge and Ambivalent Solidarities in Michelle Cliff's *Free Enterprise*

In *Free Enterprise*, Michelle Cliff employs a comparative approach that accentuates parallels between Caribbean and African American histories. On a plot level, such alliances are made through the characters, with Regina, a Caribbean woman, encouraged by the historical figure of Mary Ellen Pleasant to take on the African American mythic folk name of Annie Christmas. By imagining the Caribbean's role within African American liberation struggles, Cliff writes comparative histories of feminist revolutionary agency. At first, Regina finds the story of Annie Christmas too fantastical to be historically real—"a messianic sister with the physical power of John Henry; too much to hope for"— so Pleasant asks her, "Is Nanny too much?" (27). What shocks Regina is not that the legendary Caribbean Nanny has anything in common with African American Annie Christmas but that Pleasant is aware of "the great Maroon chieftainness" (27). Regina's surprise—"You know of her?" (28)—denotes an expectation that Nanny's story cannot travel beyond the Caribbean locale. Regina-Annie's presumption of Pleasant's ignorance about Caribbean folk histories reminds us of Camila's student in Alvarez's novel, who asks, "Should I have heard of her?" (9). In this passage, Cliff appears more hopeful than Alvarez about the circulation of marginalized knowledge and history. Pleasant asserts a shared legacy of resistance within Las Américas, responding to Regina-Annie's question by explaining, "We have maroons here too, you know" (28). Pleasant asks Regina-Annie to recognize how her assumption about Pleasant's limited knowledge signals unfamiliarity with the intersections between Caribbean and African American experiences. The narrative offers this exchange as one example of the history of Las Américas, of the links between Caribbean and US abolitionist struggles. The repetition of "you know" in this exchange is revealing, since it highlights what is at stake in the novel's pedagogical project: teaching the reader about marginalized histories requires certain, perhaps unfair, assumptions about the range of historical knowledge the reader brings to the text. Cliff expands upon Alvarez's readership depiction, noting that both reader *and* author bring a set of expectations and stereotypes that can delimit the success of a novel's ethical project. A comparative approach to teaching a history of Las Américas inevitably restricts historical information, highlighting certain parallels over others. Even focusing on comparative historiography requires the silencing of the local, the factors that distinguish Caribbean and American histories.

Critics of *Free Enterprise* remark on the novel's ambivalence about storytelling as a means for disseminating a comparative approach to historiography. As Lisa Dunick argues, "Rather than an imaginary community of oppressed voices, Cliff's text demonstrates only the distant possibility of such a community through the individual voices contained within her novel's pages" (44). Secondary sources cite the leper colony scenes of the novel to discuss the connections that Cliff draws between different cultures and their histories.[8] In a post-Emancipation United States that has not lived up to the promise of the abolition struggles, Annie visits the people confined in the leper colony for consolation and a new sense of belonging through their collective marginality. The storytelling circles at the colony expose the reader to the personal-public narratives of a Hawaiian, a Jamaican, a Tahitian, a Sephardic Jew, and a white Kentuckian. Annie's relationship to the leper colony as a collector of marginalized stories positions her as an author-double for Cliff. The leper colony stories describe transnational experiences of colonialism from different perspectives—and the dialogic form of this section mimics that of the rest of the novel, which alternates between Annie's and Pleasant's reminiscences. Both Alvarez and Cliff frame their narratives as structural dialogues that mirror the novels' comparative approach to historiography.

The alternation of voices is one way in which the novel's formal structure encourages the reader to see parallels between these different national and ethnic histories. However, the setting of the novel also alludes to an anticolonial historical context that lies in the future. Cliff creates a temporal space for dialogue between historical figures that is possible only in the world of fiction—echoing Alvarez's time line of Camila and Salomé's sections that move toward each other in time, toward a more intimate dialogue, despite being separated in historical reality (since Salomé dies when her daughter Camila is only three years old). Jeanine Luciana Lino Costa remarks on how "the treatment given by Annie Christmas to the patients of the leper colony is similar to that given to patients with the same disease given by Ernesto 'Che' Guevara and his friend Alberto Granado during their journey around South America" (143). I would add that the representation of leprosy is guided by the novel's ethical imperative of social justice, setting the stage for how the Sixties emerge as a past to the reader's present and as a future-ghost to Annie and Pleasant's present. Che Guevara, whose depiction I discuss in chapter 4, is a haunting referent for the Sixties historical legacy of the Americas—the more explicit referent in Cliff's novel being that of Malcolm X as the "hologrammatical man."

The fact that the existing academic criticism on Cliff's historical fiction overlooks the congruence between Guevara and Malcolm X is symptomatic of the text's problem-posing mode of teaching a comparative approach to history. The novel does not process and package the links but places the narratives alongside each other so that the reader is left to actively construct the connections.[9] Readers' knowledge of anticolonial and civil rights histories will inevitably shape their perception of how such histories are encoded in the novel's antislavery and postabolition setting. For instance, identifying the hologrammatical man as Malcolm X depends on whether the reader recognizes the cues given for his identity: "Homeboy, then Detroit Red, then X" (76). If the reader successfully contextualizes the hologrammatical man, the figure is an example of the temporal dialogue the novel initiates—more specifically, how the post-Sixties mourning of the civil rights movements is processed via an earlier historical period of civil rights struggle.[10] Malcolm X makes several appearances as a hologram to Pleasant, as if he has become such a powerful symbolic figure (like Christmas and Nanny) that he can defy realist conventions. His time travel highlights the potential commonalities they could have conversed about: mixed-race identity, self-defense, and liberation.[11] While the hologrammatical man is a visitor from the twentieth-century future to the nineteenth-century past, his presence for the contemporary reader is a ghostly haunting from the 1960s. He asks Pleasant, "Why didn't I know you. About you?" and Pleasant replies, "My point exactly" (142). His question echoes that of Regina, indicating that the problem of silenced histories, especially those involving female protagonists, continues to plague Las Américas. Historical erasures prevent a comparative analysis of past and present struggles for equality, as well as conversations across cultures and genders. The knowledge gap from Pleasant's and Regina-Annie's opening dialogue repeats here, with certain histories failing to be passed on from generation to generation.

The exchange between Malcolm X and Pleasant evokes the dangers of the problem-posing mode of the novel's pedagogy: if the reader does not ethically decode the historical references in the novel, then another missed opportunity can take place, with the reader unable to engage a comparative historiography because he or she lacks the information to build such dialogues. In comparison to Alvarez's *In the Name of Salomé*, the approaches of lecture versus participation-centered education are reversed in *Free Enterprise*—Cliff's novel depicts lecture as a progressive strategy for passing along marginalized histories to the next generation, but the form of the novel instead relies on the reader being a full participant in the construction of symbolic meaning. Cliff's text contains no descriptive gloss for the links between the various voices and histories depicted, while the narrative is intensely fragmented and does not provide an easy plot chronology. The thematic tension between knowledge and ignorance conveys concerns over the novel's project of historical revision and the ethical stakes of its pedagogical approach to transform the reader.

Despite the stylistic differences in the way Alvarez and Cliff structure the pedagogical mode of their historical fiction, similar symbolic elements organize *In the Name of Salomé* and *Free Enterprise*. The novels open by referencing the expectations of the reader and conclude by pairing an idealized public project of literacy with the image of a graveyard. *Free Enterprise* opens with a tree image, but rather than the family tree drafted by Camila's college student, the reader finds the "live oak and mimosa and cypress" that Annie has "decked with colored glass, clear glass" (4). These trees become a metaphor for the problem-posing structure of the novel, hinting at the expectation that the reader must actively contribute to the narrative's construction of meaning and history: "If the breeze from the river came up a certain way, and filled the spaces between bottles and branches, there might be a tune" (13). The tentative potential of the wind, which might arrive, which might create a pattern of sounds that leads to a coherent melody, conveys the novel's doubts about whether the reader will be able to make sense of the structural and symbolic gaps in knowledge and context. The tune that the trees "might" make is interpreted as "lamentation or bamboula, or something in between" and this variation in interpretation is ascribed not just to the medium of the music, "the mood of the glass, the density of the tree," but also to "the capability of the listener" (13). If Alvarez's family tree image symbolizes the types of stereotypical narratives a classroom reader might bring to a historical fiction about Dominican history, Cliff's trees express concerns about the adequacy of the novel's pedagogical approach as well as the reading lens of its audience. The questions that follow Pleasant's epitaph a couple of pages later provide an example of how the sentence "She was a friend of John Brown" leads to a multiplicity of interpretations, all containing some element of racism or sexism or homophobia, but leading up to what is the worst possible response: "Never heard of her" (18). Evoking the ignorance voiced by Camila's college student regarding Salomé's status as "National Poetess," Cliff opens her novel by mapping out the assumptions and lack of knowledge that readerships may bring to it (9).

Free Enterprise concludes with Pleasant wondering how her tombstone will commemorate her activist legacy and remembering a childhood teacher who taught her students to memorize slave narratives. Just as Camila assures herself that her tombstone wishes have been granted, that her name will be linked to the pedagogical model of her mother Sálome, Pleasant recalls her formative classroom experience as she imagines how her tombstone inscription will be interpreted and whether it will successfully align her with the historical figure of John Brown in the public imagination. As opposed to the problem-posing method of the musical bottles on Annie's trees, relying on the trained ear of the listener, the memory of the Free African School where Pleasant was educated offers a vindication of banking pedagogy. Miss Carey, the teacher, tells her students that "books are fragile things. [. . .] What they contain can easily be lost. We must become talking books; talk it on, like the Africans, children" (211). The schoolmistress's project means that "each of her students memorize[s], for recitation on command, a narrative in its entirety" (211). The difference in power dynamics between Camila as teacher and Miss Carey is striking, with Cliff's "strong-voiced woman" at the top of the hierarchy (211), commanding the children to memorize and repeatedly recite out loud narratives that she alone has selected as important enough to pass on. Here the power structure of top-down pedagogy is framed as being in service of a progressive project. This classroom scene evokes what Karla Holloway describes in *BookMarks* as the African American pedagogical tradition of recitation in southern childhood education (97–98).

However, Pleasant's reminiscence calls into question the effectiveness of this cultural practice in sustaining an oral history, in providing an alternative to the mainstream narrative that silences the African diasporic experience. As Pleasant recalls the students' oral presentations, she realizes the historical gaps that the activist lecture model cannot fill in or counter: "'Sarah?' She called out. 'Yes, Miss Carey.' 'Please come forward to recite.' And Sarah began. 'I offer here neither the history of a saint, a hero, nor a tyrant [. . .]' And Sarah continued, but Mary Ellen could no longer remember the rest of it." (211). Pleasant cannot remember the lines that follow the opening of Sarah's assigned text. Even as the passage challenges the effectiveness of the banking model of pedagogy, the novel corroborates Miss Carey's sense that the written texts the children recite are in danger of being erased from the historical record. Pleasant sees the truth of the teacher's prediction, returning as an adult to "the Vineyard, to Cuttyhunk, where the Free African School had been," and finding that the "school was decaying" and "the books were gone" (211).

While the novel mourns the failure of the top-down, lecture model of education to supplement the written word with an oral history, the final scene structurally employs a problem-posing pedagogical mode. For example, the reader is given the *words* that these children have memorized, even though *Free Enterprise* does not contextualize the recitations with publication dates, author names, or titles. These interpretive challenges stand in stark contrast to Miss Carey's pedagogical lesson of memorization.[12] If the audience wants to situate these readings in some way, the reader must take the extra step of researching the recited phrases. In so doing, the reader could discover that the students of the Free African School are memorizing texts by Gustavus Vassa and Phillis Wheatley. The form of Cliff's novel generally calls on the reader to actively construct meaning, to put the pieces of the novel's puzzle together in order to figure out what character is speaking, what time period is being imagined, and even, on a basic plot level, what exactly is happening, since the novel jumps back and forth between the past and present, history and memory. The tension between Pleasant's personal memories of her childhood banking education and the novel's problem-posing aesthetic mirrors Alvarez's pedagogical contradiction between Camila's teaching and the structure of *In the Name of Salomé*. In thinking though *Free Enterprise*'s postcolonial imperative, its ethical project of recovering lost voices, I agree with Lisa Dunick that "what remains most powerful about this text is its insistence on its own fallibility" (49). The novel's articulation of its anxieties about art as a mode of social critique is as interesting as the histories it aims to bring back into the mainstream of Mary Ellen Pleasant and others.

When discussing the representation of art in *Free Enterprise*, critics center on the unveiling of the William Turner painting and the correspondence that ensues between Pleasant and Alice Hooper, the owner of the painting.[13] The parallels between the painting and Cliff's novel are strong, since both depict slavery, and the unveiling scene provides Cliff with the opportunity to depict the different readerships her novel of historical fiction might encounter: the aesthete who focuses on artistic beauty, the white feminist who expects a person of color to act as translator of the art's true meaning, and the African American woman who looks at the bodies in the foreground rather than the beautiful background. As Noraida Agosto points out, this scene directly alludes to the reader (32). In a narrator's aside, the reader is not only informed where the painting "hangs today" but also told, "Go see it. Take the kids" (180). Agosto reads this invocation as "Cliff's address to the reader" and "a reminder that she is writing 'live' history; by enticing the readers to corroborate the fact, Cliff actualizes the history of slavery" (32). Although the narrator encourages readers to take on the responsibility of witnessing the painting themselves, I would disagree with Agosto regarding the tone of this aside to readers. The narrator's commentary contains an indictment, that the reader will perceive this painting from a position similar to that of the guests at the salon unveiling. The reader will also view the trip to see the painting as a mode of educational entertainment, as wholesome fun for the family, rather than as a troubling encounter with the violent horror of slavery. As Vivian Nun Halloran notes, this "sarcastic" recommendation "conveys the narrator's contempt for anyone who would minimize the scale of human suffering depicted in the painting by treating it as a mere novelty" (62).

Marian "Clover" Adams Hooper and Regina-Annie as author-doubles most closely embody the challenges that Cliff imagines herself facing as a Caribbean diasporic author. Cliff's *Free Enterprise* does not sustain the kind of binary distinction between teacher-authors or student-readers that is found in Alvarez's *In the Name of Salomé*. As a result, the author-doubles are not always explicitly linked to the educational literacy project associated with Mary Ellen Pleasant's memory of the Free African School. Even so, Clover and Annie are symbolic of Cliff's ambivalence regarding her subject position as a Caribbean diasporic writer and whether she can teach her reader an ethical lesson about the history of Las Américas. Suzanne Bost has pointed out that "Cliff's position among Afro-Caribbean women writers is somewhat ambiguous because of her US residence, her class advantage, her light skin, and her education" ("Creoles and Color" 119). As I discussed earlier, Cliff is by no means unaware of how her identity has been the source of criticism, challenging her authority to speak on the Afro-Caribbean experience. Her ambivalence about whether she can or should be seen as a spokesperson for Caribbean culture is allegorized in the characters of Clover Adams and Annie Christmas—and the way they oscillate between their roles as creative artists narrating the stories of others and as readerships engaged by those stories. With the controversies about Cliff's writerly authority as a context, I read her shift from writing semiautobiographical fiction like *Abeng* (1985) and *No Telephone to Heaven* (1987) to writing a historical novel about an African American historical figure as part of Cliff's ethical project to face head-on questions about the legacies shaping Afro-Caribbean identity and whether she has the "qualifications" to explore the silences in those histories.

When one is imagining the symbolism of characters like Clover and Annie, it seems easy to position them as exact opposites. Clover could be seen as Cliff's version of Alvarez's Marion, a white, female, college-educated reader who, like her cousin Alice Hooper, is fraught with white liberal guilt and has uncomfortable encounters with women of color. By contrast, Annie is often viewed by critics as an author-double for Cliff: for instance, Kim Robinson-Walcott sees Annie as Cliff's "conscious decision to foreground her blackness," which is "symbolized by the blackening of the West Indian mulatto Annie Christmas's skin" so that "the author expands her identification with blackness to politically embrace American blackness" (97). In many ways, Annie embodies a positive progressive model of the artist, since she is an activist, having participated in the abolitionist liberation struggles and continuing to collect marginal voices by trespassing into the leper colony in the 1920 present. A closer examination reveals how much Clover and Annie have in common, especially in terms of how they are haunted by the marginalized figures of Scheherezade/Sally and Industry. When Clover and Annie reflect on these Other women, their identities fluctuate between those of author and audience. This vacillation is emblematic of the novel's concerns regarding writerly authority and how readers may apply restrictive codes of cultural belonging and authenticity.

Clover meets Scheherezade, an "alley-dwelling" woman, behind Ford's Theatre, the site of Lincoln's assassination (157). Unable to enter the theater, Clover interviews Scheherezade in order to contextualize the president's violent death and "imagine its historical moment" (85). The ethnographic approach that Clover uses to collect Scheherezade's testimony is analogous to that of Annie's role in the leper colony. When Clover attempts to transform Scheherezade into a source for her art, her photography, the ethical stakes of her creative impulse are called into question. Scheherezade forces Clover to admit her ignorance, that "you know nothing about me; you don't know my name" (87). A contradiction lies at the heart of Clover's inspiration as author-photographer; despite her subject's anonymity and Clover's lack of personal knowledge about her circumstances, Clover thinks she is entitled to depict Scheherezade in a photograph: "yet you want something as intimate as my likeness to take away with you" (87). Scheherezade's commentary challenges the novel's own project in terms of intimacy and the potentially unethical grounds it may be treading upon to represent marginalized women like Scheherezade and Mary Ellen Pleasant.[14]

Although Clover begins the scene as an author-double, Scheherezade shifts the dynamics of their relationship so that Clover is an engaged audience for her story. Scheherezade's problem-posing questions and her insistence that Clover answer them lead Clover to eventually ask, "Who are you?" (90). Scheherezade uses questions during her escaped-slave narrative to perform a dialogue where Clover's personal history also becomes part of the story—specifically, how Clover's mother died in a sanatorium and her physician father later took his daughter along on tours of insane asylums, treating the "poor unfortunate gratis" (95). Clover lies to Scheherezade about the effect the sanatorium visits had on her self-development because she insists that the escaped slave is a "stranger" and she cannot expose her father, who forced her to accompany him on these visits, to the critique of an outsider (158). Clover's aside to the reader means that she reveals her secret trauma to another stranger. Clover admits that these trips give her nightmares because she is tortured by the question "What was the difference between them and her" (158). She still insists on maintaining a distance between herself and Scheherezade, since identifying with her would mean accepting the likenesses between their upbringings, between her physician father and that of Scheherezade, a plantation owner responsible for Scheherezade's enslavement. Clover's ambivalent response to Scheherezade's story, as well as the escaped enslaved woman's insistence on asking questions to paint a comparative picture of their personal histories, calls attention to the imagined power dynamics giving shape to the novel's market aesthetics.

Annie Christmas is largely read as the author-double for Michelle Cliff,[15] but the similarities in Clover's and Annie's relationships to historical subjectivity and agency render a more nuanced picture of the novel's writerly personae and, by extension, its market aesthetics. Annie's childhood nanny, Industry, is as threatening and haunting a presence as Scheherezade is for Clover. Memories of Industry lead Annie to undergo a transformation from articulating to observing history. This shift calls into question Annie's creative voice and exposes her complicity as silent witness to violence. Industry embodies an opaque, unknowable subject of history and an inaccessible readership. In the penultimate chapter of the novel, the reader finds a letter that Annie has written but never sent to Mary Ellen Pleasant. Annie reveals in the letter why her path has diverted so far from that of Pleasant after the revolt; the repeated sexual violations she suffered while on a chain gang engender Annie's isolation and withdrawal from society. Annie's trauma evokes memories of Industry, producing disturbing parallels between Annie's witnessing and that of the white woman who is audience to Annie's violation. As with Scheherezade and Clover, Annie's painful moment of intimacy with this white woman leads her to divulge a traumatic childhood event to the reader.

The memory of those repeated rapes is not what prevents Annie from sending the letter to Pleasant. After explaining that the black men on the chain gang were forced to rape Annie when her gender was discovered, she notes that "this is the point at which I usually twist the paper and lay it in the fireplace" (207). What Annie tells the reader but cannot bring herself to tell Pleasant is that the most traumatic aspect of her time on the chain gang was her encounter with a white woman. While Annie "detach[es] my nether parts from the rest of me" in order to survive her sexual violations (207), she cannot detach herself from the racialized gaze of the white woman. The dye Annie used to pass as a black man was "long dissolved in springtime," and "there I was, a light-skinned woman on a leash. A thing of wonderment to some" (208). The white woman who has "come to enjoy the daily entertainment" remarks, "She's no more a nigger than I am. What is she?" (208). The white woman claims Annie as kin in terms of whiteness but at the same time objectifies her as a "what." When Annie considers whether the woman "fear[ed] she might be next," she immediately responds, "I don't think so" (208). Evoking Clover's reaction to seeing the women on her father's tours of insane asylums, fearing the lack of distance between the self and Other, Annie refutes the possibility that the white woman would be haunted by seeing Annie in chains. The context of Clover's story seems to call this into doubt, but as the passage continues it becomes evident that it is Annie who fears an alliance between herself and the white woman who witnessed her violation so casually.

After asserting that the white woman would never fear for her safety after claiming Annie as her double, Annie proceeds to remember her childhood nanny: "I thought of Industry, the bit rusting in her mouth" (208). The only prior mention of Industry brings us back to the novel's beginning, to the conversation with Pleasant about Nanny and Regina's new namesake of Annie Christmas. Regina-Annie describes Industry as "my nurse" who "slept on a pallet next to my bed, on the floor," but she is also an author-double who narrates "tales of Nanny and her Winward Maroons" (28). As a result, when Industry "ran off I knew she had turned back into her Nanny-self" (28). The child transforms Industry from storyteller into a character of her own creation, but Regina-Annie is eventually forced to see the real consequences for an escaped slave. Industry is "caught" and "put in the stocks," and "they put the bit on her" (29). Annie is witness to Industry's violent silencing and haunted by passivity and detachment: "I couldn't save her. I saved myself instead" (29). Annie is burdened by her inability to change Industry's circumstances and Regina's own survival. This self-incrimination resembles that of Clover and ties both women to the white woman who stood by while Annie was violated. The dangers of intimacy, of sharing experiences, means that the potential of solidarity is undercut by the potential for complicity with traumatic psychological and physical violence.

When the image of Industry returns at the conclusion of the novel, it remains informed by Annie's guilt about her inability to do more than simply witness. By placing her encounter with the white woman alongside her vision of Industry presumably committing suicide, Annie invites her readers to see the intersections as well as the reasons for why "this is the story I do not tell" (208). Imagining "Industry walking into the sea, roiling in [the] tempest" of a hurricane (208), the novel mourns the stories that cannot be relayed as part of its project of historical revisionism. With "no power of nature equal to the task" of breaking the bit that silences and destroys Industry (208), the narrative acknowledges the limitations of its postcolonial ethics. The novel questions the motivations of Annie as author-double and, by extension, of Cliff. Storytelling is a witnessing informed by self-preservation, by a desire to distinguish the self from the other in order to avoid the fate of invisibility. The ethical obligations are hindered by the author-double's dependence upon the objectification of the Other in order to translate his or her story. In recalling the white woman's comment as she witnesses Annie's gang rape, Annie is not simply aligning herself as a victim in the same way Industry is a victim. Annie is both subject and object in the white woman's gaze, just as Industry is in hers, just as Scheherezade is in Clover's. Scheherezade and Industry also recall Camila's Duarte in that they symbolize readerships whom the novel cannot reach, who are subjects of history but not participants in the readership process. In *Free Enterprise*, the themes of sexuality and intimacy are intertwined with the representation of author-double and reader.

Part of the violence that Scheherezade locates in Clover's request for her photograph is a demand for undeserved intimacy, the intimacy of photographing her body. As in Alvarez's novel, the intimate sphere evokes the challenges of an ethical encounter between readerships and the projects of historical revision; queerness is central to allegorizing this problem. Interestingly, while Cliff's prior works like *Abeng* and *No Telephone to Heaven* explicitly portray sexual encounters between women, *Free Enterprise* does not. The historical novel hints that certain characters and historical figures are queer women, but *Free Enterprise* follows a mandate of discretion, since it does reference or illustrate any sexual encounters. The censoring of sexual intimacy is evocative of the offstage depiction of sex in *Fruit of the Lemon*, which I discussed in chapter 2. Queer sexuality is rendered as a site of impossible intimacy, with Cliff's novel acknowledging same-sex desire alongside the missed opportunities for historical figures due to the logic of el secreto abierto. Alice Hooper "admit[s] to a fantasy" of joining homesteading women: "She'd read of female couples, the most daring of pairs, [. . .] friends or cousins, traveling" out West (97). These historiographies provide Alice with a model for what her relationship with her cousin Clover might have looked like, but the euphemism of "friends or cousins" for these same-sex relationships indicates that a public queer identity must be closeted within the asexual framework of familial friendship. Alice Hooper notes that her relationship with Clover involves "spectating life" and "never—but that glorious once—becoming real, descending into it, striding through it with intent" (97). Witnessing and documenting the Civil War via Clover's photography is a proxy activity for Alice and Clover, who cannot live reality fully and publicly as women desiring women. The reader doesn't know exactly what that "glorious" exception is, but the prior passage relates how Alice and Clover are left alone on the battlefield of Antietam: "They lay there after a meal of oyster loaf and white wine, while Patrick strolled the sunken road" (96). Cliff perhaps finds herself in the same position as Alvarez with Camila, that bringing such historical figures explicitly out of the closet could be potentially unethical. However, the novel's ambivalence about how history ends up being forgotten, silenced or not passed on, suggests that these sexual intimacies are rendered visible silences to allegorize the challenges of historical recovery.

The idea that certain historical subjectivities, like those of queer women and men, would not be passed on or would be censored if incorporated by mainstream histories also ruptures the dialogue between Pleasant and Annie that organizes the novel. Pleasant's first-person narrative reinforces her public identity as a heterosexual woman, since she mentions being "loved by my dear husband James" (139). However, Pleasant's husband provides more than just love. Annie remarks to Rachel that after the failure of the revolt coordinated with John Brown, Pleasant became a public activist while Annie "withdrew" (197). Pleasant can become a public avenger precisely because of her marriage: "She had promised her husband, right before he died, that she would use his money [. . .] solely for the furthering of the race" (197–98). The financial stability provided by heterosexual marriage enables Pleasant to take on a more public role, to become "a liberator by marriage, and by inheritance" (198). However, the rift between Pleasant and Annie, between the public and the private routes they take after the revolt, also stems from the unspeakable queer intimacy they share. In a letter to Annie, Pleasant tells her that "you are to me like an old lover; don't be shocked. I mean you know me very well and can read between the lines. There is no one left who can" (133). Knowledge returns as a theme in Pleasant and Annie's correspondence, this time framed by a special intimacy that Pleasant ascribes to lovers. While Kaisa Ilmonen points out that "the narrator hints many times to Annie's lesbianism" (189), I would add that the critical reception has not addressed the novel's depiction of Pleasant as a queer subject. Using the "shocking" metaphor of same-sex desire to describe their relationship as one of reader and text, of Annie reading between Pleasant's lines, allows the novel to queer the intimate encounter with its audience. Pleasant's translation of Regina to Annie Christmas also models the silencing of queer identity, since Pleasant explains that the need for a name change is based on how the name Regina "sounds too much like a royal orifice" (25). "Regina" is too close to "vagina" and must be sanitized. The trauma of cloaking her birth name and silencing its linguistic reference is repeated when Annie reveals how gang rape led her to "detach my nether parts from the rest of me" (207). Nevertheless, the contradiction between Pleasant's public heterosexual identity and private queer desires remains unexplored. The reader is left to make sense of el secreto abierto and the silences encoded in the description of Annie's relationship to Pleasant.

Unlike Camila's, Pleasant's mode of activism is not teaching literacy. Pleasant is a capitalist, investing her husband's "fortune" from "the China trade" into "her own enterprises," such as "bringing a lawsuit against a cable car company" to force "the integration of public services" (198). The lesson that she teaches about the market being a space that can facilitate and sustain civil rights activism is not one that Annie can imitate. "Know[ing] she wanted me to join her" in "the Cause," Annie explains to Rachel that her inability to take on an activist role is due to her selfishness in "seeking my own redemption" (198). Much as Alice frames her witnessing of the Civil War with Clover's photography in opposition to becoming "real" with "intent" (97), Annie positions Pleasant's public activism as more valuable and transformative than her inward turn. Nevertheless, Pleasant's marketplace is no more open to the articulation of a queer identity than the photography that Clover creates to document her and Alice's historical context. The novel cannot imagine a public for a sexual queer woman, so the potential for a relationship between Pleasant and Annie must be relegated to the spaces between the lines of the text.

Counterpoint: Depicting Violence Ethically in Marlon James's *The Book of Night Women*

Like other Caribbean diasporic historical fiction, Marlon James's *The Book of Night Women* negotiates between the demands to entertain and teach, to simplify and complicate, to make history both palatable and challenging. The historical revisionism of Alvarez and Cliff highlights the interconnectedness of Las Américas, of the social movements in the United States and the Caribbean, focusing on abolition and feminist struggles. James's novel instead aligns itself with the African American tradition of neo-slave narratives. *The Book of Night Women* is inspired and informed by an ethical imperative: how to ethically depict a history of slavery without falling into the pitfalls of flattening out or reinforcing its violence. As I have discussed, *In the Name of Salomé* and *Free Enterprise* are pedagogical historical novels that contain a curious contradiction between the way the characters teach their students and the way the novels teach their reader: there is a tension between memorization or banking models of education that are information based and the more egalitarian power structure of problem-posing education, where the students are active subjects rather than passive consumers of knowledge. Cliff's Annie Christmas and Clover Adams Hooper alternate between the roles of author-artist and audience-witness. James also creates a continuum between these identities by depicting the mixed-race Lilith as the mirror-subject of the reader at the start of the novel who undergoes a learning process that transforms her into an author-double by its conclusion.

Depicting slavery in Jamaica, *The Book of Night Women* contains second-person allusions to the reader's presence and uses an invented patois to both defamiliarize and train the mainstream market audience. The novel encourages the reader to mimic the process by which the main character, Lilith, becomes literate. Lilith is trained to read by the house slave Homer using Henry Fielding's eighteenth-century novel *Joseph Andrews*. Literacy entails not simply reading but also reading beyond the surface, determining how a cultural product can be instructive about the cultural logic of its historical context. My earlier discussion of Glissant's forced poetics maps out the creative potential and limits of articulating desires within oppressive discourses. Homer attempts to teach Lilith the skills of interpretation via a banking approach, lecturing Lilith about how to read. The novel shows Lilith rejecting Homer's mentorship and developing a problem-posing method of self-education, but ultimately opting for violent action and narration as modes of historical agency.

In his blog, Marlon James discusses the challenges involved in the ethical project of training the reader to view the violence of Caribbean slavery anew: "What does one do when the absolute brutality of truth would stretch the boundaries of plausibility in fiction?" ("Books I Was Reading," par 10). The beginning of *The Book of Night Women* addresses the problem of historical realism when it asserts that "blood don't got no colour" and proceeds to list the factors shaping the traumatic event of the main character's birth (3). The layering of violence, the excess of blood spilled, imitates the process by which blood comes to have no color, in other words, how the system of slavery desensitizes in order to normalize a vicious cycle of violence. After this third-person narrative, which acts as an impersonal review of the circumstances surrounding the birth of "the lone baby of 1785," the narrator emerges as a first-person voice at the same time that the main character and the reader are also named: "I goin' call her Lilith. You can call her what they call her" (3). As Sam Vásquez notes, the name of Lilith "invokes the archetype of female sexuality, fecundity, and horror from mythology and midrashic literature" (50–51). In the opening frame, the narrator emphasizes his/ her rhetorical power, not only in naming Lilith, but also in aligning the reader with "they." The readership is affiliated with an unknown, abstract community that is defined in opposition to both the narrator and Lilith. I extend Vásquez's analysis of Lilith's name to argue that the "perception of horror" is "evident in descriptions of white men's perceptions of Lilith throughout" (50–51) and is associated with the *reader's* perception of Lilith. The antagonism of the narrator versus the reader, Lilith versus "them," symbolizes the tension that James imagines between the objectives of his historical fiction and the demands of his audience, between the historical contextualization of the enslaved who have been erased from history and the commodification and decontextualization of such narratives within the book market. Despite the contentious relationship that the opening sets up between narrator and reader, the novel imagines an economy of knowledge that situates the reader as a student seeking information from the narrator: "Two thing you should know if you want to know her" (3). The narrator's voice becomes one of authority, a gatekeeper for the reader who doesn't know Lilith but who has become enticed to learn more about her.

As the story continues, the first-person voice of the narrator disappears and Lilith's perspective takes center stage. The reader as knowledge seeker is symbolized by Lilith herself, who struggles with her ignorance about her parental history (who is her father, who was her mother) as well as her ignorance about how slave society works. Lilith is in an unusual position because she has been safeguarded from any type of slave labor. Up until she is about fourteen years old, she lives under the care of the only two slaves on the plantation who do not work: Circe and Tantalus. Lilith is the reader's representative, since both are removed from the gruesome violence of enslavement. This relatively safe haven is violated when puberty marks Lilith as an attractive conquest and a Johnny-jumper sexually attacks her. She manages to save her life by killing him, but this act of self-defense ushers in a new set of circumstances; in order to escape the vengeance of the other Johnny-jumpers, Lilith is taken from the field to the master's house and hidden in the basement for months on end. The reader is also spared the drudgery and everyday violence experienced by the field slave and drawn into the intimacy of the great house's close-knit interactions between master and slave. While there, Lilith comes under tutelage of the head house slave, Homer, and begins the transition from memorizing literacy to producing knowledge, from a banking model of education to that of problem posing. The great house is also the most realistic space where such an allegory of literacy can emerge to address the historical novel's market context.

When Homer shows Lilith the novel *Joseph Andrews* for the first time, she explains how illiteracy is a facet of bondage: "As long as you can't read this white man will have all sort of power over you" (56). Homer outlines the material and psychological freedom facilitated by literacy, mainly that reading gives a slave leverage, that "when a nigger can read, she can plan" (56). Homer credits her literacy as the reason why she is prepared to receive the new master, Humphrey, since she knew in advance about his return to Jamaica from England. Homer tells Lilith that reading this novel will also help her "get free" in her mind, "chang[ing] plenty 'bout you," and will help her acquire knowledge so that "nothing the massa can do will surprise you" (56–57). Homer frames Henry Fielding's novel as a cultural artifact that can provide insight into slavery's cultural logic. Interpretation will transform the inner self of the reader, Lilith, by giving her a better understanding of her historical context. While Homer argues that literature has the potential to liberate the mind, *The Book of Night Women* appears equally interested in exploring the limits of that potential. Homer does not recognize how her literacy project is confined by the discursive dynamics of the European texts she reads. Certainly, Homer's didactic lectures alienate Lilith even as she succeeds in teaching Lilith to read and exposing her to new ideas about the power of literacy.

James's novel highlights two obstacles to the ethical imperative of literacy: the unpredictability of interpretation and the negative influence of the culture industry. Within Caribbean diasporic historical fiction, sexuality is the trope used to articulate a writerly anxiety about the effectiveness of the pedagogical directive. The progressive definition of reading is first troubled when Lilith begins to read between the lines to interpret Homer's goals. Noting that Homer "look at her too long" and is "touching her face," Lilith "start to wonder what Homer desire" (59). The specter of queer desire haunts the margins of the teacher-student encounter, linking James's historical novel to the work of Julia Alvarez and Michelle Cliff. When invited to attend the night women's clandestine meetings to plan a slave revolt, Lilith reveals how much she feels threatened by Homer's pedagogical goals: "Morning, noon and night you in me business, now you all coming down in the cellar, 'bout you teaching me to read. You must really be a sodomite" (73). Lilith's homophobic fears point to how the reader's interpretation matters as much as a text's content. Lilith assumes that Homer's attentions involve some measure of self-interest and that this motivation is sexual, blurring the line between mentorship and exploitation. The dangers of the ethical imperative are clear in how Lilith responds to Homer's facilitation of her literacy and introduction to the sisterhood of night women: "Me no have to tell you nothing. [. . .] So keep you woman secret and you woman loving to youself" (75). Homer's banking model of teaching Lilith about community building and consciousness-raising prompts Lilith to abandon the education offered because of the power dynamic it rests upon. Lilith rejects Homer's pedagogical project by insisting that such a relationship with Homer must entail sexual submission.[16]

Lilith turns toward what might be termed the Disney version of art, seeking a heterosexual union that will bring an end to her limbo status in the great house. European fairy tales provide her with a paradigm of upward mobility, based on the "page with the sleeping princess" that Tantalus shows her as a child (103). The page is devoid of any historical or plot context since it is "t[orn] out from a white girl storybook with picture and word" (76). Lilith emphasizes how the image symbolizes a heterosexual romance encoded by race and class: "The white boy look at the white girl like she be the beautifullest, preciousest thing" (76). The fairytale romance is one narrative that Caribbean diasporic fiction battles against for attention in the marketplace. In rejecting Homer's version of literary criticism, Lilith interprets this Sleeping Beauty narrative as a script for how to "get the love she want" (103). The implications of her misinterpretation, of ignoring the storybook's racist, classist, and sexist implications, are catastrophic. Lilith unsuccessfully tries to seduce her master, Humphrey, aspiring to move up the chain of servants to become mistress of the house. Instead, her inexperience as a house servant leads Lilith to accidentally spill boiling hot soup on one of the New Year's ball guests, which prompts a harsh punishment from Humphrey: she is gang raped, whipped every day for several weeks, and then exiled to the estate of Coulibre.

Lilith's struggles as a student-reader illustrate the obstacles that James imagines his historical novel encountering. At the Coulibre library, Lilith returns to the novel *Joseph Andrews*, seeking consolation after losing the companionship of Dulcimena, the house slave murdered by her lecherous master, Roget. The absence of her mentor Homer means that Lilith must become her own source of knowledge and transition into a new mode of problem-posing education. However, the banking model that Homer represents still shapes Lilith's self-education, since Lilith positions *Joseph Andrews* as a replacement mentor, shifting to a more egalitarian power relationship even as that dynamic continues to be framed in relation to sexual conquest. To create a different source of community, Lilith personifies the novel so that it stands in for the heterosexual intimacy that she seeks: "There be only Joseph Andrews. There be only one man, one soul, that can make her laugh and he be neither black nor real" (210–11). Lilith's lens of interpretation changes, critiquing how this alternative literary tradition has limitations, since it cannot imagine the existence of a reader like Lilith: "Joseph want her to look at him, to laugh like a white woman who have the right to. But she not a white woman. [. . .] This not England. [. . .] There be no love for the nigger" (225). Lilith cultivates a cultural critique of the novel, precisely the type of interpretive engagement that Homer lectured her about. *Joseph Andrews* turns out to be another escapist fantasy that cannot speak to the reality of an enslaved black woman: "*Joseph Andrews* lying to her, making her wish for a place and time that never goin' come" (225). Through her problem-posing mode of engaging with the novel as mentor, Lilith condemns the text's alignment of her gaze with that of a white reader. Lilith becomes self-aware of how *Joseph Andrews* trains a reader like herself to adopt self-destructive desires. After rejecting the alternate reality of Henry Fielding's novel, Lilith goes on a murder rampage, killing Roget after he tries to beat her, then killing his wife by pushing her down the stairs, and finally setting the entire house on fire, killing the Rogets' child and house slave. Violence turns out to be the only available alternative for survival left to Lilith, and as a result, *The Book of Night Women* appears to foreclose the possibility of a literary space for liberation and education.

The next mention of *Joseph Andrews* (which will not be cited again for another two hundred pages) marks the beginning of Lilith's romance with the overseer of Humphrey's plantation, Robert Quinn. This transition is the logical conclusion to the personification of *Joseph Andrews*, since Lilith remarks on the resemblances between the fictional character and Quinn, especially his "*wanton ringlets*" (212). The introduction of heterosexual romance with the relationship of Quinn and Lilith directly addresses the readership's hopes for a happy ending to the novel. Just as the page of *Sleeping Beauty* is pivotal in Lilith's search for love, so is the novel's audience seduced into hoping that Quinn will be the exception to the rule of white manhood in the novel. Instead, their romance has a hyperviolent ending à la Quentin Tarantino. The novel scripts the trajectory of Lilith and the reader along similar lines: violence becomes the mode by which a passive reader like Lilith becomes an active agent of history. In this moment, the novel appears to concur with Frantz Fanon that the mission of uncovering the past or historicizing the present cannot be a goal for the Afro-Caribbean intellectual.[17] Rather, only violent struggle can liberate. Nevertheless, violence has a different function for the market aesthetics of the novel than it does for Lilith. The gory violence that historically contextualizes the novel's beginning is central to Lilith's emplotment, and the reader also embarks on a process of becoming anesthetized to violence. If Lilith's transformation from reader to author is initiated by violence, then readers find that they are not immune to its power: readers are not free from the desensitizing effects of slavery. The novel undermines the market's emplotment of romance and calls into doubt Homer's earlier lesson for Lilith, advocating that literature frees the mind.

The last pages of the novel finally reveal the narrator's identity: the first-person voice of the novel turns out to be Lovey Quinn, Lilith's child with the overseer. The inheritance of literacy is central to the formation of Lovey's writing voice: "Me was but nine year in age when me mother start to teach me how to read. The book she teach me to read was *Joseph Andrews*" (426). This maternal inheritance is complicated by self-interest: "She didn't teach me for me but for her, for when the time come to write her song she have somebody true to be her witness" (426). Just as Lilith suspects Homer's motivations, the narrator recognizes how self-interest informs Lilith's literacy project. However, the narrator is unsure about Lilith's goals in teaching Lovey to preserve her legacy: "Mayhaps she 'fraid of how the time was goin' judge her. Mayhaps she don't care, for she tell me everything as if me was a stranger and not blood" (426). Lilith's strategy in relaying her story to her child as if she were speaking to a stranger reminds us of Clover's tactic in relaying to Scheherezade the experience of insane asylum tours with her father. Lilith avoids intimacy and does not acknowledge any shared bond with her audience. In framing Lovey as a stranger, Lilith shares Clover's motivations for censoring some aspect of her narrative, especially anything that could evoke a troublesome connection between narrator and reader, in this case mother and daughter. The novel's conclusion hints at the threat that such intimacy presents for both mother and daughter, since the power dynamics between Lilith and Lovey have problematic implications. Lilith's story becomes ventriloquized by her child, a narrator who must erase aspects of self-identity in order to write Lilith's story. Lovey is unable to distinguish the narrating self from its subject, and writing requires the silencing of individuality and racial background: "In the dark with no skin I can write. [. . .] The first time me write, me wanted to tell a different story, a story 'bout me, not a story 'bout her" (427). The narration of the novel, primarily in the third person, symbolizes the writer's self-effacement, reminiscent of Camila's voice in Alvarez's novel and Faith's covered mirror in *Fruit of the Lemon*. What Lilith's story reveals about Lovey is that s/he is the inheritor of a forced

poetics, a discursive legacy that does not allow Lovey to formulate a subjectivity distinct from that of Lilith. The European discourse that negated
the Afro-Caribbean subjectivity and experience of Homer and Lilith as
readers *continues* to delimit the creative imagination of future generations.

The foreclosure of Lovey's gender ambiguity is emblematic of the violent silencing necessitated by the mandate of discretion that s/he must
follow in narrating Lilith's story. Only one line at the novel's conclusion
alludes to Lovey's gender: "Any niggerwoman can become a black woman
in secret. This is why we dark, cause in the night we disappear and become
spirit" (427). Lovey's narrating "I" takes on a gender association only as
part of the "we" of night women, and this communal affiliation is based
on a shared experience of erasure and invisibility. Granted, the invisibility of el secreto abierto allows for a life of privacy and secrecy necessary
for survival within the totalizing system of slavery, but it contributes to
Lovey's inability to tell what is presumably "her" or even "his" story. The
novel's ending reverses the order of its opening phrase: "This was the first
thing me write: You can call her what they call her. I goin' call her Lilith" (427). The first line Lovey writes does *not* turn out to be the opening
line that we read in *The Book of Night Women*. The naming of Lilith by
others comes first, which consequently frames Lovey's decision to call the
main character Lilith as a rebellion against the norm. The shift in sentence
order indicates that at some point in the novel Lovey has lost some narrative power in relation to her readers, that she now ranks second to how
the reader names Lilith. The revision alludes to Lovey's transformation in
the course of narrating Lilith's story, but it remains unclear what has led
to this loss of voice aside from the act of narration and Lovey's ambivalent
claim to the night women community. Since the gender ambiguity of the
narrator is maintained until the last page of the novel, the "revelation" of
Lovey's gender is potentially a sign of forced poetics, that Lovey is forced
to articulate a self in terms of choosing a side of the gender binary. Telling Lilith's story has inhibited Lovey's fluidity as a subject, and in order
to belong to the narrative of the nightwomen, Lovey must gender his/
her writerly authority.[18] Lovey's position as author-double then speaks to
the conundrum at the heart of the Caribbean diasporic writer's project
to articulate counterhistories within a marketplace that commodifies and
privileges certain voices over others.

In the Name of Salomé (2000), *Free Enterprise* (1993), and *The Book
of Night Women* (2009) are historical novels that situate themselves as

pedagogical interventions. The project of counterhistory sees education as a tool, as a goal, and as a fraught encounter. The market aesthetics of Caribbean diasporic historical novels link their contemporary contexts to particular pasts in order to comment on the processes of dehistorization, the way certain stories are excluded from mainstream historical narratives. For Alvarez, it is the histories of the famous Salomé and her less-than-famous daughter Camila; for Cliff, it is the stereotyped and maligned Mary Ellen Pleasant and the invisible others like Annie who contributed to the cause of abolition; for James, it is the revolts that were orchestrated by anonymous female slaves in the Caribbean. The mission to reeducate the reader about Caribbean histories of slavery and revolution is tempered by the tension between the depiction of education and the fiction's stylistic form. By engaging Paulo Freire's pedagogy and Édouard Glissant's forced poetics, I read these educational encounters as places where the novel imagines and troubles its relationship with its readerships. The language of sexuality and intimacy that encodes the relationships between teachers and students serves a dual function: to evoke the vulnerability of certain subjectivities when entering a public and to illustrate the tensions caused by the contemporary market discourses that the historical fiction feels compelled to engage in order to gain access to readerships.

The ambivalence that Caribbean diasporic historical novels display about their ability to transform the reader with their historical lesson plans is key to understanding the market aesthetics of the fiction. The ethical imperative of such cultural production is responsible for the self-conscious manner with which the historical fiction explores the benefits and challenges of circulating its counternarratives via the multicultural book market. The first half of this book has discussed the historical content and structural forms that Caribbean diasporic historical fiction adopt and how gender and sexuality are the sites for processing concerns about the effectiveness of the pedagogical imperative. The second half of this book focuses on how Caribbean diasporic writers engage specific historical legacies in the Caribbean, revolution and dictatorship. By localizing my discussion of historical fiction in terms of these historical contexts, I show how Caribbean diasporic writers identify the histories of anticolonial revolution and postcolonial dictatorship as relevant to the construction of diasporic identity in Britain, Canada, and the United States. At the same time, the works of Ana Menéndez, Dionne Brand, Michelle Roffey, Junot Díaz, and Edwidge Danticat continue to foreground sexual intimacy as a way of allegorically working through the relationship between art and audience.

4 Messy Intimacies

Postcolonial Romance in Ana Menéndez, Dionne Brand, and Monique Roffey

CARIBBEAN DIASPORIC HISTORICAL FICTION engages with anticolonialism as a historical and rhetorical legacy from the home island that shapes the diaspora and the Global North. The historical novels *Loving Che* (2003), *In Another Place, Not Here* (1997), and *The White Woman on the Green Bicycle* (2009) signal how anticolonial discourses about politics and revolution continue to have purchase in the contemporary moment. Additionally, the postcolonial romances of Ana Menéndez, Dionne Brand, and Monique Roffey explore the problem of gender and historiography. Focusing in on the Great Men narrative of anticolonial history by highlighting the figures of Ernesto 'Che' Guevara and Eric Williams, the novels are concerned with the discursive boundaries imposed on historical action, which often relegate women to the roles of silent witnesses or objects of history. The investigative journeys of the main characters in the novels thereby engage with two rhetorical legacies of anticolonialism, the political ideology of romance and the scientific approach of calculating historical experience.

The postcolonial romances of Ménendez, Brand, and Roffey are less concerned about "what happened" and more interested in the language used to chronicle anticolonial thought and the postcolonial vacuum of vocabulary left when revolutionary movements did not fully deliver their promise. Despite lacking the traditional markers of historical fiction, *Loving Che*, *In Another Place*, and *The White Woman* historicize the ideological struggles of the anticolonial period as it is foreclosed, ushering in the postcolonial era's pessimism about social movements. In a 2004 interview with Robert Birnbaum, Ana Menéndez asserts that *Loving Che* is "not a novel about Che Guevara" and that "it's not a historical novel" (par. 54) The description that one of Brand's characters, Verlia, applies to her writing could very well describe both novels: "Well, this diary will not be a chronicle of anything that has happened. [. . .] I was going to write about the revolution; instead this book is full of loneliness" (220). The characters in the postcolonial romances process the contemporary legacies of anticolonialism; like Sabine in Monique Roffey's novel, they "witnessed that powerful potential" and are "still mourning its failure" (113).

Che Guevara and Eric Williams are the principal historical figures embodying the political ideology of romance in *Loving Che*, *In Another Place*, and *The White Woman*. As Rosamond King notes, "Caribbean men of color are largely portrayed in the Cariglobal imagination as heteronormative, patriarchal heroes," and "This is true in historical narratives of Great Men who fought or defeated slavery (for example, Toussaint L'Ouverture and Cuffy), colonialism (Eric Williams, Frantz Fanon, and José Martí), or imperialism (Che Guevara and Maurice Bishop)" (161). The fictional depiction of Great Men seeks to reconcile the romantic promise of anticolonialism with the postcolonial crisis regarding such hopes for liberation in the Caribbean. A legacy of anticolonialism is, borrowing King's words, "a spectacular failure of male leadership, if not of Caribbean masculinity" (162). Guevara and Williams are the male historical voices and actors to whom the characters in the novel must somehow connect in order to claim anticolonial revolution as part of their historical heritage. In so doing, the novels address how the "strategies of these specifically male and heteropatriarchal regimes and ideologies failed" (King 194). Ménendez's title references a loving Che who is being recuperated and also invokes the act of loving him, in either case framing romance as an inheritance from anticolonial discourse. The novels of Ménendez, Brand, and Roffey also incorporate personal forms of writing, such as diary entries and letters, employing a sentimental tradition of women's writing as a medium for Teresa, Verlia, and Sabine to inscribe themselves into the Caribbean nation-state's narrative of anticolonial male heroism.

The postcolonial romances critique the legacy of anticolonialism's approach of calculating historical experience via the investigative journeys of their characters. The market aesthetics of the novels are encoded in the search for historical truth and justice, which is a metaphor for the readership's lens of interpretation. In *Loving Che*, the nameless narrator embarks on a research project of collecting photographs and documents to historically contextualize her origins. When this project fails, she is left with the hybrid narrative of Teresa de la Landre and her romantic rewriting of Che Guevara's image and words. *In Another Place* sees

Verlia attempting to understand her historical subjectivity using anti-colonial methods. Like Teresa, she repeats and revises Che's words to arrive at a more scientific and rational approach to interpreting her revolutionary potential. These methods lead Verlia to sacrifice her body and romantic desires—passing on this legacy of calculation to Elizete. In both novels, we have a postcolonial community of women struggling to understand their worth within an anticolonial history and ideology. *The White Woman* provides a counterpoint to these historical novels by depicting a white male wrestling with the legacy of a romance between his wife and Eric Williams, with George reading Sabine's unsent love letters to Williams. The investigative journey entails a European man responding to a European woman's fascination with the Caribbean Great Man of history, which underscores the postcolonial inheritance of paternalism and homosocial filiation.

The investigative journeys of the narrators engage not only the anti-colonial discourse of scientific calculation but also the evaluative context of book market. The market aesthetics of the novels speak back to the critical reception encountered by Ménendez, Brand, and Roffey. The critiques leveled at the writing preceding *Loving Che, In Another Place*, and *The White Woman* often assert that the language, subject matter, and style of the authors border on "excess" (Whitfield 31). For instance, Ménendez's *In Cuba I Was a German Shepherd* is described as having characters that are "didactic" and "extravagantly childish" (Eder 14), with storylines that are pervaded by an "indulgent magical realism" (Eder 14) or the "contrived feel of exercises done for a writing class" (Kakutani, "As the Day Wanes" E8). Even the novel's title is considered "too beguiling" (Sutherland 31). The market aesthetics of *Loving Che* addresses these critiques by depicting the narrator's frustrated attempts to objectively locate her authentic or "real" historical origins. The challenges of making a Caribbean woman central to anticolonial history is evidenced in the harsh comments leveled by one reviewer at Brand's *Primitive Offensive*, who credits the "exhausting" writing style to a "limited range of subject matter, which can sustain a short reading but not a 60-page book" (Russell 76). The problem, of course, is actually the validity of queer black women as literary subjects, much less historical ones. The discourse of excess is also deployed in the reception of Roffey's *August Frost*. The novel is disparaged for its narrative tempo and magical realism, following "a pace far too leisurely" (Rev. of *August Frost* [*Kirkus*] 1727) and "slow-moving" ("August Frost" [*Publishers Weekly*] 55), as well as a plot that makes it appear "as if the book [. . .] were simply reluctant to deal with reality" (Bolick 24). The discursive projects of the historical novels that I discuss in this chapter are responsive to the reviewers' labeling of the authors' prior works as immoderate in style, fantasy, and insignificance of subject matter.

The market reception of Caribbean diasporic writing shapes its emplotment of romance. Positive reviews tend to describe such writing by referencing sexual intimacy and food consumption. Ménendez's writing is described as passionate (Rev. of *In Cuba* [*Library Journal*] 135; Sutherland 31), "bittersweet" (Kakutani, "As the Day Wanes" E8; Zaleski 221), and providing "food for thought" (Sutherland 31). Roffey is likewise lauded for writing "with colour and exoticism" stories that are "full of sensuality" (Owen 14). Caribbean diasporic authors understand the market appeal that romance has in the global book market and the access it provides to certain readerships. The positive reception of *In Another Place* and *The White Woman* indicates the benefits of this writerly strategy, since reviewers highlight the way that the genre creates an intimate relationship between the text and reader. Reviewers argue that Brand's novel successfully "seduces the reader" and is "easier to digest," especially since she depicts the romances "in a way that does not smack of lesbian propaganda" (Carter 24). Meanwhile, Roffey's text is said to depict "the island itself—seductive, mysterious, unpredictable" ("White Woman" 35) and is credited with a "terrific sense of place: heat and languor, politics and passion, tropical smells and the heady music of the local patois" (Woodhead 26). The market logic privileges facile consumption in opposition to explicit political ideology.[1] The market aesthetics of historical fictions by Ménendez, Brand, and Roffey imagine the dangers of such market appeal with the messy intimacies of their characters' investigative journeys. The market aesthetics appear especially prescient when reviewers insinuate that mainstream success problematizes the ethical imperative of the novels, for example, remarking on "Brand's 'anoinment' by a major publisher, for a novel whose writing was subsidized by a grant from the Ontario Arts Council" (Thorpe 446), or praising a text for providing the readership with unmediated access to anOther world—"She writes realistically enough to make readers feel they have visited the island" (Birkett 80). The market aesthetics engage the contemporary context of the neoliberal marketplace and its rhetoric as the novels explore the postcolonial inheritance of anticolonial discourse.

(En)gendering History: Men as Agents, Women as Witnesses

Before delving into the novels' representation of anticolonialism's legacies, I frame the discursive work of the postcolonial romances by reviewing how male historiographies periodize the shift from anticolonial to postcolonial, from the Sixties to the post-Sixties. Bringing Caribbean, US Latino, and African American studies into dialogue makes it evident not only that the narration of such a historical shift continually references a nostalgia for a resistant and revolutionary subject always already in the past but also that these narratives are gendered. The representation of the female body and femininity is central to these postcolonial and post-Sixties historiographies, even as women are constructed as objects rather than public agents of history. By resignifying symbolic figures like Che Guevara and Eric Williams through intimacy, both familial and sexual, the novels speak back to the masculine theorizations of post-Sixties postcoloniality to show their gendered limitations and also explore the contemporary implications of the ideological approaches and blind spots inherited from anticolonial movements. The postcolonial romances employ intensely personal narratives about decolonization to negotiate the shift between the anticolonial revolutionary past and the postcolonial present.[2]

Prominent male historiographies that explicitly engage with the anticolonial and civil rights movements constitute the gendered emergence of a consensus periodization. The theorists I discuss as models of this trend are concerned with the foreclosure of those progressive movements of social justice and with making that past speak to the present. While using different terminology—David Scott's *futures past*, Flores's *political horizon*, Dyson's *automortology*—they each express a sense of loss regarding a historical transition. The mourning of the anticolonial, Sixties past is tied to the way the critics imagine the role of women within that history. Women are not merely minor characters in influential male historiographies about the transition from anti- to postcolonialism, but they remain on the margins because of the symbolic value ascribed to their bodies and femininity. In each scholar's work, there emerges a binary opposition between masculine models of historical agency and their female counterparts that facilitates, if it does not rationalize, the nostalgia for a revolutionary past. Against a backdrop of negative femininity, the postcolonial male agent of history inherits the mantle of Sixties public intellectualism—suggesting that the postcolonial critic must imagine a negative inheritance that is inevitably associated with women.

Scott, Flores, and Dyson believe in the necessity of creating a new vocabulary for the post-Sixties and postcolonial present. These scholars articulate a rhetorical problem facing the contemporary public intellectual: how to honor the progressive legacy of the Sixties while avoiding its ideological pitfalls. In *Conscripts of Modernity: The Tragedy of Colonial Enlightenment* (2004), David Scott argues that a new postcolonial vision of history should be understood as "futures past." The task at hand entails "identifying the difference between the questions that animated former presents and those that animate our own" (3) in order to identify a different set of "visionary horizons" (29). A new set of questions is necessary because the anticolonial model of understanding the relationship between the past, present, and future is not applicable to the postcolonial public sphere. For Scott, the anticolonial futures of "nation and socialism" are no longer "new beginnings" but "tangible ruins of our present" (29). Since these futures are a past horizon of progressive hope, Scott argues that the postcolonial present must be reoriented toward a new set of goals. Scott focuses on the rhetorical task of articulating this loss of anticolonial vision for a first-person plural community, as opposed to generating new discursive models for progressive movements.

Juan Flores articulates a similar discursive gap created by the shift from the Sixties to the post-Sixties in *From Bomba to Hip-Hop: Puerto Rican Culture and Latino Identity* (2000). The Sixties were "watershed years in the construction of a new language of Latino identity" whose vocabulary was "inspired by the Civil Rights movement" (201). Flores sees this Sixties "political horizon of the Latino imaginary" as "hardly even a living memory" by the 1990s: "The importance of that foundational period in the story of Latino identity-formation [has been] minimized or erased" (201–2). It is not simply that the Sixties rhetorical model has been forgotten; it appears to be out of step with a post-Sixties present that lacks "the momentum of the Civil Rights movement to build on" (215). The political horizon has changed because of decontextualization, with the institutionalization of Latino studies programs disconnected from "the activist relationship" that previously tied such programs to "their social contexts and communities" (214). The use of the first-person plural is central to Flores's analysis of institutionalization, which notes that a "charged revolutionary aura does not surround the Latino Studies agenda in our time" (207). The conception of "our" post-Sixties present relies on the formulation of a communal identity as the link to anticolonial struggles, making it possible to imagine a horizon where "ebbs and flows may eventually connect the university-based struggle to such systemic types of social confrontation" again (207).

In *April 4, 1968: Martin Luther King, Jr.'s Death and How It Changed America* (2008), Michael Eric Dyson looks to King as embodying the shift in vision and horizons that Scott and Flores address, emphasizing the distance between the Sixties past and the future it imagined. Dyson uses the term *automortology* to describe how King's last speeches "look[ed] back on a self whose past lies in the future" (25) in order "to open a historical window onto his role as actor and observer in the civil rights drama" (37). King's final public speeches offer a rhetorical model for the contemporary intellectual. King becomes a figure who encapsulates the crisis of imagination that key male historiographies describe: "What we make of [King's] death may determine what we make of his legacy and our future" (75). Dyson invests the possibility of articulating a new discursive model for the future of "our" collective project into the rhetorical project of unpacking the symbolism of King's assassination.

For all of these critics, there is a tension between honoring the Sixties models for a progressive politics and addressing how the present has not lived up to the future horizon that the anticolonial and civil rights movements worked toward. Scott, Flores, and Dyson gender historical action in order to resolve this tension between the past and the present, the promise of Sixties social movements and the realities of the postcolonial present. Underlying the postcolonial, post-Sixties vision of the relationship between the present and the past is a gendered construction of historical action. Dyson is especially useful in pointing out a critical tension in how the historical subject is imagined: "There has been a big debate among scholars of the civil rights movement about whether it is Great Men—and the inherent patriarchy of the term has been increasingly criticized as the years have added up to feminist consciousness—who shape history, or whether such figures are molded by the movement" (148). Dyson's voice expresses some ambivalence, on the one hand wishing to discuss the relationship between the individual leaders identified by history and the largely invisible grassroots community, and on the other hand acknowledging that such a discussion necessarily relies on masculinist conceptions of public figures as Great Men. The rhetorical invocation of "we" and of "our" political mission is a discursive strategy connecting the critics' approaches. The historiographic voice as an implicitly male first-person plural makes these terms of community identity inaccessible to certain subjectivities, constructing the plural self as a society of heteronormative Great Men, relegating the Others of women and sexual minorities to the margins.

Major male historiographies are attuned to and reference feminist analyses in their texts, yet the examples they cite to foreground this historical shift can be read as a set of Great Men acting with women as witnesses. In each scholar's work, there is an opposition between masculine historical agents and their female counterparts. In David Scott, Caliban and Hamlet are central symbolic figures for distinguishing the anticolonial from the postcolonial, while romance as a genre for anticolonial history emerges as the only space where potentially feminine markers are invoked. Scott portrays romance as a genre of historiographic writing that is out of place with the postcolonial present, which must be replaced by the more masculine narrative of tragedy. Juan Flores reiterates this opposition of masculinity and femininity in terms of Caribbean-Latino writing styles. Flores traces a pure civil rights lineage of US Latino/a literature from the Sixties writer Piri Thomas to contemporary author Abraham Rodriguez, while framing the work of women writers such as Julia Alvarez as a negative literary model that is assimilationist because of its nostalgic thematics. The gendered discourse used to describe different modes of historiography and narrative has implications for how women and men are depicted within histories of the anticolonial Sixties. Dyson establishes Martin Luther King Jr.'s historical significance by arguing that he embodies the shift from Sixties to post-Sixties, at the same time as he positions women such as Coretta Scott King and Michelle Obama as silent witnesses to or victims of history, for instance, labeling Michelle as portable authenticity for Barack (*Can You Hear Me Now?*, 6). Heteronormativity is implicitly the code for relating women to the Great Men of history. Highlighting the way that paradigmatic male historiographies identify sentimental or tragic genres of writing history as well as how they distinguish between feminine and masculine modes of historical subjectivity is useful in addressing how Caribbean diasporic historical novels imagine the shift "from past to post." The gendering of historical discourse, voice, and nostalgia informs the market aesthetics of Caribbean diasporic writing as it maps out and deconstructs the discursive terrain of historiography.

Feminist critics such as Ileana Rodríguez and María Josefina Saldaña-Portillo provide a nuanced approach to how the privileging of Great Men finds its origins in the gendered stakes of anticolonial rhetoric. In *Women, Guerrillas, and Love: Understanding War in Central America* (1996), Rodríguez notes that the conceptualization of the New Man in anticolonial writing necessarily defines the collective as male. Within narratives of revolution, "the revolutionary wanted to speak, not in the name of, but as, a collective subject" (35). The rhetorical authorization of the anticolonial male writer depends upon "the conflation of the two narrative subjects, the lyrical masculine I of Romanticism and the collective subject of revolutionary-ism" (35). The use of the first-person plural, "formulated in a masculine I" (xvii), precludes women from being identified with the collective, the revolutionary masses as well as the anticolonial speaking subject. Voice is of vital importance in the postcolonial romances that I analyze in this chapter. The discursive strategy of having an individual, male "I" stand in for and embody a heterogeneous "we" is not without its tensions in anticolonial discourse. The postcolonial romances of Menéndez, Brand, and Roffey attend to precisely this rhetorical conflict between the self and the other, between the first-person singular and the first-person plural. Anticolonial discourse defines this relationship as one of love and intimacy. As Rodríguez points out, a "paradox forms the center of the dilemma revolutionary definitions struggle with in finding the New" (46). For example, if "disciplining the troops is defined as *tendresse*, love," then love becomes articulated as "an exercise of power, authority, violence" and "violation" (46). Additionally, if the collective is defined as male, then the homosocial project of revolution is haunted by the threat of queer desire and intimacy: "The New Man is born with an injunction, that he is not to be a 'little woman,' he is not to be a 'faggot'" (46). Relegating love to the public sphere and the social project of revolution, loving and liberating the masses, means "making the emotive personal-social expressions clandestine" (48). Anticolonialism's public project of intimacy domesticates the masculine collective and excludes women from the project of revolution. When women do appear, they can be articulated only as objects that reassure the heteronormative subjectivity of the male revolutionary; they are depicted as the "realization of erotic desires, 'revolutionary pussy'" (94). The postcolonial romances that I discuss here reimagine the relationship of women to a Caribbean history of revolution while also engaging with anticolonialism's paradoxical and tense (dis)articulation of intimacy and sexuality.

Feminist critics also offer the context of neoliberalism as an important framework for understanding the calculating economy of anticolonial discourse. Rodríguez frames her project "within the chaos of neoliberalism," which she sees as presenting a particular challenge to contemporary cultural production (xx). She argues that "today's coupling of schooling and industry, intelligence and management, commits the intelligentsia to think of best possible performance scenarios, and to swaying back and forth between input/output, cost/benefit ratios—binding culture to technical and financial criteria" (xx). For instance, neoliberalism promotes the evaluation of pedagogy and educational institutions by metrics alone. These metrics privilege one type of assessment, overvaluing data performance analysis and documentation as the sole means of verifying or "credentialing" teaching expertise. In *The Revolutionary Imagination in the Americas and the Age of Development* (2003), María Josefina Saldaña-Portillo explains how the contemporary rhetorical economy of calculating cultural value is inherited from anticolonial discourse. Or rather, Saldaña-Portillo makes the case that the postcolonial era is informed by a "discursive collusion between the age of development and the revolutionary movements" (6). This perspective insists that anticolonial movements not be simply viewed as reactions against the contexts of "colonial and neocolonial capitalism" and claims that those movements were informed and shaped by "a racialized and gendered developmentalism" (7). For Saldaña-Portillo, the failure of the anticolonialism is rooted in a rhetorical problem that undermines its stated goals of liberation and consciousness-raising. The problematic legacy of anticolonialism lies in its acceptance and promotion of a "developmentalist model of history" and a "developmentalist model of revolutionary subjectivity, consciousness, and agency" (6). The limitations of anticolonialism's imaginary derive from its emerging neoliberal contexts, for example, its emplotment of historical progress and its discursive dependence upon a gendered collectivity.

Caribbean diasporic writers identify romance as a genre that facilitates a feminist revision of anticolonial movements while also tackling the rhetorical shortcomings of revolutionary discourse. Feminist revisionist histories are a dominant trend within Caribbean diasporic historical fiction. Often these take the form of generational histories, following a matrilineal genealogy, as in the case of Cristina García's *Dreaming in Cuban* (1992) and Dahlma Llanos-Figueroa's *Daughters of the Stone* (2009). Within the broader category of feminist revisionist narratives, postcolonial romances emerge as a trend that articulates the shift from coloniality to postcoloniality and forms a response to both the erasure of the Caribbean from dominant historical narratives and the global decontextualization of the contemporary public sphere. Postcolonial romances can be read as fusing male historiographies' expression of the public intellectual's longing for anticolonial revolution with anticolonial discourses' ambivalent framing of revolution as an extension of personal love.[3] The novels of Ana Menéndez, Dionne Brand, and Monique Roffey engage the historiographic narrative of Great Men by depicting how the female characters try to build intimate relationships of solidarity within the historical context of decolonization. The writers also encode investigative characters in their novels who embark on an anticolonial approach to historical research that focuses on "scientific" methods, which value documentation and testimonials as means by which to calculate the truth about a historical event or person. The novels depict the anticolonial approach to recovering such facts as unreliable and delimited. Calculating historical truth entails physical and/or psychological trauma for these investigators, since the rational scientific approach they adopt cannot reconcile desire with the archive of history expressed by the female body and subject. Additionally, the novels depict how calculation fits into the developmental model of neoliberalism. The historical texts appear to concur with Vanessa Agard-Jones that "fiction captures something that social science often cannot" because "it moves beyond what can be readily observed, measured, and tabulated to more ephemeral phenomena that empirical methods often fail to capture" (331). Nostalgia emerges as a productive mode by which to contest the gendered boundaries of the historical archive.

Romantic Fictions and Archival Gaps in Ana Menéndez's *Loving Che*

The antihistorical form and plot of Ana Ménendez's *Loving Che* evokes the challenges of historiography. The novel is divided into three sections alternating between two first-person narrators. The text opens in the present, with a nameless female narrator in South Florida whose maternal grandfather and only guardian has recently passed away. This opening section has no title or clear time setting, establishing the absence of history as its context. The narrator embarks on a search for the mother that she never knew, making several trips to Havana, Cuba, in order to locate her, but is unable to do so. In this sense, the journey of Menéndez's narrator echoes that of Camila in her attempt to recover a connection with her dead mother in Alvarez's *In the Name of Salomé*. In *Loving Che*, the narrator unexpectedly receives a package containing letters from her mother, with no return address. Since the packaged narrative forms the second section of the text, providing flashbacks to pre-Revolutionary Cuba and the Cuban Revolution, the novel situates the narrator's introduction within a present that is absent of history. The narrator begins as a reader-double, identifying the audience's similarly dehistoricized condition as a hallmark of the postcolonial era, recalling my discussion of Chariandy's *Soucouyant* in chapter 2. The package of letters introduces the voice of Teresa de la Landre, with Teresa's section sharing the same title as the novel, "Loving Che." The mother's letters are a remembrance of her affair with Ernesto Guevara during the Cuban Revolution, hinting that el Che is the biological father of Teresa's daughter.[4] The contemporary circumstances of Teresa are unknown, leading this anticolonial past with Che to be more vivid than the postcolonial present. With the third section of the novel, entitled "Letter on the Road," the narrating daughter returns, this time within the context of Cuba's Special Period of the 1990s, and her new goal is to determine the veracity of her mother's romance. The nameless narrator's desire to shift from rootlessness to belonging via an investigation of her mother's archive does not produce the self-assured closure of Andrea Levy's Faith, which I analyzed in chapter 2. The narrator moves from reader of her mother's letters to storyteller, taking on the role of author-double. The postcolonial crisis of the daughter as historiographer is clear as she wrestles with the question of whether to claim a relationship to her mother's archive of the anticolonial past, to the revolutionary figure of el Che, and if so, how. As Menéndez states in her interview with Birnbaum, the novel is "about this myth [of Guevara] that people have appropriated and that people have fallen in love with in a way that is ultimately destructive" (par. 78). The postcolonial romance of Che's mythology is an entry point for representing the tragic limits of the postcolonial period.[5]

The narrative structure echoes the concerns of prevailing male historiographies regarding the relationship of the anticolonial past to the postcolonial present by focusing on the inheritance of anticolonial longing, through the revolutionary figure of el Che. In the concluding chapter to *The Latino/a Canon*, Raphael Dalleo and I discuss how *Loving Che* is representative of a post-Sixties trend in US Latino/a writing that is concerned with a contemporary renegotiation of the Cuban American relationship to anticolonialism. The conclusion of Teresa's packaged narrative speaks directly to the narrator's crisis of inheritance. Teresa reverses the traditionally anticolonial calculation of worth. Whereas her daughter wants factual verification of her origins, Teresa's letters valorize the personal over the public, sexuality over politics, and the emotional over the scientific. Teresa acknowledges that she and the narrator are "past forgiveness or understanding," partly because of her abandonment of the narrator as a child and her more recent refusal to meet the narrator in person (155). Teresa also notes that reconciliation is impossible because of the decontextualization she has forced upon the narrator as well as the narrator's repeated attempts to make Teresa clarify their mutual past: "I took a history from you and you returned carrying his memory in your dark eyes" (155). As Isabel Alvarez Borland notes, Teresa employs the strategy of decontextualization *in order* to narrate her romance: "When Teresa finds a picture of Che Guevara in a magazine, she tears it out and places it in a box with other pictures; she literally *removes* the historical figure of Guevara from his official context and places him in the realm of the 'personal' or private story" (38). Rather than give the narrator some clarity regarding the veracity of her parentage and historical origins, Teresa appears to have decided that her personal narrative of an affair with Che Guevara will address the divide between the public project of revolution and the narrator's private reality of her birth.[6]

Teresa contextualizes a photograph of the narrator as an infant with the following note: "I leave you our failures together and also the private triumph of your own life, the beating in your chest of a love that endures. Farewell" (155).[7] The first-person plural legacy of love in the public sphere, of anticolonial revolution, is a failure that must be continually juxtaposed with the more minor, "successful" product of love within the sphere of sexual intimacy: the individual life of the narrator-reader. Teresa implies that one cannot be understood without the other. The private accomplishment of engendering love via procreation is so tenuous that Teresa supplements her farewell with a second image, one of Che Guevara peeking around the corner of a wall at an empty room, followed by a second goodbye: "Farewell but you will be with me" (156). Teresa's good-bye acquires the double valence of the novel's title. One layer of interpretation could intuit that the new photograph of Che means that it is he who is saying farewell to the narrator as his daughter. On the other hand, if the Che photograph supplants that of the narrator as child, Teresa could be addressing Che as the "you" who will always be with her. The public image and myth of Che Guevara then appear to hold such heavy symbolic value that the closure of the narrative cannot be completed with merely the narrator's minor, personal success of existence but must be bookended by the more public imaginary of anticolonial revolution. The novel bids farewell to the historical narrative of Great Men even as it remains a ghostly presence informing the postcolonial present. The second farewell text and photograph in Teresa's narrative allude the postcolonial failure of vocabulary to sufficiently heal and resolve the traumatic foreclosure of the anticolonial project and its ideology. The additional legacy passed on to the daughter, "the beating in your chest of a love that endures," is defined by both the postcolonial failures of the revolutionary project and a romantic conception of love and intimacy (155). This crisis of imagination and inheritance differs from how critical male historiographies articulate the postcolonial problematic, in terms of both how the present relates to the past and how romance is defined.

Menéndez's novel associates the contemporary moment with an inability to reconcile the history lesson presented by the anticolonial era, in this case the Cuban Revolution. The first divergence from the dominant definition of the postcolonial problematic relates to the role of nostalgia, or what David Scott calls "longing for anticolonial revolution" (7). Whereas leading male historiographies echo the anticolonial calculation of facts over myth by framing nostalgia as part of the postcolonial problem, Menéndez depicts nostalgia as a strategy used to mediate or counter the problem of global decontextualization. Nostalgia is an active mode of memory that processes the anticolonial rhetorical inheritance of the postcolonial era. The novel depicts nostalgia as valuable lens for accessing a more ephemeral archive of memory, even if it does not meet the requirements of a "scientific" calculation of historical worth. This lack of context or this gap in history prevents the postcolonial subject from delineating a clear relationship to the anticolonial past, so that he or she resorts instead to the productive vagaries of nostalgia to fill in the gaps of historical knowledge. The personal context of Menéndez's narrator is defined by a lack of historical grounding, beginning with the character's nameless status throughout the novel and extending to the lack of information about her parentage. The daughter states at the opening of Menéndez's novel that, "of my own origins, I know little," and she is especially frustrated that her existence cannot be verified with historical documents (3). This is the criticism she applies to her caretaker grandfather: "I don't understand how you have not one photograph, not one letter, not one document. [. . .] What's to keep me from thinking you didn't kidnap me, or even that you're not really my grandfather?" (6). For the narrator at the opening of the novel, relation can be proven only via such archival documentation;[8] without material evidence obtained by a scientific investigative process, she feels she must categorize the little she does know of her context, including her grandfather, as a complete fiction.[9] The novel therefore opens with the narrator asserting that fiction has no truth-value.[10]

The personal gap of context is mirrored in the public sphere as well. The daughter's hobby of collecting photographs is motivated by her desire to "play a game with history" where she imagines potential modes of relation with the person depicted: "I will take out one of my photographs and imagine the stranger caught there is a half-forgotten old aunt, or a great-grandmother who smoked cigarettes from a long silver holder" (1). She decides to organize an official archival project based on this personal pastime and encounters several obstacles in the course of planning a public photography exhibit:

> Some years ago, I became interested in the photographs that exiles had taken out of Cuba. It was common, I found, to frame the photos or place them in albums, to be taken out now and again in the company of friends. I thought that I would construct a traveling exhibition of these photographs, and was even able to secure funding for the project. But I ran into delays and other problems. Many families, I was dismayed to learn, would not give up their photographs, not even for a few days. And when, in a purely innocent gesture, I agreed to accept the photographs of exiles who had fled Batista, my political motivations were put in question and the entire project fell apart. (2)

Her project of translating a personal mode of relation into a public project fails for two reasons. First, most families are unwilling to lend their private documents for a communal archival project, echoing Faith's mother's warning from chapter 2 about the dangers of sharing personal narratives in the public sphere. The families approached by the narrator prioritize safeguarding intimate images of family over the construction of a diasporic community through art. Additionally, the narrator's attempt to broaden the historical range of her project to include Batista-era refugees is viewed as a politically suspect gesture. The daughter's challenges point to another layer of problematics facing the postcolonial subject. The gap between the private and public sphere appears to exacerbate decontextualization because the alternative of a grassroots communal history is thwarted. The crisis of ideology inherited from the anticolonial moment continues to haunt and silence alternative definitions of community, in this case of Cuban American exiles. While key male historiographies frame the predicament of the postcolonial moment in terms of a need to put the anticolonial past behind us, Menéndez's novel points to that very desire to disconnect from the past as the problem, producing a lack of public and personal historical context in addition to an inability to place those spheres of the private and the public in dialogue.

The second distinction in terms of the postcolonial problem relates to the romance genre. Romance, love, and revolution become inextricably connected in Menéndez's novel, blurring the line between the (male) public and the (female) private spheres of the characters' lives. The personal history of romance takes precedence over the public historical archive, particularly in the representation of Che Guevara as a lover rather than an anticolonial icon. Much of what Che says in the novel is derived from verbatim quotes of his published political writings, but these are reframed in the text as intimate conversations between himself and Teresa. Also, the photographs that are included in the text as part of the package that Teresa sends to her daughter can be easily accessed by a reader on the Internet. The structure of the novel runs counter to the daughter's earlier assumptions regarding material documentation as the only true source for determining historical truths and familial relation. The investigative process that the daughter embarks on in the third section of the novel, "Letter on the Road," reveals that the challenges of archival research are a problem not simply in Cuba but in Miami as well. The narrator interviews numerous experts, such as the Cuban history professor Dr. Caraballo, the Cuban photographer Jacinto Alcazar, and the curator consultant Ileana, to verify the historicity of her mother's packaged memoir.[11] Not only do the academic institutions of Florida International University and University of Miami refuse to cooperate or ignore her requests altogether, but the narrator's interviews reveal more about how she processes the archive through the lens of romance than about whether Teresa existed. For instance, after receiving from Jacinto a copy of a 1957 letter addressed to Guevara, the narrator reproduces it in the text without quotes because she feels that the writer's defense against Guevara's accusations of political betrayal reads like "the pleadings of a spurned lover," with "the ghost of [Teresa's] betrayal [. . .] already hovering about Che's dealings" (168). As the novel concludes, the daughter, despite collecting these photographs, interviews, and historical documents, still remains nameless, without a sense of who her mother really is, and questioning the veracity of the package she receives. The implication seems to be that the daughter might even have created Teresa's narrative herself, on the basis of her prior experience coordinating a photograph exhibit as well as the lens of romance she uses on her investigative journey through Miami and Havana.

A significant shift occurs in the daughter's formulation of relation, even though she remains unmoored from the historical archive, unable to verify her personal history via documentation. The novel concludes with the daughter packing a picture of Ernesto Guevara into her suit-case, a photograph that also accompanies her narrative. The narrator's conclusion consequently mirrors that of Teresa, completing a personal story with the packaging of an image: "I began to pack my bag. [. . .] And when I was done, I lay across the top the tightly wrapped photo-graph of a man standing alone with his camera, the future not yet a darkened plate; a beautiful stranger who, in a different dream, might have been the father of my heart" (228). The daughter's worldview is transformed by the calculation's failure to satisfy the quest to determine her origins.[12] She accepts the person in the photograph as a stranger, unlike her previous readings of her photograph collection. Yet this read-ing is laying claim to an inheritance of failure as the link and divide between the anticolonial and postcolonial eras. The dream that might have been, the future soon foreclosed, these phrases allude to a nostalgia that mourns the loss of an anticolonial hope that could look optimisti-cally forward to the horizon of the future, still undarkened by our post-colonial knowledge. The narrator leaves this nostalgia as a productive inheritance for the reader, linking postcolonial romance and tragedy. As Marion Rohrleitner points out, "Both the nameless daughter and the readers of the novel find themselves in the predicament of being required to actively use their imagination in the reconstruction of Teresa's and her daughter's past" (147). I would add that the reader of *Loving Che* is drawn to identify with the nameless Cuban American narrator in Miami as she seeks to verify the history of her mother, Teresa, a Cuban during the Revolution. In so doing, the historical novel calls into question the definition of nostalgia as necessarily an intellectual blind spot, an irra-tional desire that must be overcome.[13] Rather, *Loving Che* points to the inextricability of the past and present, with this longing for revolution as a *working through* of the anticolonial past and the postcolonial inheri-tance of anticolonial rhetoric.[14] Menéndez frames nostalgia as a by-prod-uct of the shift from past to post, one that must be engaged in order to understand the logic underlying the postcolonial problem-space.

"Now I Calculating": Re-membering Revolution through Romance in Dionne Brand's *In Another Place, Not Here*

As in *Loving Che*, Dionne Brand's *In Another Place, Not Here* out-lines the relationship of the anticolonial past to the postcolonial present by engaging Che Guevara's voice and writing. Brand's novel wrestles with the legacy of romance as an anticolonial genre for writing history, mapping out its gendered assumptions about emotion, affection, and intimacy. The novel alternates between the perspectives of three women, the cane-field worker Elizete in Grenada, the community activist Abena in Toronto, and the revolutionary Verlia who travels from Toronto to Grenada. Dionne Brand's novel demonstrates the disastrous implications of anticolonial discourse's heteronormative logic for the queer subject. Like Menéndez, Brand rescues romance as a postcolonial genre capable of addressing the blind spots of anticolonialism. In narrating the fallout of the Grenada Revolution via the romances between the three women, Brand exposes the anticolonial and developmentalist calculation of worth assigned to personal versus public, emotional versus scientific, sexual versus political, folk versus intellectual. The novel articulates a postcolonial ethics via the tragic depiction of these women's inability to escape their marginalization within the narrative of anticolonialism.

Pamela McCallum and Christian Olbey reference Verlia as an archival model when they describe her as "possibly the most densely articulated figure of history in the novel," explaining that "Verlia's collection of clippings, carefully saved in a shoe box under her bed, constructs and represents the pressures and possibilities that shape her moment" (161). The shoebox contains newspaper articles about heroes of revolutionary decolonization such as Mahatma Gandhi and Fidel Castro, including a drawing of Dessalines. Verlia's shoebox archive is analogous to the disorganized packet mailed by Teresa in *Loving Che* and Sabine's boxes of clippings and letters about Eric Williams in *The White Woman on the Green Bicycle*. The investigative trope of *In Another Place* allegorizes how historiography rhetorically processes the archive to identify what voices are worthy of inclusion and bearing witness, and the negative effects of applying a heterosexist lens to historical action. The novel encodes the mainstream reader as another investigative figure, attempting to make sense of the fractured narrative in much the same way that Elizete mourns the gaps in Verlia's archive. By following the trajectory of Verlia as a reader-double, the market aesthetics of the novel explore the damaging effects associated with the reader's inheritance of the anticolonial and neoliberal calculation of worth as a lens of analysis.

Verlia's youthful encounter with Che Guevara's writings shapes her decision as an adult to escape the tragic post-Sixties present of Canada and participate in Grenada's anticolonial project. Verlia's romantic nostalgia for anticolonialism is a context for the tragic failure of the Grenada Revolution. As a teenager in 1960s Canada, Verlia initially reads Guevara's writings as offering rebellion against her family's conception of how the present relates to the future. Anticolonial discourse offers a story about overcoming the present and creating a new horizon, a narrative that her family instead derives from religion: "She at seventeen could deliberately misunderstand her family saying go make something of yourself. And think perhaps they wanted her to read Fanon and Nikki. [. . .] Go sit into the early morning plotting your salvation, she could read them as saying; study Che, Ho Chi Minh, [. . .] learn guerilla tactics from Mao. These being the things that she needed to know to make something of herself" (160). Verlia sees anticolonial discourse as transforming her consciousness in a way that will satisfy her family's romantic goals of salvation. Translating the second-person call of "make something of yourself" into the third-person mission of "something of herself" reveals that this new self-definition will entail a certain distance between the personal, familial context and her new public revolutionary persona. Anticolonial discourse is a new religion for Verlia, a fresh worldview that still follows the same plotline of redemption but offers the possibility of a different future horizon. The family sees formal higher education as the entry point for domesticity, for finding the marriageable man who will engender a nuclear family: "Yes, the college to study physiotherapy and then the skinny Black man and the house on a street in Sudbury where there are no trees [. . .]. She is terrified at this seduction" (150). The bourgeois family narrative emplots a utopian future of a nuclear family that is frighteningly appealing, so much so that Velia worries she is "as much in danger of accepting the perfect picture as her uncle" (150). With the "seduction" of a domestic utopia, Verlia's coming to consciousness is encoded in terms of intimacy and sexuality.

Fearing that she will be enlisted into her family's regime of complicity and passivity in the face of oppression, Verlia runs away to "Toronto to join the Movement" (165). Guevara's writings offer an alternative trajectory of education and romance, with Verlia memorizing the following sentence: "At the risk of seeming ridiculous, let me say that the true revolutionary is guided by great feelings of love" (165). Verlia is citing Che Guevara's "Letter to Carlos Quijano," and she positions his letter to the Uruguayan magazine editor as a model for her ideal writing voice. Using this famous citation, Verlia attempts to root herself in the first-person "me" of Che's language: "There is a way she lands in the middle of that line, falls as if in love with herself. She wants to live in all the poetry and all the songs, all the revolutionary words shooting the bus double time down the highway leaving her uncle's life of capitulation and dying" (165). Verlia invests a transformative power in language and creative writing (poetry, songs). She imagines that art and rhetoric will allow her to escape from the path of submission charted by her family. Guevara's discursive model of the first-person voice offers Verlia the possibility of a different trajectory. However, Verlia's anticolonial education turns out to be equally conscripted in terms of gender and sexuality, creating a split self in Verlia. Verlia's desire to "live in Che's line" reinforces (165), rather than deconstructs, the tension between the intimate personal and the public historical voice, with Verlia alternating between the first-person "me" of Guevara and the intellectually distant third-person voice.

Dionne Brand complicates anticolonial discourse by breaking down the conceptual binaries it sets up between the personal and the public, the emotional and the logical, the mind and the body. Anticolonial values are shown to be unstable and ambiguous, undermining Verlia's romantic narrative of overcoming the obstacles of her body and cultural past. Verlia defines her self-education as a "struggle for a more 'scientific' understanding of the place that she's from" (165). Acquiring "this new language" of empirical analysis requires a war against the body, "knock[ing] her head against the books" because political inaction is blamed on "the sloth the body feels if we can't do anything about life" (165–66). Verlia identifies ideological commitment to a political cause as a way to save herself from her body's apathy. So while Greg Mullins argues that Brand's novel "suggests ways of thinking about the politics of love—and especially the sexual love of two black women for each other—as a challenge to the political and economic structures that limit the capacity for human flourishing in our contemporary era" ("Dionne Brand's Poetics" 1100), I maintain that Brand articulates the challenge of a queer politics of love within a more specific historical and rhetorical context: anticolonial revolution. What Verlia learns is that the desires of the body run counter to anticolonialism's intellectual aims, and she finds the ideological opposition between mind and body to be particularly problematic as she explores her sexuality.

Verlia outlines the romantic goals of her alternate education using another quote from Che Guevara's letter: "It is impossible to think of the genuine revolutionary lacking in this quality. . . . Our vanguard revolutionaries must make an ideal of this love of the people, of the most sacred causes, and make it one and indivisible. . .one must have a big dose of humanity, a big dose of a sense of justice and truth in order not to fall into dogmatic extremes, into cold scholasticism, into isolation from the masses. We must strive every day so that this love of humanity is transformed into actual deeds. . . ." (166). Verlia chooses a passage that continues in the same vein as the previous citation from Che, describing love as the motivation for revolutionary commitment. However, this passage no longer employs the first-person singular. Instead the collective "we" is used to conflate the revolutionary subject with the masses. At first, this quote disapproves of the distance between a love of humanity and cold scholasticism. Verlia adopts Guevara's solution to ideological extremism: an intellectual balancing act that requires the transformation of thought into action, of emotion into reality. The ellipses that Verlia inserts into this passage from Guevara are as important as the terms she highlights. She leaves out Guevara's derogatory comments about "ordinary" love and its inferior practices of "daily affection" (Dalleo, "Post-Grenada" 68). This censorship indicates that contradictions are already emerging between Verlia's lived experience and the anticolonial lens she adopts. For Verlia, physical affection denotes the ordinary family life she left behind: "This is why she'd joined the cell not wanting to limp home in the embrace of where she used to be" (183). That embrace would mean being seduced by the heterosexual domesticity that her family advocates. The negative invocation of physical affection augurs the challenges that intimacy with Abena and Elizete presents to Verlia's definition of a politically committed revolutionary.

When she uses Guevara's language to deal with the trauma of her imprisonment in a Canadian jail, the censorship that Verlia performs in order to conceive of herself as a revolutionary becomes especially visible. Verlia is "arrested for kicking a cop" and spends the weekend in jail, "keeping quiet under their 'Black bitch! Black whore! Nobody's coming to get you out'" (183). Verlia credits her psychological strength during an imprisonment compounded by racist and sexist diatribes to a mantra: "They didn't know but she'd kept herself quiet repeating Che's words to herself. 'At the risk of seeming ridiculous . . . at the risk of seeming ridiculous . . . let me say that the true . . . true revolutionary is guided . . . the true revolutionary is guided by great feelings of love . . . ' Over and over taking the sentence from the middle or wherever her thoughts happened on it, ' . . . guided . . . true . . . of seeming ridiculous . . . great feelings . . . at the risk . . . of love'" (183). Verlia's meditation reveals a more accentuated fracturing of her language, with the ellipses used to reorganize the sentence structure from Guevara so that the great feelings of revolutionary action come at the risk of romantic love. Verlia's equation of political action with the sacrifice of personal relationships presages her later choices to leave Abena in Canada for the Grenada Revolution as well as to leap off the cliff and

leave Elizete behind when the United States invades Grenada, marking
the end of the Revolution.

Verlia's anticolonial goal is to emerge from jail a different person and
use Che's language to imagine "who it would take to say those words,
who she would have to be" (184). Nevertheless, Brand does not allow
Verlia to make a clean break from her past persona. There is no trium-
phant jail cell transformation for Verlia as there is for other Sixties icons
like Malcolm X, the ghostly figure in *Free Enterprise* that I analyzed in
chapter 3. Verlia's ideal versus actual behavior when she is released from
jail hints that she cannot completely purge the past, especially the influence of her personal relationary context:

> When she was finally released [. . .] she wanted to say something like Che,
> something tippling off the tongue full of all her anger but peaceful in the
> end, reconciled to his instinct. *You are nothing but an instrument of the rul-
> ing class, a brutish automaton lacking humanity, used to repress the body
> and spirit of the people.* Something like that. [. . .] When it came out of her
> mouth it wasn't only out of her mouth but first her finger marking his face,
> an old gesture marking an enemy, and then she spat on the floor in front of
> him. "Never have a day's peace. Look for me everywhere." Such an old curse
> creeping out of her. She did not remember learning the gesture. And this too
> then, Che, wrath. Look how it raised her hand in an old sign, look at how it
> sprang water from her mouth. (184)

Verlia goes from wanting to be *like* Che, mimicking his discursive analysis, to conversing *with* Che, asking him to evaluate how her body betrays
her intellectual intent. Verlia seems disembodied here, with her perspective rendered in the third person as she imagines a conversation with
Guevara. She asks Che to look at her finger, hand, and mouth as carrying an unconscious cultural memory that undermines her calculated
speech.[15] The rhetorical move Verlia performs as she leaves jail does
not fulfill her goal of reducing the policeman to his place, as a pathetic
cog within a larger system of oppression. Instead, Verlia threatens the
cop with her individual gaze—look for me—and then asks Guevara to
turn his gaze against her—look at me. Verlia appears to be asking, how
could this finger-pointing gesture, which she does not remember learning, spontaneously silence her studied memorization of anticolonial
discourse? The Afro-Caribbean-inflected verbal putdown supplants the
anticolonial critique of the police state's repression of body and spirit.
Verlia's concern about this unconscious displacement makes visible
not only her desire to police her body but also the impossibility of any

complete break with one's past cultural context. While Verlia blames her body for this betrayal, she does not acknowledge how her family may have productively shaped her psyche in offering alternate forms of rhetorical self-defense and social critique.

The dialogue with Che continues in the first-person diary that Verlia writes as she participates in the Grenada Revolution, where she hears him "tell[ing] me how much harder I have to work" (213). The diary shifts Verlia's position from reader-double to author-double as she becomes an active narrator of revolutionary history. Raphael Dalleo argues that "in keeping a diary, this most personal form of writing, Verlia shows the potential function of the private" and that "the novel deconstructs the opposition of the intellect as public and emotion as private by framing solidarity through the passage from Che Guevara that Verlia returns to" ("Post-Grenada" 68). Notwithstanding the testimonial mode of the diary, I would argue that Verlia's difficulty with embodying Che's revolutionary persona and narrative voice becomes tied to overcoming the obstacle of her flesh and its private desires. While reading Che teaches her that revolutionary activity "comes to an end only with death unless the construction of socialism is accomplished on a world scale," she also hears her "family crawling through, saying be satisfied with being alive" (213). Guevara's version of the first-person voice from his letter to Quijano does not provide a model for Verlia to reconcile that familial past with her revolutionary present, other than as a betrayal of political commitment. Verlia's personal failures—"It weakens me to think of them"—become amplified by the collapse of the Grenada Revolution (213). Given this choice between death as political fulfillment and life as complicity, to remain alive would mean confronting the public failure of the anticolonial project as well as facing the threat of intimacy in relation to her queer female body.

Verlia's journey to Grenada and her suicidal jump off a cliff are escapes from the challenges that her intimate relationships with Abena and Elizete pose to her cultivation of a revolutionary anticolonial persona. When Verlia joins the radical cell in Toronto, her intellectual commitment negatively affects her body. As Dalleo notes, the novel's "split of the intellect and feeling is nowhere clearer than when Abena worries that Verlia's nervous breakdowns come from working underground" ("Post-Grenada" 68). Anticolonialism requires the sacrifice of Verlia's body, and she performs a rhetorical violence to discount her physical disintegration: "It's just my body. My head's straight" (191). The anticolonial binary that Verlia maintains between her body and mind also operates on a heteronormative logic: reason is privileged as the "straight" norm that will override the threatening queer desires of the body. Verlia's invocation of rhetorical violence is most explicit during a conversation with Abena, precisely because their relationship straddles the border between romantic and political passion.

The clean break Verlia tries to maintain between her past personal life and her present political activism becomes endangered by her relationship with Abena, which is the backdrop for, if not the means by which, she becomes an active member of Canada's civil rights or Black Power movement. Verlia criticizes Abena's more "minor" commitment as community organizer by arguing that Abena's motivations are dubious: "Maybe Abena was hiding something, maybe there was some reason that wasn't really about the struggle at all but personal" (186). Velia not only thinks that Abena is secretly harboring a problematic attachment to intimacy but also questions the depth of Abena's political passion. Because Abena is cautious about "armed" activism, Verlia accuses Abena of not engaging in a meaningful dialogue "because we fuck" (186). In her derogatory reference to sexuality, Verlia positions their romantic relationship as a barrier to an intellectual debate about how to accomplish social change. Abena contests this binary between the personal and the political by reminding Verlia, "Who taught you anything? Including fucking?" (186). Verlia's anticolonial self-education is not really an individual project, calling into question the idea of a heroic anticolonial subject (the Great WoMan) changing the course of history. Rather, Verlia's education is tied to some messy intimacies, with sexual power dynamics shaping the relationship between teacher and student, revealing the tensions between the roles of mentor and lover. These tensions recall the student-teacher dynamic of Camila and Marion's romance in Julia Alvarez's *In the Name of Salomé* that I examined in chapter 3.

Verlia reinstates the pedagogical dynamic of queer sexuality when she becomes Elizete's lover and works to change the conditions of the sugar estate workers in Grenada. Verlia positions Elizete as an ideal representative of the folk, but Elizete refuses to reduce their relationship to one of political activism. Elizete exposes the testimonial nature of their talks and rejects Verlia's objectification by declaring, "I not no school book with she, I not no report card, I not no exam" (77). Elizete understands what she represents to Verlia and how she essentially is Verlia's research project, a means for Verlia to test her ability as a revolutionary to become one with the people. As Ileana Rodríguez notes in her analysis of guerrilla narratives, this fusing of the revolutionary subject with the collective is a central concern of anticolonialism. Elizete offers an insightful critique of this goal, pointing out that the pedagogical paradigm for their relationship erases her personhood and her body. Despite her critique of Verlia, Elizete adopts these same tenets of anticolonial ideology once Verlia commits suicide. The deepest transformation, how Elizete internalizes a split self like Verlia, is visible on the discursive level of the text. Elizete is the opening first-person voice in the novel, but the novel closes with Elizete's perspective in the third person. Elizete's journey from first person to third person is due to her adoption of a research project after Verlia's suicide, of traveling to Canada to understand Verlia. Elizete becomes the investigator of an archive of history and intimacy that Verlia leaves behind. Elizete adopts the same testimonial mode as Verlia, erasing herself in the third person as she quotes Abena in the first person, collecting Abena's narrative about her immigration to Canada and facing her mother's disappointment and physical abuse (234, 236). Elizete is ambivalent about her relationship to Verlia, particularly the significance of their queer romance in the context of the Grenada Revolution. If Verlia's leap makes her the Great WoMan of history who sacrificed her life for the Revolution, then what is Elizete's relationship to Verlia: that of reader-witness or author-historian?

Elizete most concretely identifies the problem that ties all of the novel's women together, the troubled relationship between self and other, history and intimacy: "And after the first moment she didn't care anyway if the woman did not know that it was she, Elizete, lover to Verlia who was lover to her. What did it matter anyway, she had only wanted to see her to see what Verlia meant by 'not enough,' to measure if she was not enough too and if that was why Verlia left her, lying on stones" (235). Elizete follows the same discursive logic of privileging reason over emotion, mind over body, that Verlia initiated with her reading of Che Guevara. Elizete attempts to evaluate her own worth even as she judges irrelevant the loving sexual encounters inspiring her investigative journey to find Abena. Elizete feels an affinity with Abena because Abena was Verlia's lover, seeking her out in order to make sense of Verlia's suicide. Like Verlia, Elizete rejects a relationary web of intimacy in order to understand her individual identity as a queer Caribbean woman. When Elizete and Abena lie together after a moment of sexual intimacy, they both struggle to define their relationship to each other and to Verlia, the anticolonial revolutionary. Elizete ends their conversation by explaining that her coping mechanism for dealing with Verlia's death is to "count the endless names of stones" (241). Elizete reveals that the scientific discourse of interpreting the world remains a legacy of anticolonialism, even if the future it sought to imagine has been foreclosed by the tragic conclusion to the Grenada Revolution. Elizete adopts Verlia's model of historiography in order to imagine herself as something other than a witness but is delimited as an author—she is relegated to counting names, rather than imagining new ones for her stones of mourning. The United States' invasion of Grenada is an explicit context for anticolonialism in Brand's novel, but the text's attention to the discursive problem of calculation—through Elizete's postcolonial inheritance—suggests that neoliberalism also informs and delimits the potential of anticolonial discourse, particularly because of its developmentalist approach to subjectivity and historical progress.

In Another Place, Not Here is a discursive hybrid, rather than a novel that weighs in on the side of either romance or tragedy. Critics gloss over the tension embodied by Brand's text, often articulating positions akin to Verlia's anticolonial calculation. For example, Pamela McCallum and Christian Olbey read the "romantic relationship between Verlia and Elizete" as a minor element of the novel that Brand "resists" by privileging the "possibilities of resistance at this historical juncture" over "the individualistic subjective realm of the romantic" (171). Kaya Fraser sees the ending of the novel as "the symbolic death of one sort of poetics and the imagining of another" (291), evoking an anticolonial conception of revolutionary history, clearly distinguishing "past from post." At the same time, Joanne Saul argues that "this vision of history as inescapable makes the novel a tragic one" (61), giving us a sense that Brand depicts the present as overshadowed by the past. The academic discourse on the novel unconsciously adopts the dominant tropes of Verlia's narrative, such as the struggle between public good and personal passion as well as the romance of imagining new horizons for the Caribbean and its people on the islands and in the diaspora.

The rhetoric of value and intimacy in *Loving Che* and *In Another Place, Not Here* represents a broader allegory about cultural production with regard to social change. Addressing opposite ends of an anticolonial time line, the Cuban and Grenada revolutions, these historical novels share an interest in how the characters read and interpret Che Guevara's writings and persona. Menéndez and Brand employ the genre of romance as a way to reimagine the role of women in the Great Man narrative of anticolonialism. At the same time, their texts express concerns regarding the value of art and fiction in a postcolonial era. The power of anticolonial voices from the past, whether in the form of Teresa's collection of Che's photographs or Verlia's revolutionary mantra from Guevara, have more discursive authority than those of the contemporary world. For instance, *Loving Che*'s narrative is mainly composed of Teresa's packet, with the narrator's significantly shorter sections opening and closing the novel. Abena is never structurally integrated into *In Another Place* in the way that either Elizete or Verlia is, since they have separate sections and subtitles dedicated to them. Revolutionary Velia's narrative of suicide gets the final word. The novels depict the inability of anticolonial language to describe the postcolonial present, but art in the contemporary world is also unsure about how to bridge the gap between that past and the present. The postmodern experimental style of Menéndez's and Brand's novels speaks to these silences while also expressing an ambivalence about whether postcolonial literature measures up to the anticolonial ideal of writing as an instrument of progressive politics. Additionally, the postcolonial context of neoliberalism challenges the worth of cultural production through what Ileana Rodríguez calls the "binding [of] culture to technical and financial criteria" (xx).

Counterpoint: Postcolonial Police States and the Legacies of Anticolonial Masculinity in Monique Roffey's *The White Woman on the Green Bicycle*

Roffey's *The White Woman on the Green Bicycle* (2009) complements the postcolonial romances of Menéndez and Brand. Roffey's novel engages the Great Man narrative of Caribbean history by depicting a woman's intimate dialogue with Eric Williams's legacy. There are two key differences in the way Roffey emplots this encounter. Whereas *Loving Che* and *In Another Place, Not Here* are concerned with the way women process the historical legacy and archive of anticolonialism—the narrator with her mother's diary, Elizete with Verlia's scientific discourse of revolution—*The White Woman on the Green Bicycle* is more interested in the models of black masculinity passed on from colonialism to anticolonialism to postcolonialism. Mighty Sparrow, Brian Lara, and Patrick Manning make appearances in the novel's postcolonial world, and the anticolonial figure of Eric Williams contextualizes these masculinities. Additionally, while Menéndez and Brand focus on recuperating the voices of Caribbean women within their postcolonial romances, the main character of Roffey's novel is Sabine, a European woman who does not consider Trinidad her home.

It is not unusual for feminist revisionist histories to be articulated through the perspective of a non-Caribbean character or even a colonial lens. These texts force the reader to adopt the uncomfortable position of viewing the world through a racist, sexist, and heteronormative lens. At the same time, the historical fiction works against the biases of the narrator, encouraging the reader to learn to read against the grain of the narrating voice. One example is Beryl Gilroy's *Inkle and Yariko* (1996), which rewrites Ligon's history of Barbados and the many seventeenth- and eighteenth-century literary interpretations that were inspired by that historical narrative. The novel takes the form of a diary, narrated in the first-person by Thomas Inkle, a colonial traveler who is shipwrecked and captured by a tribe of Caribs and who then escapes to Barbados to become a prosperous slave owner. Despite Inkle's desire to depict himself in a positive light, the novel encourages an "against the grain" reading that undermines his interpretation of indigenous and slave culture, for instance, in his expression of nostalgia for his days as a captive (130). With this narrative strategy in mind, I supplement my reading of the postcolonial romances I have discussed thus far with my analysis of *The White Woman on the Green Bicycle.*

The form of Roffey's novel, its alternation between first-person and third-person narrative, evokes the tension between the historical contexts of the public and the personal, mapping the transformation of reader-doubles into investigative author-doubles. The novel opens in 2006, with an omniscient third-person perspective that is able to access the individual thoughts and feelings of only the characters with a semblance of power: the corrupt police who beat Talbot for reporting on them as well as the expats Sabine and George Harwood. By contrast, the novel rarely gives the reader or Sabine a glimpse of the thoughts of the Afro-Caribbean women servants—Jennifer, Venus, or Lucy—and the most vocal advocate of Black Power, Granny Seraphina, is the ultimate figure of opacity. This first half of the novel depicts a decontextualized postcolonial present, with the actions of the characters disconnected from their motivations. The reader never knows why the police are corrupt, why George and Sabine are in Trinidad, or even why the government blimp appears to be following the characters' movements.[16] The second half of the novel reverts to the past as the central context by which to reframe the postcolonial present of 2006, with sections set in 1956, 1963, and 1970. In contrast to the third-person perspective of first half of the novel, the second half is devoted to the first-person voice of Sabine. In this sense, it shares a great deal with the feminist historical fiction of Menéndez and Brand, since Sabine's narrative maps out Eric Williams's rise to power during the anticolonial period, imagining one white woman's relationship to that public political movement.[17] Sabine's voice is also very different from the detached narrative voice that opens the novel since it personalizes the romance of anticolonialism. Her foreignness as a colonial unfamiliar with Trinidad also positions her as a reader-double for a mainstream British and US readership that might find the Caribbean to be equally foreign. As a result, the chapters from the past have an explicit pedagogical function, educating the reader with Sabine's explanations of historical context, for example about the presence of the Indo-Caribbean population on the island or the landscape of Caribbean plants and food. I discussed this type of descriptive gloss in chapter 3 as typical of the postcolonial pedagogical imperative, a writerly strategy adopted by Caribbean diasporic writers in response to the assumed reader's lack of knowledge about the Caribbean past.

The dehistoricized first half of the novel offers a depiction of romance different from that of Menéndez or Brand. In contrast to the second half of the novel, the historical context that is given remains superficial: an opening subtitle of "Trinidad, 2006" marks the setting and time of the narrative, as well as events like the earthquake and the World Cup of soccer. In this section, Eric Williams is a disembodied ghost who haunts Sabine and her husband, George (18). When George discovers her shoebox archive of articles and unsent letters dedicated to Williams, he is transformed by this secret personal history. George symbolizes the novel's aspirational hope for an activist reader, rehabilitated by the pedagogical imperative of the text. In contrast to Verlia, who sees intimacy as undermining her revolutionary persona, George is politicized by reading Sabine's intimate thoughts and desires. Like the narrator of *Loving Che* and Elizete of *In Another Place*, George embarks on an investigative journey to recontextualize the present. However, this journey is concerned not so much with the place of women within anticolonial revolution as with how anticolonialism haunts postcolonial masculinity. In chapter 5, I discuss how Junot Díaz and Edwidge Danticat frame dictatorship as another legacy for understanding the development of postcolonial masculinity. After a failed confrontation with the superintendent of police who orchestrated the violence opening the novel, George interviews the other postcolonial "Fathers of the Nation" (107): Mighty Sparrow, Brian Lara, and Patrick Manning—contemporary historical figures whom Roffey connects to the legacy of Eric Williams.

As the "Soft News Man" at the recently conglomerated *Trinidad Guardian*, George has made a name for himself as the reporter who writes "fluffy stuff" and "upbeat stories, the good-news stories the younger men on the paper refuse to touch" (15). The neoliberal context of multinational corporations informs the business of writing in the postcolonial moment. George is politicized after reading Sabine's shoebox archive and engages in confrontational interrogations, motivated as much by his desire to recuperate the admiration and love of his wife as by a desire to determine the contemporary legacy of Eric Williams. These interviews are conducted at the intersection of romance, fatherhood, and nation. While interviewing the Mighty Sparrow, George finds himself inquiring whether the entertainer acknowledges a crippled choirboy as his illegitimate son, and in the next breath asking why Sparrow attended the fiftieth anniversary celebration of the PNM, the political party founded by Eric Williams in 1955. George sees Sparrow and Williams sharing their roles as "Fathers of the Nation" (108), with the implication that both abandoned or betrayed their parental responsibilities. Despite his critique, George seeks advice from Sparrow on how to recuperate his lost intimacy with Sabine. In the course of the interview-confession, Sabine's letter-writing devotion to Eric Williams becomes metaphoric: "There had been a love affair going on for a short time, when Williams was alive: Williams and the whole damn island" (110). Sparrow advises George to embark on a romantic endeavor of artistic production for the purpose of repairing his relationship with his wife, Sabine: to "win her back" (112).

George's interpretation of his new mission follows the anticolonial romance of political activism. He reconfigures his job as a reporter, invigorated by his desire to rekindle his romance with Sabine. George begins by politicizing his interview, asking Sparrow to share his most recent song, a satiric take on the blimp that is "vintage Sparrow, not his usual party stuff of late; old-school calypso, critical, political" (118). As he records and listens to the song, George hears two layers within Sparrow's voice: the voice of the boy who Sparrow will never concede is his progeny and Sabine's writerly voice, sharing with Williams "intimacies she's never shared with" her husband (112). The harmonizing theme that George hears connecting these voices is one of disillusionment. The boy's "purer" voice is a creative inheritance that belies his crippled body, while Sabine's letters reveal another legacy of the anticolonial period: "Sabine had encountered a scholar, a player, a man poised to mean something and be someone. She'd witnessed that powerful potential and she was still mourning its failure" (113). Neither Sparrow nor Williams has lived up to his symbolic potential as a father of the newly independent nation of Trinidad, and its postcolonial realities testify to their tragic inability to fulfill the rhetorical potential of their liberatory masculinity. George is inspired to respond this gendered tragedy by "writ[ing] something which might actually matter, for once" (121).

George attempts to resolve Sabine's postcolonial disillusionment using the investigative technique of interviews, collecting the contemporary postcolonial male's perspective on the past and the present, on Eric Williams and the blimp. His article on the Mighty Sparrow prompts the first written correspondence that George has received from Sabine in years, and he opens the note "hoping that it might say something of love" but finds instead Sabine's handwritten question for George's next interview: "*Can you ask Mr. Lara what he thinks of the blimp?*" (130). George reinvests his reporter role with the urgency of political activism, focusing on decoding the blimp's significance as a symbol of the postcolonial police state. Connecting the blimp to the legacy of Eric Williams is an attempt on the part of George and the novel's author, Roffey, to historicize the postcolonial state of Trinidad. Interviewing Brian Lara, a legendary cricket player, George is prompted not only to ask Sabine's question but also to give her credit for its origins (132). The result is a meditation on the blimp, with Lara calling into question its stated purpose as a "crime-busting initiative" (13), "watching the bandits" in low-income neighborhoods (132). Instead, Lara proposes that the blimp is "watchin' the coast" and "oil installations," as part of the United States' strategy to prevent any alliances between Trinidad and Venezuela: "They think he the new Castro in the Caribbean; they hate the way Chávez and Castro are friends. Imagine if Manning and Chávez paired up, too, eh? Then trouble for the US. Two oil-rich countries and a big ol' mudder-arse Communist like Fidel—that would be something to worry about" (132–33). With George acting as mediator, Sabine's question and Lara's response reveal that the anticolonial legacy of the Cuban Revolution continues to haunt the United States and the Caribbean in the postcolonial era, despite its tragic failure to live up to the promise of decolonization. At the same time, the postcolonial moment is shadowed by the profit-motivated surveillance, implying parallels between the neoliberal political alliances and the novel's book market context.

Lara critiques neoliberalism and US cold war ideology in terms of its perceived effects on the next generation: "The blimp change the view, man. It stick up in de eye and it stick up in de stomach. Children growin' up with this kinda nonsense hangin' over them? Like the crime problem is their fault? Their Daddy's fault? How it go help dem? How it go make them proud, break out?" (133). Lara mourns that his trajectory through cricket will not be an accessible avenue of upward mobility for the next generation of poor, and implicitly male, children. Lara also expresses concern for how the blimp will affect the perception of "Daddy" in these poor neighborhoods. Anticolonial horizons have been foreclosed for *male* children, with the postcolonial state delimiting and even emasculating the role models of masculinity and paternity. When George asks Lara to "imagine what your life would have been if your father hadn't the gumption to put you forward," the readership is encouraged to interpret postcolonial violence as symptomatic of a vacuum of paternal responsibility. George and Lara see on the horizon the "vexed" and "disappointed" men these orphaned boys will become, knowing that these are the "kinda man the blimp suppose to be watchin' all now" (134). The blimp's surveillance evokes the reader's complicity in consuming diasporic fiction and watching poverty as if it were on display in a fishbowl. The blimp in Roffey's novel recalls my discussion in chapter 2 of how David Chariandy's *Soucouyant* depicts the narrator and the reader as "professional knowers."

George's final interview confronts the ghost of Eric Williams in the guise of the most direct inheritor of his legacy, Patrick Manning, the PNM prime minister of Trinidad in 2006: "People said that Manning has worshipped Eric Williams, was in awe of him. People said that whenever Manning was in a tight spot he asked himself: *What would Williams have done?*" (159). Comprehending that he has been chosen to do a "PR job" because of his reputation as a "silly white fool in love with Trinidad," George sees his interview with Manning as his chance to critique the postcolonial powers that be. Failing to draw Manning into any serious statements about the blimp, George instead discusses a recent football match in order to segue into discussing Eric Williams: "Eric Williams was a keen footballer. What do you think he'd make of Trinidad and Tobago in the 2006 World Cup?" (162). The anniversary of "fifty years of the PNM" is an important historical context, a way for Roffey to reference the transition from anticolonial to postcolonial using the metaphor of paternity. George quotes Manning to his face in order to point out the divide between political leadership and orphaned male population, between the title of "the *Father* of the Nation" that both Williams and Manning invoke and Manning's public admission that "between 1991 and 1995 the PNM did not spend enough time looking after its own children" (163). George mourns the loss of the "revolutionary" opportunity that came with decolonization, noting "everything could have been rethought" (164). George acknowledges his complicity with the failure of anticolonialism, noting that his critique of Manning as a "colonial" is based on the knowledge that "it takes one to *know one*" (165). The metaphor of fatherhood and its limitations is depicted as a negative inheritance of anticolonialism: "Trinidad needs a good government. Not a bad father. Not a father at all. Leave that to the man in the street. Stop patronizing the people of Trinidad" (165). Roffey acknowledges another gendered legacy of the Great Men of decolonization, a historical narrative that not only excludes women from its story but also conscripts masculinity, setting up the state as the patriarchal overseer of social norms, without admitting that the state's motives have nothing to do with the loving guidance of parenting and are instead concerned with the consolidation of power through control and surveillance.

Male historiographies in Caribbean, US Latino/a, and African American studies often construct a romantic narrative of overcoming in theorizations of post-Sixties postcoloniality by implying that the anticolonial past (as well as its questions and answers) can be cleanly left behind. In *Loving Che*, *In Another Place, Not Here*, and *The White Woman on the Green Bicycle* the past cannot be left behind: it continues to haunt the present and yet remains inaccessible as well. The romance of anticolonialism, with its aspirational horizons and political solutions, cannot simply be replaced with a more "rational" acceptance of the tragedy of postcoloniality. Just as prominent male historiographies employ a masculinist conceptualization of the postcolonial problematic by writing romantic tragedies, Menéndez, Brand, and Roffey insert the female subject of Caribbean history into the postcolonial moment by narrating tragic romances. These Caribbean diasporic writers map out the legacy of the anticolonial period in terms of gender, of how the Great Men narrative of decolonization shapes postcolonial ideas about political activism and artistic creativity as well as gender and sexual identity.

The symbolic authority of such anticolonial figures cannot be simply debunked. In the final passage of *Loving Che*, the prototypical subject of history remains a man, standing alone, center stage in the photograph, with a woman as witness and armed with only imagination as the means to narrate a relationship to that historical figure. The self-reflective nature of these novels, the way in which they draw attention to voice in relation to historical narration, marks the novels of Menéndez, Brand, and Roffey as intellectual projects that recuperate women as agents of history. Equally important, Caribbean diasporic historical fiction speaks back to the masculine theorizations of post-Sixties postcoloniality by revealing how the contemporary moment is shaped by the type of masculinities that anticolonialism privileged and silenced.

Menéndez, Brand, and Roffey's historical novels call into question the definition of nostalgia as necessarily an intellectual blind spot, an irrational desire that must be overcome. *Loving Che, In Another Place, Not Here,* and *The White Woman on the Green Bicycle* posit the inextricability of the past and present, with the longing for revolution as a *working through* of the anticolonial past. Nostalgia is a by-product of the shift from past to post that must be engaged in order to understand the logic underlying the postcolonial problem-space. This chapter's conceptualization of nostalgia as a productive context enables a transition into my next chapter, which continues to analyze novels concerned with the nation-pasts of the Caribbean islands and how the diaspora negotiates those legacies. I return to the themes of gender and sexuality in chapter 5, with my discussion of dictatorship as a national context that shapes diasporic belonging in the work of Junot Díaz and Edwidge Danticat.

5 Dictating Diaspora

Gendering Postcolonial Violence in Junot Díaz
and Edwidge Danticat

JUNOT DÍAZ's *The Brief Wondrous Life of Oscar Wao* (2007)
and Edwidge Danticat's *The Dew Breaker* (2004) are historical novels
whose narrative forms seek to mimic the diversity of the Caribbean diasporas they depict. *Oscar Wao*'s discursive heterogeneity incorporates
black urban slang, Spanglish, comic books, and science fiction, while
Dew Breaker focuses on a diasporic community orphaned by postcolonial violence, alternating between the perspectives of the Tonton
Macoutes and their male and female victims. The multiple discourses
in Díaz's and Danticat's novels call to mind Timothy Brennan's description of the novel as a genre that "mimic[s] the structure of the nation, a
clearly bordered jumble of languages and styles, and a rhetorical space
where previously foreign languages [meet] each other on the same terrain, forming an unsettled mixture of ideas and styles," themselves representing "previously distinct peoples now forced to create the rationale
for a common life" ("National Longing" 49–50). Whereas Brennan
addresses the novel's role in imagining the nation and incorporating different subcultures into one community, I propose that Díaz's and Danticat's historical novels embody the cultural and linguistic diversity of
the Dominican and Haitian American diasporas rather than the nation.[1]

Oscar Wao and *Dew Breaker* wrestle with the problem of how to best
narrate the histories of these diasporic communities, composed of immigrants from the Caribbean and those born in the United States, as well as
the perpetrators and victims of postcolonial violence. Díaz and Danticat
concentrate on the historical context of dictatorship and tackle the ways
in which its legacy shapes diasporic belonging and artistic production.
The novels question the ethical imperative of narration and art in a postcolonial world, where dictatorships have left an indelible mark on public
discourses about belonging, nation, and history. Both authors blur the

lines between narration and dictation, calling into question whether diasporic storytelling can heal the wounds of postcolonial violence, especially when it derives narrative strategies from the Trujillo and Duvalier dictatorships. For Díaz and Danticat, a major legacy of these dictatorships is the formulation of community as patriarchal and homosocial, where discourses of cultural authenticity marginalize alternative diasporic identities. Dictation becomes gendered as a masculine endeavor shaped by dictatorship's history of sexism and heteronormativity.[2]

Díaz and Danticat see dictatorship as an inescapable cultural and historical context. In their respective works of fiction, the diaspora does not achieve a clean slate of history with its immigration from the island of Hispaniola; rather, the characters are haunted by their experiences of postcolonial violence. *Oscar Wao* and *Dew Breaker* express ambivalence regarding their postcolonial ethics, depicting diasporic cultural production—including oral storytelling, sculpture, and writing—as relying upon models of dictation inherited from postcolonial authoritarian regimes. Both novels remain uncertain about the motivation behind as well as the efficacy of educating their readerships about the Caribbean diaspora's history. Highlighting the shared etymologies of *dictation* and *dictatorship*, the novels align the desire to record Caribbean histories with the regulation of diasporic subjectivity. In *Oscar Wao*, Lola notes that the diaspora is composed of "ten million Trujillos (324)," while *Dew Breaker* depicts a diasporic community where the dew breaker and his family circulate among the victims of his past torture.

The haunting of diasporic art by the past does not signify an apolitical throwing up of hands, an abdication of the pedagogical imperative. The authors' ambivalence about their ethical projects translates into a warning about the dangers of consuming any narrative uncritically, without thinking through the historical context of its artistic form and culture. The authors do not unequivocally position art or storytelling as capable of healing the wounds of postcolonial violence and dictatorship; rather, they see such modes of cultural production as forms of *processing* historical trauma that do not escape or erase that violence. Díaz and Danticat embrace their roles as public intellectuals in the United States, which are shaped by the multicultural marketplace for their writing. They also voice concerns about the privilege of representation that has been bestowed upon them. *Oscar Wao* and *Dew Breaker* place storytelling within a local and international context, depicting artists who ambivalently embody the tensions and contradictions of diasporic culture and history. With the retelling of stories understood as potentially another form of violence, Díaz and Danticat posit a critique of their unusual and exemplary roles as cultural ambassadors—if one voice is chosen to represent a diasporic community, how many are silenced?

In contextualizing narration within the workings of a US multicultural society, Danticat and Díaz isolate gender and sexuality as primary focus points by which to articulate the diaspora's relationship to the homeland's history of dictatorship. The nation-state's heteronormative and patriarchal structure immigrates along with the diaspora. In *Oscar Wao*, Abelard's fall initiates the dispersal of the de León family, while *Dew Breaker* shows the Duvalier regime creating a diaspora of orphaned boys in the United States. Unlike much of the academic criticism written about these authors and their fiction, neither historical novel equates diaspora's hybridity with justice and equality. The diaspora's inheritance of a masculinist model of dictation exposes how cultural production depends on the silencing of other voices. For example, Yunior's narration censors Oscar's queerness, and Michel's tape-recorded message suppresses the influence of his wife. In each case, one individual is empowered to translate the history of a Caribbean diaspora to an audience, with Yunior directly addressing his reader and Michel speaking to his newborn son. Through the male author-doubles, Díaz and Danticat deconstruct the process of narration and how it defines community through the emplotment of a particular history, identifying key historical actors and events that must be passed on to the next generation—for instance, Lola's daughter, Isis, and Michel's son.

The diasporic male-male discursive relationships of Yunior and Oscar as well as Michel and his son relegate women to the margins. In turn, both Díaz and Danticat express concern about the influence of *readerships* on the construction of heteronormative and masculinist histories of the past. The complicity and vulnerability of the reader constitute a dominant thread in the representation of narration. The pedagogical thrust of *Oscar Wao* and *Dew Breaker* supports my thesis that Caribbean historical fiction aims to teach the reader about Caribbean history while also exploring how the dominant narrative of that history is gendered. The lesson that Díaz and Danticat impart is that histories encode the rules of masculinity, of how to become a man (via sex and/or violence), marginalizing women from that public narrative despite their strong voices (Lola is the only first-person voice that interrupts Yunior's narrative, just as the wife also interrupts Michael's oral recording).

Though *Oscar Wao* and *The Dew Breaker* share a concern about the possibility of reconciliation between the victims and the perpetrators of dictatorship's violence, Danticat's novel uniquely addresses the experiences of women artists. Both Díaz and Danticat present first-person narrators as author-doubles who embody the inheritance of patriarchal storytelling from the Trujillo and Duvalier dictatorships. However, in addition to mapping out a homosocial diasporic community, Danticat emplots women as author-doubles who encounter rhetorical challenges in their ability to inherit and pass on models of historiography and art. The characters of Ka and Freda are women who inherit their artistic visions from their fathers and process the violence of the Duvalier dictatorship, through either singing or sculpture. The public market for their art places gendered restrictions on the way these author-doubles can express themselves artistically, and their interpretation of these patriarchal models eventually becomes untenable in the diasporic context. Ka and Freda are placed on similar trajectories, forced to choose between creative expression and cultural identity, ultimately moving from their public modes of art to a minor and marginalized community of women. Danticat's representation of women artists provides a counterpoint to Díaz's exclusively male world of narration, especially since the women in Díaz's novel are not fully developed as potential author-doubles.

Díaz, Danticat, and Diasporic Contexts

Oscar Wao and *Dew Breaker* speak back to celebratory theorizations of diaspora that frame the concepts of diaspora and nation in opposition to one another. By opening with an epigraph from Derek Walcott, Díaz's novel references the labeling of the diasporic subject as either "nobody" or a "nation," while Danticat's title figure of the dew breaker indicates that the legacy of the dictatorship continues to haunt the Haitian diaspora in the United States. Academic discourse often defines diaspora as a more inclusive community operating on less oppressive identity politics than those set by the nation-state.[3] Carole Boyce Davies refers to how "diaspora assumes expansiveness and elsewhereness" and thereby parallels the "migrations of the Black female subject [who] pursue[s] the path of movement outside the terms of dominant discourses" (37). These dominant discourses are specifically nationalist, since it is "the unproblematic, sacred homeland definition on which nationalist discourses turn [that] is oppressive" (51). Stuart Hall also constructs diaspora as a counterculture to nationalist logics of exclusion, aligning "the diaspora experience" with "the recognition of a necessary heterogeneity and diversity" that stands in opposition to the nation's "essence or purity" ("Cultural Identity" 235). The "nature" of diaspora is defined by diversity. In foregrounding heterogeneity as the foundational element of diaspora, Hall argues for a "conception of 'identity' which lives with and through, not despite, difference" (235). The distancing of the diaspora from the nation sets up a parallel opposition between liberation and oppression, diversity and homogeneity. To structure the relationship of the diaspora to the nation in binary terms, the essence of diasporic consciousness becomes defined as Other, as purely marginal.

It makes sense, then, that the academic reception of Díaz's and Danticat's writing often depicts their fictional texts as works of diasporic activism that can undermine the oppressive power structures of nation and empire. *Oscar Wao* is described as a heroic literary text—Anne Garland Mahler titles her essay on the novel "The Writer as Superhero"— that breaks through oppression to posit an ideally marginal but resistant diasporic subject, whether it be Yunior or Oscar (or Junot Díaz).[4] The discourse surrounding *Dew Breaker* makes comparable claims, arguing that the power of the text lies in its accurate depiction of marginalized diasporic communities. Trauma studies are a popular lens of analysis that isolates Danticat's novel as an anthropological artifact "rais[ing] awareness" (D. Smith 139).[5] Yet the novels can be read as a challenge to such academic formulations of diaspora, critiquing these as narrow definitions of belonging. Yunior's internal conflict in *Oscar Wao* is over Dominican cultural authenticity; he is torn between identifying either himself or Oscar as a model diasporic subject. Danticat's chapter "Night Talkers" also points to the ways in which the diaspora produces different Haitian American experiences; Dany encounters Claude, a young man deported from the United States to a Haiti he barely remembers having lived in as a child.[6] Díaz's channeling of Oscar's life through Yunior's narrative lens and Claude's disidentification with his Haitian family by labeling them "backward-ass peasants" reveals that even within the diaspora a silencing can occur, because the diaspora is also conditioned by the logic of the nation (102).[7]

The relationships between Yunior and Oscar as well as between the dew breaker's family, the male roommates, and isolated Haitian American women are not ones of solidarity but of competing diasporic identities.[8] Díaz and Danticat emphasize the contradictions of diasporic communities, revealing how they remain informed by institutional violence and the ideology of dictatorship. *Oscar Wao* contests the binary opposition between diaspora and nation, showing how a common inheritance of exclusion and oppression links these communities. *Dew Breaker* equally blurs the line between the macoutes and their victims, primarily with the main plotline of Ka's discovery of her father's identity. Ka believes her father was imprisoned during the Duvalier dictatorship, inspiring her to depict him in a statue as an honorable survivor. However, he turns out to have been a prison guard responsible for the torture of civilians. The author-doubles in Díaz's and Danticat's novels address the complicity of ordinary diasporic individuals in sustaining the oppressive influence of postcolonial regimes.

Junot Díaz's *The Brief Wondrous Life of Oscar Wao*

Oscar Wao is a transnational text that blurs the opposition between diaspora and nation by making clear that for US-born Oscar to be a diasporic subject he must be domesticated according to the code of nationalist belonging, as enforced by the Dominican Republic–born Yunior. *Oscar Wao* delves into the intersections and conflicts between the Dominican nation and its periphery, as Yunior goes from embodying both resident and immigrant Dominican American men in *Drown* to embodying a Dominican-born Latino in *Oscar Wao* who dictates the life of US-born Oscar de León. I complicate the accepted reading of *Oscar Wao* as a transgressive text that challenges the oppressive structures of the nation-state by explaining how the novel is responsive to the values of an academic readership, particularly in relation to diasporic discourse. Díaz historicizes the origins of diasporic identity, positioning Oscar de León as a subject that the Dominican nation cannot assimilate. Despite its title, the true protagonist of *Oscar Wao* is author-double Yunior, and the relationship between Yunior and Oscar calls attention to how narrating a diaspora's history also entails domesticating difference. While Oscar is endearingly inauthentic, Yunior's mission to identify him as a representative subject who can embody the Dominican diaspora leads him to silence Oscar's points of queer Otherness—his virginity and sentimentality. Yunior's insecurities as narrator reveal that his investment in telling Oscar's story is motivated by an inability to tell the full story about himself. Just as the ending of the novel projects onto Oscar a transformation into full-fledged heterosexuality, it also hints at el secreto abierto of homosocial romance that cannot be rendered as part of a Dominican diasporic history.

Yunior's narration suggests that the "fukú," or curse of the diaspora, is to reproduce the trauma of violence that engendered its existence, which for Oscar's family originates in "the Fall" of his grandfather, Abelard (126). Because the formation of the Dominican diaspora is intimately tied to the violence that the Trujillo dictatorship used to forcibly silence opposing voices, *Oscar Wao* offers itself up as a foundational fiction of the Dominican diaspora, with all of the positive and negative connotations that the term suggests.[9] Yunior plays a pivotal role in Díaz's novel because of his dictation of Oscar's life and his intertextuality as a character from *Drown*. In a 2007 interview in *Slate* magazine, Díaz suggests that "one of the questions that a reader has to answer for themselves is: Why is Yunior telling this particular story?" ("Questions," par. 8). Yunior, as sole narrator of *Oscar Wao*, establishes a link between storytelling and dictatorship. By pulling back the veil of an omniscient voice and revealing Yunior as the narrator, Díaz underscores the dangers involved in accepting the authenticity of any historical narrative, even the fiction that he himself writes. The novel thus echoes Linda Hutcheon's equation of history and fiction as narratives with similar functions: "Historiography and fiction are seen as sharing the same act of refiguration, of reshaping our experience of time through plot configurations; they are complementary activities" (100). The writing of history and the writing of fiction have the same goal of ordering the past and dictating which key events should be seen as shaping our present. Díaz goes one step further than Hutcheon to construct the relationship of historical agency to literary narration as a rivalry.

In Díaz's view, rather than performing "complementary activities," the writer and the dictator compete over who gets to shape the public imagining of a national and diasporic identity. In a substantial footnote, the as-yet-nameless narrator of *Oscar Wao* helpfully points out the parallels between fictional dictation and political dictatorship: "Rushdie claims that tyrants and scribblers are natural antagonists, but I think that's too simple; it lets writers off pretty easy. Dictators, in my opinion, just know competition when they see it. Same with writers. *Like, after all, recognizes like*" (97). In the *Slate* interview, Díaz extends this analysis further and applies it to the desires of a reading audience by arguing that the "real dictatorship is in the book itself" ("Questions," par. 13). When asked to clarify his statement, Díaz explains: "We all dream dreams of unity, of purity; we all dream that there's an authoritative voice out there that will explain things, including ourselves. If it wasn't for our longing for these things, I doubt the novel or the short story would exist in its current form. I'm not going to say much more on the topic. Just remember: In dictatorships, only one person is really allowed to speak. And when I write a book or a story, I too am the only one speaking, no matter how I hide behind my characters" (par. 15). In this context, *Oscar Wao* appears as a corrective to the critical success of *Drown*, cautioning against the uncritical consumption of a narrative packaged to give anthropological insight into a "wondrous life." Yunior is the "one person" whom Díaz warns of, since he is the authoritative voice in *Oscar Wao*.

At first glance, the novel appears to have a polyvocal structure, but Yunior is the individual consciousness filtering the narratives of the other characters, regardless of whether they are in first, second, or third person. He presents Beli's history to the reader after researching her past: "I'll give you what I've managed to unearth" (119). Even the first-person voices in the novel turn out to be funneled through Yunior. He quotes from Oscar's diary, and one of Lola's narratives is directly relayed to Yunior (205–11). Yunior's dictatorship extends beyond the fictional lives he narrates to include his power to relay or withhold information from the novel's readership. At times this censorship is rationalized in terms of protecting the reader from excessively harsh realities. For example, Yunior makes a point of emphasizing his insider knowledge about Abelard's imprisonment, that he can narrate "a thousand tales to wring the salt from your motherfucking *eyes*" but instead chooses to "spare you the anguish, the torture [. . .] spare you in fact the events and leave you with only the consequences" (250). Yunior makes transparent his rationale of making the *ends* more visible and relevant than the *means*. The comforting and yet threatening tone conveys the position of authority that Yunior assumes in relation to the reader and, by extension, the power that he has over our sense of what Oscar's life means. Yunior testifies to his role in silencing other perspectives as he narrates Oscar's story, foreshadowing how Yunior's ending for Oscar will violently censor his queerness.

Yunior's role as dictator is a product of his intertextual migration from *Drown* to *Oscar Wao*. When the coincidence of relation is discussed, critics agree that the Yunior in *Oscar Wao* is the Yunior from *Drown*, who immigrated to the United States at a young age with his brother Rafa.[10] The discussions of intertextuality trace one line of inheritance for *Oscar Wao*: same name, must be the same character. In an essay published in *Contemporary Literature*, I analyze the dynamic of narrative voices in *Drown* and *Oscar Wao*, emphasizing how the Yuniors from *Drown* embody at least two different diasporas, those of immigrant Dominicans versus Dominican Americans born in the United States. Because it is uncertain whether any of the Yuniors return from *Drown*, the Yunior in *Oscar Wao* symbolizes a change in diasporic power dynamics that is responsive to the interpretive assumptions made by readers of *Drown*.

Drown makes it easy for readers to confuse the Yuniors, since it equates the experiences of Dominican-born and US-born diasporic communities through the Yuniors' shared abandonment by their father Ramón and the anonymity of the other short-story characters.[11] The novel points to the danger behind readers' misinterpretation of *Drown* by imagining the consequences of having one type of diasporic subject stand in for and hold court over another individual's authenticity.[12] Instead of being one of many in *Drown*, Yunior emerges as the sole, subjective arbiter of authenticity in *Oscar Wao* and narrates a singular historical legacy, that of dictatorship. The power relations between diasporas similarly shift, with Yunior as the Dominican-born narrator establishing the terms of US-born Oscar's belonging. The relationship between the resident and immigrant diasporic communities therefore goes from one of egalitarian marginalization in *Drown* to a hierarchical power structure of dictatorship in *Oscar Wao*. Perhaps because so many readers assumed that the Dominican Republic–born Yunior was the only Yunior in the short story collection, Díaz gives Yunior's double a different name in *Oscar Wao*. Readers cannot ignore Oscar's difference and how he represents a diaspora that does not fit the established norm. The novel lures readers into thinking that it is an inclusive, progressive project whose aim is to show how marginal diasporic histories and subjects have a place within the Dominican community. One reviewer remarks that the novel is also a corrective for an ignorant American audience, a "cure" for the "woeful myopia" of Díaz's readership in terms of the Dominican Republic's history (Asim BW03). The novel's pedagogical imperative requires that the ostensibly more authentic Yunior violently de-Other Oscar in order to make him fit into this historical narrative.

Unsentimental Education

The critical reception of *Oscar Wao* largely focuses on Oscar and his family as exemplary models of a diasporic community. The prevailing interpretation of the novel overlooks how Yunior's ability to dictate, first as an invisible presence and then as an embedded reporter, shapes the story of Oscar's brief life.[13] As readers become invested in seeing Oscar achieve some measure of happiness for his own sake, they become blind to and even complicit with the role Yunior plays in determining the means by which Oscar will finally feel that he belongs. As dictator of the novel (or co-dictator, if you wish to count Trujillo as a character), Yunior takes on the task of domesticating the tension of Oscar's inauthentic Dominican diasporic identity. The novel defines authentic identity in much the same way that the reception of *Drown* does. *Oscar Wao* is the imaginative outcome of what would happen if the Yuniors from *Drown* wrote the rules of authenticity, applying them to Dominican diasporic subjects unable to meet that same definition of representative identity, such as Oscar de León. *Drown*'s Yunior collective of decontextualized, disaffected, downwardly mobile men stands in stark contrast to the earnest Oscar, who is obsessed with the historicity of his family. Yunior's individuality makes possible a more direct confrontation with the national codes of masculinity through his relationship with Oscar as subject of his narration. The challenge that Yunior faces in telling Oscar's story is how to render him as belonging to the Dominican diaspora while also attending to his unique individuality. Yunior sacrifices Oscar by relying upon a restrictive definition of diasporic identity and silencing Oscar's critiques of Yunior's masculinity. In so doing, *Oscar Wao* calls into question the notion of a diasporic foundational fiction that can escape the rules of national belonging and sexuality. In the novel, the seductiveness of dictatorship, whether political or literary, is an inheritance that Díaz's readership and the Dominican diaspora must wrestle with.

For Yunior, the shift from witness to participant in the story is structured by a writerly imperative that is responsive to readers' desires. The hypersexualized and unsentimental author-double Yunior assimilates his Other, Oscar, into Dominican belonging, fulfilling readership demands for authenticity. Oscar's inauthenticity as marginalized nerd and "fat-boy" is actually incidental (176); what troubles Yunior's narration is reconciling Oscar's queer attributes—his sentimentality, virginity, and tears. *Oscar Wao* is a self-referential text haunted by the historical violence making that authenticity possible. Oscar's progression from tearful margins to unsentimental center parallels Yunior's transformation from anonymous outsider to a named participant. By aligning Oscar's evolution with that of Yunior, Díaz exposes the conflicted process that situates a diasporic male subject as an agent of history. Through Yunior, sexuality becomes a barometer of belonging that continues to shape the nation-state and diaspora.

The sentimentality that contributes to Oscar's inauthenticity as a Dominican male is intimately connected to his thwarted heterosexuality. Oscar's virginity, arising from his inability to find a willing sexual partner, delegitimizes his masculinity and his identity as a Dominican. The narrative opens by affirming that Oscar "never had much luck with the females," which is "very un-Dominican of him" (11). At first, it seems that his lack of luck in the romance department results from his physical appearance. The narrator emphasizes Oscar's unattractive physique, compounded by a combination of "antipussy devices" such as his "Puerto Rican afro" and "Section 8 glasses" (20). The narrator's reasoning in alleging the unsightliness of Oscar's hair appears to be that even Oscar's blackness is derived from the wrong source, from Puerto Rico rather than the Dominican Republic. His overweight body is also unable to perform what is considered masculine movement. In addition to "thr[owing] a ball like a girl" (20), Oscar finds that "kids of color, upon hearing him speak and seeing him move his body, shook their heads" and told him, "You're not Dominican" (49). Oscar's cultural inauthenticity is not derived simply from his physical body: after all, his childhood obesity did not prevent him from being a "'normal' Dominican boy" (11), meaning "lov[ing] himself the females" and having "girlfriends galore" (12). It is the childhood tears Oscar sheds after Maritza dumps him that initiate the process by which "everything he had in the girl department" would be "burned up that one fucking week" (17). Oscar's childhood fall from hetero-grace and his resulting sexual abstinence are attributed to his sentimentality. Such sentimentality functions as part of el secreto abierto of Oscar's queer identity: "People 'know' the 'secret' without being told, through any combination of factors such as behaviors, speech, or dress" (King 64).

Oscar's failure to meet the rules governing sentiment is demonstrated by the number of tears he sheds throughout the novel, "often for his love of some girl or another" (23–24). Oscar normally knows well enough to follow a mandate of discretion and keep these tears hidden by crying "in the bathroom, where nobody could hear him" (24), understanding that such a public display of emotion is forbidden. Oscar learns this lesson when his visible sentimentality is first punished. Beli discovers her seven-year-old son crying "por una muchacha" (14) and promptly grabs Oscar by the ear, throws him to the floor, and instructs him on the more proper response to heterosexual rejection: "Dale un galletazo . . . then see if the little puta respects you" (14). Beli identifies unsentimental violence as the appropriate masculine response to frustrated heterosexual desire, in opposition to Oscar's tears. Crying feminizes and infantilizes Oscar's body, signifying inappropriate behavior that is equated with homosexuality. On another occasion, Oscar is unable to suppress his emotions after encountering Maritza at school with her new boyfriend Nelson, and his tears garner him the moniker "the mariconcito" from his fellow students (16). Sentimentality is again equated with homosexuality, foreshadowing Yunior's linguistic queering of Oscar later on in the novel. Oscar also cries while watching the happy endings to science fiction movies, when the hero is "finally hooked up" (47) with "the love of his life" (307). These cinematic narratives—*Robotech Macross* and *Virus*—model the romance that Oscar unsuccessfully seeks. His tears correlate with his unconsummated sexual longing and the violent consequences of these illusory relationships (186). Oscar cries in reaction to both self-inflicted violence, like his failed suicide attempt (191), and the external violence that comes as punishment for trespassing upon the territory of others, as in the beating ordered by the Capitán in the Dominican Republic (297, 305). Instead of following the dominant script of active, unsentimental violence, Oscar cries when his heterosexual aspirations are thwarted. Oscar's virginity is a product of his sentimentality, and together these factors invalidate his claim to Dominican masculine identity. Yunior's college friends tease Oscar by repeatedly asking him, "You ever eat toto?" (180). Oscar's reply in the negative, that he has never performed cunnilingus on a woman, is taken as a sign that he has failed to meet the ultimate standard of Dominican manhood: "Tú no eres nada de dominicano" (180).

Despite what appears to be an insurmountable inauthenticity, the novel's conclusion recuperates Oscar as a Dominican man through the body of Ybón, a prostitute in the Dominican Republic. Oscar understands Ybón's potential: "He was sure, [she] was the Higher Power's last-ditch attempt to put him back on the proper path of Dominican male-itude" (283). After all, a woman with a career in sex work would be the most realistic point of access for poor, pathetic Oscar. However, their relationship is not based on the typical power relations and economy of prostitution that I discussed in reference to Chariandy's *Soucouyant* in chapter 2. Rather, Oscar falls in love and gets a makeover. Meeting Ybón physically marks Oscar, in part because of the beatings he receives for courting her, but also because he decides to diet and lose "all the weight" (312). In addition to the fatboy becoming thin, the relationship provokes an inner transformation, one that allows Oscar to disregard the authority of his grandmother's "Voice" and continue endangering his life by pursuing Ybón: "Something had changed about him. He had gotten some power of his own" (319). The most dramatic evidence of this psychic shift and new strength comes when Oscar faces his second beating by the Capitán's goons. The narrator tells us, "This time Oscar didn't cry when they drove him back to the canefields" (320). His lack of tears is the principal indication that Oscar has finally learned either to rein in or to purge that feminine weakness that dominated his body, behavior, and mind. Facing his death, Oscar is unsentimental and lectures his killers on the transformative power of Ybón: "He told them that it was only because of her love that he'd been able to do the thing that he had done, the thing they could no longer stop" (321). What is this "thing" that Oscar has accomplished? After describing Oscar's murder, Yunior discloses that just prior to his death "Ybón actually *fucked* him. Praise be to Jesus!" (334). With a miracle of divine intervention, Oscar emerges as a devirginized, unsentimental hero who is delivered into authenticity through Ybón's body. Oscar's speech to his murderers reveals that even death cannot undo his newfound belonging through sex.

Yunior's Narrating Eye

Yunior is instrumental in convincing the reader to accept this plot resolution, a romantic ending of consummated love. Yunior narrates Oscar's progression from inauthentic diasporic male to assimilated, unsentimental un-virgin. Whether as nameless narrator or named character in the story, Yunior is exceptionally responsive to the reader's presence. At the start of the novel, the nameless "I" has a heightened awareness of his audience, predicting a desire for information: "You want a final conclusive answer to the Warren Commission's question, Who killed JFK? Let me, your humble Watcher, reveal once and for all the God's Honest Truth" (4). In calling himself the Watcher, a character from Jack Kirby and Stan Lee's comic *The Fantastic Four* who acts as Historian to the Universe, the narrator claims to be an objective witness to History and an expert on the Truth. Díaz reinforces the narrator's guise of objectivity by having him substantiate the narrative with excessively detailed footnotes about historical contexts. Since the novel opens with a promise of fulfilling the readership's expectations, the anonymous narrator depends upon a specific articulation of his identity: first, as distanced enough from the novel's subject to be objective, and second, as familiar enough to be able to provide access to unmitigated and unmediated truth.

The narrator maintains his anonymous, all-knowing persona up to the point that he is identified as Yunior; after revealing himself, the narrator is exposed as an imperfect and subjective source of information, and the footnotes become less frequent.[14] Once the appearance of objectivity is shattered by this revelation of identity, Yunior's storytelling also shifts. As the nameless narrator, Yunior plays the part of a confident and trusted informant, but he becomes plagued with doubts about his ability to tell this story. For instance, he admits to the impossibility of knowing everything: "Which is to say if you're looking for a full story, I don't have it" (243). This self-consciousness turns defensive as Yunior confesses his concerns about the reader's demands for information and realism, as well as his ability to fulfill those expectations. The crisis of authority comes to a head when "A Note from Your Author" interrupts the story (284). Yunior is frustrated by the fact that he may not be meeting his audience's standards for plot development: "I know what Negroes are going to say. Look, he's writing Suburban Tropical now. A puta and she's not an underage snort-addicted mess? Not believable. Should I go down to the Feria and pick me up a more representative model?" (284). The question of authenticity arises in regard to the prostitute's body as the territory chosen to recuperate Oscar and whether Ybón can be the foundation for a true story.

Yunior assuages these readerly concerns by stating that to choose a younger, more exploited body would mean that he would "be lying," and that "this is supposed to be a *true* account of the Brief Wondrous Life of Oscar Wao" (285). Ybón's appearance is a writerly choice, and Yunior realizes that the romance between her and Oscar requires some stretch of the imagination: "Can't we believe that an Ybón can exist and that a brother like Oscar might be due a little luck after twenty-three years?" (285). Yunior's logic for narrating Ybón into existence is not to posit the prostitute as an authentic subject but rather to give Oscar his "due." Yunior wants to demarginalize Oscar, to cure him of the obstacle that prevents him from claiming belonging as a Dominican male. Yunior references the novel's audience and its desires for realism, identifying the narrative as the product of a tense negotiation between himself and the reader.[15] Yunior capitulates to the readership's expectations for Truth by continuing to disguise his role in shaping what is purportedly the "real" story. Yunior encourages the reader to accept the romance of sex as a realistic ending for Oscar so that the reader (following the novel's metaphor) swallows "the blue pill," accesses Truth, and leaves a Matrix of illusion behind (285).[16]

Yunior is attuned to the reader's desire for a favorable conclusion because of his investment in the story he tells. The prologue indicates that the unnamed narrator wants to exorcise his ghosts: "Even now as I write these words I wonder if this book ain't a zafa of sorts. My very own counterspell" (7). Oscar's story haunts Yunior, a story that the book seeks to both resolve and purge via its contrived romantic ending. Yunior at first tries to dictate Oscar's progress by civilizing his body and behavior. In the chapter "Sentimental Education, 1988–1992," the narrator explains to the reader that "it started with me" and a couple of pages later discloses that "me" as Yunior (167). Yunior's explicit entrance as a character coincides with his failed reeducation of Oscar. Yunior can no longer hide behind his anonymity at this point in the story, and his role in Oscar's college experience says more about Yunior's pathos than Oscar's. By taking on "Project Oscar" (176), Yunior seeks to "fix Oscar's life" (175). The steps toward fulfilling this task include the miraculous accomplishment of getting the "dude to exercise" and "fucking run," as well as modifying his behavior, "to swear off the walking up to strange girls with his I-love-you craziness" and "stop talking crazy negative" (176). Yunior's project fails because Oscar eventually refuses to comply. At first, Yunior believes that his good will has gone unappreciated: "Here I was, going the fuck out of my way to help this fucking idiot out, and he was pissing it back in my face" (178). Upon further reflection, Yunior recognizes that his anger may come from a different place: "What made me angrier? That Oscar, the fat loser, quit, or that Oscar, the fat loser, defied me?" (181). The constant is Oscar's identity as a "fat loser," and what troubles Yunior is his choice to remain one, to remain inauthentic and reject Yunior's impulse to enlighten him. Oscar's defiance haunts Yunior, explaining why "I got the motherfucker for the rest of my life" (181). Yunior is narrating out of a desire to resolve the tension between himself and Oscar, between Yunior's version of the prototypical Dominican male and his inauthentic Other.[17]

Exposed publicly for cheating, Yunior is attacked on the bus by his ex-girlfriend. His social life temporarily ruined, Yunior faces a couple of choices: either forget himself in a series of meaningless relationships, what he terms "Bootie-Rehab," or focus "on something hard and useful like, say, my own shit" (175). Instead, Yunior creates a third alternative. He altruistically decides to save Oscar: "I focused on something easy and redemptive. Out of nowhere, and not in the least influenced by my own shitty state—of course not!—I decided that I was going to fix Oscar's life" (175). The sarcastic tone reveals how Yunior's heightened awareness as narrator includes extending a critical eye to himself. In retrospect, Yunior connects the fierce attention he paid to reeducating Oscar with his desire to avoid thinking about his problems with the ladies: "I really must have been in a dangle over Suriyan—which is why I threw myself something serious into Project Oscar" (176). By his account, an "ill sucio" (180) and "the biggest player of them all" (186), Yunior has his own fukú to worry about. Yunior's last conversation with Oscar is about Yunior's pathological infidelity:

[Lola] loves you.
I know that.
Why do you cheat on her, then?
If I knew that, it wouldn't be a problem.
Maybe you should try to find out. (313)

Oscar defies the dominant model for male subjectivity through his disapproval of Yunior's hypersexuality. Moreover, Oscar acutely critiques Yunior's lack of action and responsiveness to his identity crisis. The conversation is one moment when Oscar's voice is faintly heard beyond Yunior's narrative veil, and Oscar's insightful clarity belies Yunior's depiction of him as a befuddled and naive loser. Yunior shows himself to be aware of his failings and doing all he can to avoid addressing them. His narrative about Oscar's brief wondrous life is therefore an extension of Yunior's strategy of denial and disavowal. Yunior as author-double uses Oscar as a diversion from the failed narration of his insecurities about sexual intimacy.

Yunior's counterspell strives to make Oscar's defiance and critique irrelevant. Not only does Yunior fulfill the reader's desire to see Oscar achieve a measure of belonging by the novel's conclusion, but he also manages to narrate a happy ending for himself. With a lovely, adoring wife and a job at a community college, Yunior insists that he is "a new man, a new man" (326). It is questionable whether this neat wrap-up for Oscar and Yunior has succeeded in saving them both. A certain anxiety underlies Yunior's attachment to hypersexuality as instantiating an imagined community, as the foundational element of diasporic identity that roots it in the Dominican nation. The project of saving Oscar incorporates him into a specific history and culture, into the ancestral lineages of Abelard and Beli, fixing the diaspora within a history of la Patria. The reinsertion into cultural authenticity through the female body comes with a great deal of historical baggage. The link between nation and sexuality occurs in the novel's first footnote, which describes Rafael Leónidas Trujillo "for those of you who missed your mandatory two seconds of Dominican history" (2). The footnote describes the dictator's reputation for "fucking every hot girl in sight, even the wives of his subordinates, thousands upon thousands upon thousands of women," as well as for the "forging of the Dominican peoples into a modern state" (2–3). The hypersexual description of Trujillo resonates with Yunior's boasting of his prowess and his concurrent resentment that Oscar should have any romance not enabled by Yunior: "I mean, honestly, who was

I to begrudge Oscar a little action? Me, who was fucking with not one, not two, but three fine-ass bitches *at the same time* and that wasn't even counting the side-sluts I scooped at the parties and the clubs; me who had pussy coming out of my ears? But of course I begrudged the motherfucker" (185). If Yunior sees Oscar as imprisoned by excess sentimentality, Yunior is tortured by his dependence upon sex to authenticate himself. In explaining why he must police Oscar's romantic activities, Yunior gives a cartoonish, almost parodically misogynistic description of his sexuality. Yunior seems to be arguing that Oscar is no competitor, that he cannot infringe upon Yunior's very active sex life, so that readers understand Yunior to be all the more selfish in his desire to dictate to Oscar. Yunior reveals his fascist tendencies via his sexual excesses and identifies hypersexuality as the primary source of his authority, enabling him to tame the threat that Oscar represents. Perhaps Yunior's failed reeducation of Oscar aligns him more closely with Porfirio Rubirosa, who is deemed "the original Dominican Player" for having "fucked all sorts of women" (12).[18] These male agents of history are the postcolonial problem of authoritarian regimes, whose power is derived from the violence and exploitation of female bodies like those of Ybón and Beli. Yunior acts as the spokesperson for a disturbing model of diasporic masculinity that the novel figures as a by-product of dictatorship.[19]

In keeping with his hyperheterosexual definition of Dominican identity, Yunior inserts Oscar into Dominican history by saving him from his sentimental and virginal condition. That narrative is nevertheless fractured by Yunior's discomfort with the similarities between his sexuality and that exemplified by Trujillo's regime. Despite "the beauty" of sex that Oscar finally experiences (335), the novel's ending cannot reconcile Oscar's inauthenticity with the nation's definition of masculinity. Rather, the narrative emphasizes the structures of feeling that organize the reading experience and how much power the dictating voice and its values hold over our understanding of Truth and History. The institutional violence used to enforce the nation's social codes haunts the diaspora, shaping its formation in the United States. Yunior, despite his claims to be a new man, follows his assertion that "I don't run around after girls anymore" with the qualification "Not much, anyway" (326). Before closing the novel with Oscar's final letter about his joyous sexual experience, Yunior tries to end his narrative by reading from Oscar's copy of the graphic novel *Watchmen*. He quotes from the last panel, where Veidt asks for reassurance that his destruction of a major US city was the price worth paying to guarantee world peace: "I did the right thing, didn't I? It all worked out in the end" (331). Dr. Manhattan's reply is the final warning before readers enter the matrix of Oscar's satisfied sexuality: "In the end? . . . Nothing ever ends" (331). The dialogue indirectly references Yunior's growing insecurities and the novel's structural difficulties in providing the finally final conclusion to its plot. Yunior remains uncertain whether the romance he has imagined for Oscar, the violence he performed to authenticate Oscar as a diasporic Dominican, will provide closure and satiate the public demand for authenticity. The counterspell that Yunior weaves does not accomplish what it seeks; he cannot exorcise the ghost of Oscar.

Oscar's romantic conclusion is ostensibly a fiction, accomplished by Yunior "sew[ing his] balls back on" (168). The final letter transforms Oscar from inauthentic sentimental nerd into a courageous man who accepts death as just punishment for having sex. Oscar accepts his curse, evident in a family history of postcolonial violence, in order to be initiated into Yunior's community of compulsory heterosexuality. However, there is another layer of suppressed desire within the narrative of *Oscar Wao*. In the *Slate* interview, Meghan O'Rourke inquires after Díaz's "unconventional plot device" of unveiling the narrator and garners a cryptic warning from Díaz: "Yunior's telling of this story and his unspoken motivations for it are at the heart of the novel and can be easily missed" (par. 10). The goal of Yunior's Project Oscar is to purge the Otherness within himself.[20] After all, the narrator evinces an in-depth understanding of the very same nerdy knowledge about comic books and science fiction that marks Oscar as an outcast. The final "curing" of Oscar through sex also attempts to resolve Yunior's desire for Oscar de León. In *Oscar Wao*, the true romance, the one that cannot be explicitly narrated, is between Yunior and Oscar. Yunior's sexuality is so hyperperformative that it rationalizes his cultural authority as narrator.[21] The specter of homosexuality looms at the margins of Oscar's narrative, and if Yunior seeks to dispel it by declaring Oscar an un-virgin, his motivations stem in part from an anxiety about his embodiment of heteronormative values.

Yunior's relationship to Oscar's queerness is most evident in the linguistic politics of the novel, with a sexual difference that is made (in)visible by Yunior's rhetoric. For example, the "Oscar Wao" of the title is derived from Yunior's identification of Oscar with homosexuality. After Yunior's unsentimentalizing education project fails and he violently punishes Oscar for his rebellion, Yunior encounters Oscar dressed for Halloween as Dr. Who. Yunior points out the queerness of Oscar's outfit by comparing him to the ultimate literary figure of the dandy: "I couldn't believe how much he looked like that fat homo Oscar Wilde, and I told him so. You look just like him" (180). Yunior's comment aligns that visible queerness with the English language and its literary lineage. Yunior's "outing" of Oscar also produces the Spanish mistranslation that becomes Oscar's nickname: "Melvin said, Oscar Wao, quién es Oscar Wao, and that was it, all of us started calling him that" (180). The translation of Oscar Wilde into Oscar Wao closets the queerness that was at first visibly recognizable to Yunior. What Yunior finds particularly tragic is that Oscar eventually accepts this queer label of Oscar Wao, a mispronunciation, as part of his identity: "After a couple of weeks, dude started *answering* to it" (180). Oscar is capable of resistance, so his choice to identify with the translation and respond to the name Oscar Wao signifies a quiet acceptance of a queer identity, an acknowledgment of el secreto abierto.

The discursive (in)visibility of Oscar's queerness is evident in the US locale of the Rutgers University campus as well as the Dominican Republic. Oscar's uncle is described as joyous regarding the appearance of Ybón because she contains the threat of homosexuality that Oscar symbolizes within the family: "His tío seemed thrilled that he no longer had a pájaro for a nephew" (286–87). As E. Antonio de Moya notes, the term *pájaro* is "regularly used to designate in a pejorative way men who are homosexual *by choice*" (90; emphasis added). Oscar's uncle reduces homosexuality to a choice rather than a core facet of one's identity, an act rather than a state of being. The "fact" of Oscar's homosexuality is not doubted here; rather, his uncle is celebrating Oscar's translation into heterosexual belonging: "I can't believe it, he said proudly. The palomo is finally a man" (287). Yunior reinforces the uncle's definition of homosexuality with Oscar's final letter of heterosexual reunion, following the logic that homosexuality could presumably be unchosen. The linguistic distance between *palomo* and *man* is not accidental. De Moya identifies *palomo* as a term associated with "men who are at the bottom of subordinate heterosexual categories of masculinity" (86). Since the uncle and Oscar are in the Dominican Republic, we can assume that Yunior's role as narrator involves making certain linguistic choices about representing conversations in this location. Oscar's queerness is left untranslated by Yunior, a queerness that is marked by Spanish alone. Yunior reiterates the uncle's epithet, emphasizing its visible truth as well as the valuable consequence of Oscar's upward mobility into "real" manhood due to Ybón. At the same time, Yunior closets Oscar's sexuality by leaving it untranslated, perhaps indicating that there is no cultural equivalent in English, but also pointing to Yunior's concerns regarding the linguistic visibility of queerness.[22] Yunior's linguistic performance follows a mandate of discretion that sustains el secreto abierto of Oscar's sexuality.

The novel's conclusion supposedly resolves the ambiguity of Oscar's sexual identity as a virgin, since he engages in a heterosexual act, having sex with Ybón. But in light of the fact that this act (like the novel as a whole) is a fiction constructed by Yunior as narrator, the motivation for "resolving" Oscar's queerness is tied to the threat that identity represents to Yunior's sexuality. Oscar's authenticity comes from his ability to identify with a diaspora of marginal outcasts: "Every day he watched the 'cool' kids torture the crap out of the fat, the ugly, the smart, the poor, the dark, the black, the unpopular, the African, the Indian, the Arab, the immigrant, the strange, the feminino, the gay—and in every one of these clashes he saw himself" (264). Oscar aligns himself with the gay students at Don Bosco, last but not least on this list of marginalized communities. The linguistic divide between Spanish and English, between the feminino and the gay, remains a visible tension, and yet this passage acknowledges that a continuum between the two distinct conceptions of queerness exists through Oscar's affinity with these identities. Even so, we also have to recognize that Yunior constructs these multiple kinships. Instead of contesting another identification as a means of ushering Oscar into mainstream belonging, Yunior zeroes in to counter and "cure" his sentimentality, his femininity—in other words, his queerness. That cure necessitates murdering Oscar's identity as a queer subject. Oscar's physical death at the hands of the Capitán's hired killers is simply the logical conclusion to sex with Ybón. Oscar's death is dictated by Yunior's standards of authenticity, silencing other potential narratives for Oscar's becoming a Dominican American man.[23]

By isolating sexuality as the site by which to recuperate Oscar, Yunior also identifies queerness as the most threatening point of difference embodied by Oscar. Just as Yunior shares with Oscar a passion for science fiction (not to mention Elvish), Yunior's choice to dispel the queerness of Oscar is also an effort to abject the "*gay-hay-hay*" within himself (172). Yunior's veneer of hyperheterosexuality cracks open at times to reveal these queer desires. His concealed desire is the reason that "years and years" have passed and Yunior "still think[s] about" Oscar (324). The most overt articulation of Yunior's secreto abierto comes at the novel's end, when he fantasizes about the day Lola's daughter will ask him for the whole story, the story that presumably he has just relayed to the reader. Yunior describes Iris as "the beautiful muchachita" who "could have been my daughter if I'd been smart, if I'd been _____." (329). This blank regarding the reason behind Yunior's failed paternity connects with Yunior's comments about his current marriage and "how sometimes we even make vague noises about having children" (326). Taken together, these passages potentially refer to biological infertility, but the silence that Yunior is unwilling to bridge also signifies a fundamental insecurity about his ability to meet his own criteria of authenticity in terms of heterosexual reproduction.

The beauty that Iris embodies and that gives purpose to Yunior's continued role as narrator is a beauty that reconciles Yunior's queer desires with those that Dominican masculinity dictates he should have. Iris is the ideal representative subject, and since "she's her family's daughter," she will eventually "stop being afraid and she will come looking for answers" (330). In the fantasy encounter, Yunior, convinced of his centrality to the history of the de León and Cabral families, imagines a "knock at my door" (330). Yunior's certainty comes from his access to all of Oscar's "books, his games, his manuscript, his comic books, his papers," which are stored like cadavers in "four refrigerators" (330). Yunior still wants to shape and control the future narrative of Oscar. Iris represents that future, and her body is marked by Yunior's queer desires. Yunior imagines himself evaluating Iris's body: "She has her mother's legs, her uncle's eyes" (330). The "eyes of Oscar" are finally located in a body that is appropriate for Yunior's desire (327). This fantasy consequently plots the meeting of Iris's Oscar-eyes with Oscar's writing and words, so that the ghosts can be laid to rest: "She'll take all we've done and all we've learned and add her own insights and she'll put an end to it" (331). Yunior's dream of reunion is located at the margins of his home, an occasion that must occur "when it starts getting late" and he "takes[s] her down to my basement" (330–31). Access to the corpus of refrigerator contents is possible only in the sole company of Yunior, after dark. Once Iris and Yunior descend to the basement of his happily married home, they can together lay bare the cracks in Yunior's foundation. The dream's tension of sexual intimacy is so threatening that the fantasy of encountering Iris's Oscar-eyes is followed by the final entry, in which Yunior "reveals" Oscar's final letter declaring "the beauty" of heterosexual sex.

By extension, "fukú" is a thinly disguised obscenity directed at the reader of *Oscar Wao*. The novel opens with the reader being told, "one final note, Toto, before Kansas goes bye-bye" (6). In a reference to both *The Wizard of Oz* and *The Matrix*, the reader is warned that the narrative that follows will have tenuous connections to reality. With "*Toto*" inflected by the sexual connotations of lowercase *toto*, which the novel repeatedly uses as Dominican slang for female genitalia, Yunior defines the reader as a "pussy." The novel follows a heteronormative logic of penetration in relation to its audience, and the conclusion entails a voyage home by "fucking" (with) the reader. The narrative thrust of the novel is grounded in the same heteronormative logic that Yunior applies to violently expunge Oscar's Otherness and his own queer desires. The various discourses employed in *Oscar Wao* draw in a heterogeneous reading audience, and the novel's market aesthetics seek to seduce these readers into the position of a subjected woman (124), perhaps as stand-ins until the fantasy Iris appears. The heteronormative strategy of seducing the reader does not resolve the sexual crises permeating the novel. Since the reader might be conceived of as male, female, or transgendered, Yunior's potential intimacy with the reader is fraught with the same ambivalence and contradiction as his suppressed romance with Oscar.

However, this toto-logic also highlights the reader's vulnerabilities as a participant in the project of nation and narration. As Díaz points out in an interview, "Yunior's such a scary narrator [. . .] because he's so incredibly charming" ("Junot Díaz" [Miranda] 36). If readers accept Yunior's narrative without question, without interrogating Yunior's narrative authority, without asking how Yunior's desires and values shape the moral lessons implied by the ending, then they are left with a curse of ignorance and are vulnerable to the dictations of others.[24] Or perhaps it is the same inheritance of intimacy that Yunior struggles with, the curse of being complicit. Yunior's narration is his attempt to strike back at the system that marginalizes Oscar, rendering him an inauthentic diasporic subject.[25] What Yunior succeeds in doing is merely reinstating the very standards of masculinity and Dominicanness that alienate Oscar and himself. Yunior is drawn to disciplining Oscar's sexuality because of his investment in his self-policing. Oscar's magical recuperation into heterosexuality is an attempt to resolve Yunior's anxieties regarding el secreto abierto, a utopian fantasy narrated as the "real" story in order to silence the threat of Oscar's queerness. Fractured by Yunior's attempt to reconcile his audience's desire for accessing Truth with his desire to resolve both his and Oscar's crises of authenticity, the novel is a testament to the dangerous lure of beautiful endings.

Edwidge Danticat's *The Dew Breaker*

Like Junot Díaz, Edwidge Danticat comments on the uncomfortable position she occupies as a public representative for the Haitian diaspora in the United States. In her nonfiction book *Create Dangerously* (2010), Danticat explains how the expectations attached to this role place an impossible burden upon her creativity. She recounts the requests for her to translate the Haitian American experience to a mainstream public immediately following the 2010 earthquake in Haiti: "Even before the first aftershock, people were calling me asking, 'Edwidge, what are you going to do? When are you going back? Could you come on television or on the radio and tell us how you feel? Could you write us fifteen hundred words or less?'" (19). Danticat discloses that her role as public intellectual comes with its privileges and limitations. One the one hand, she is expected to take on an activist role, to initiate and embody the outreach initiatives for the victims of the earthquake. On the other hand, she is expected to speak for the Haitian people, to reduce the emotional toll of the earthquake into a digestible media clip. Danticat's awareness of how she is framed as the authentic body and voice of Haitian experience shapes her creative writing.

Edwidge Danticat experienced a backlash to her novel *Breath, Eyes, Memory* (1994) that was comparable to the negative reception of *In the Time of the Butterflies*, which I discussed in chapter 3.[26] Danticat addresses in *Create Dangerously* the consequences of this reaction to the novel's depiction of virginity testing. Repeatedly told she was performing a disservice to the Haitian people by writing the novel, Danticat sees such criticism as the product of mainstream portrayals of Haitians in the United States: "Maligned as we were in the media at the time, as disaster-prone refugees and boat people and AIDS carriers, many of us had become overly sensitive and were eager to censor anyone who did not project a 'positive image' of Haiti and Haitians" (32). Highlighting the circulation of stereotypes about Haitians, Danticat acknowledges the legitimate fears of reinforcing those negative images. She defends her right to write, to even potentially feed into the mainstream images of Haitians,[27] but she admits that such critiques touch upon her insecurities: "Anguished by my own sense of guilt, I often reply feebly that in writing what I do, I exploit no one more than myself" (33). That sense of guilt and fear that her writing may at times be complicit with restrictive definitions of Haitian identity, whether they are positive or negative, feeds into the market aesthetics of her writing. In *Create Dangerously*,

Danticat imagines a chorus of readers evaluating the authenticity of her words: "I can hear now as I write this cries of protest from other Haitians my age (and younger and older too) shouting from the space above my shoulders, the bleachers above every writer's shoulders where readers cheer or hiss or boo in advance" (60).

The author-doubles within *Dew Breaker* narrativize Danticat's relationship to an imagined readership, and the novel processes the negative response to *Breath, Eyes, Memory* by depicting the tense power relations between multiple Haitian diasporas. Discussing the backlash in *Create Dangerously*, Danticat asks, "Besides, what is the alternative for me or anyone else who might not dare to offend? Self-censorship? Silence?" (*Create* 33). It is no coincidence that *Dew Breaker* opens with an epigraph from Osip Mandelstam, a Russian Jewish writer who supported the Russian Revolution but opposed Joseph Stalin's totalitarian leadership. In 1933, Mandelstam published a poem critiquing Stalin that resulted in his arrest and eventual death at a work camp. Danticat cites the following words from Mandelstam's poem: "Maybe this is the beginning of madness . . . / Forgive me for what I am saying / Read it . . . quietly, quietly." Dictatorship acts as a historical context for the Haitian diaspora and a metaphor for the ambivalent influence of readerships upon a writer's creative work. Danticat's epigraph from Mandelstam alludes to Haiti's history of dictatorship and references the intersecting demands of narration, audience, and politics. The citation from Mandelstam's poem positions art and storytelling as dangerous activities, asserting that the public revelation of certain truths carries risks because of the intimacy it requires between the writer and the reader.[28] Just as Mandelstam requests forgiveness from his reader for trespassing onto precarious territory via narration, he also instructs the audience on how to respond and read his poem, desiring the collusion of silence.[29] *Dew Breaker* similarly tackles the tragedy of Haiti's postcolonial violence by depicting art's fraught role in processing the historical trauma of dictatorship. The novel has chapters set in Haiti during violent historical transitions such as that of Jean-Claude Duvalier's exile in 1986, while also indicating that such threats of violence are present in the United States. For instance, the novel references the assault on Abner Louima in 1997 (38) and the death of Patrick Dorismond in 2000 (45), both victims of New York City police brutality. Danticat's novel is very much concerned about the function of art within the context of state violence.[30] The novel's epigraph from Mandelstam initiates an engagement with a question that Danticat poses in *Create Dangerously*: "How do writers and readers find each other under such dangerous circumstances?" (10).

Danticat's comparative lens of history, drawing links between the Caribbean and the Global North, is a strategy that she shares with diasporic writers such as Julia Alvarez and Michelle Cliff that I discussed in chapter 3. Danticat's historical novel also deploys the lens of gender to draw parallels between the historical contexts of the nation-state and the diaspora, with the authoritarian state instantiating a code of masculinity for a homosocial community. The epigraph's reference to the dangers attached to storytelling in the context of dictatorship allows Danticat to also elaborate upon Mandelstam's concept of forgiveness: Not only must the original sin of dictatorship be forgiven, but the retelling of that tragedy is a form of trauma that must also be forgiven. The market aesthetics of *Dew Breaker* introduces several author-doubles who model the gendered challenges of artistic expression in processing the postcolonial tragedy of dictatorship as the originary site of diaspora.

Edwidge Danticat's *Dew Breaker* underscores the importance of storytelling to the historical formation and formulation of a Haitian American community in the United States. Danticat represents storytelling as a tool for processing political violence with the goal of creating diasporic kinship bonds beyond the nation-state's borders. *Dew Breaker* does not idealize either the diaspora or art as free of oppressive tendencies; rather, the novel highlights how the narration of this community remains tied to the Duvalier dictatorship and its definition of the nation-subject. Just as Junot Díaz's *Oscar Wao* depicts a process of domestication and exclusion in terms of heterosexuality and ethnic purity, Danticat's novel calls attention to masculinist codes of national belonging that shape diasporic identity and render women as marginal within the newly dispersed communities in the United States. The diaspora that Danticat describes is a homosocial community of lost boys and dew breakers that can potentially forgive and overcome the inherited binary of victim versus victimizers. Women, on the other hand, remain excluded from this development of an artistic consciousness that aims to reconcile the baggage of postcolonial violence. I focus on the chapters "Monkey Tails," "The Book of the Dead," "The Dew Breaker," and "The Funeral Singer" to show how the author-doubles of Michel, Ka, and Freda offer different experiences of diasporic community.

Paternities of Diasporic Relation

In the "Monkey Tails" chapter of *Dew Breaker*, storytelling is depicted as a homosocial strategy for imagining reconciliation between the perpetrators and victims of political violence. Michel speaks to his unborn son on the eve of his due date in 2004; Michel's narration mirrors the broader structure of Danticat's historical novel in that it is narrated from a contemporary setting that looks backwards to process a trauma set in the historical past. Michel's oral storytelling remembers the 1986 fallout of Jean-Claude Duvalier's sudden self-imposed exile from Haiti, but from the perspective of an adult. As Michel notes in his analysis of the historical moment, "I wasn't thinking like this back then but rather I only think all this now, as a thirty-year-old man, lying in bed next to my pregnant wife watching as the clock moves towards midnight, towards her due date" (147). With an adult's hindsight, Michel describes the transition from a nation under dictatorship to one without leadership in terms of waking up from one nightmare into another: "We had fallen asleep under a dictatorship headed by a pudgy thirty-four-year-old man and his glamorous wife. During the night they'd sneaked away" (140). Michel's contemporary context of imminent paternity, waiting for his son to be born, shapes his interpretation of this historical event, with fatherhood as a metaphor for understanding how dictatorship shapes the history and culture of the Haitian nation.[31] I discussed a similar political metaphor of paternity in relation to Monique Roffey's novel in chapter 4.

Jean-Claude Duvalier's nickname of Baby Doc, referencing his position as son to the elder dictator, François "Papa Doc" Duvalier, is one way that the Haitian public sphere defines the dictatorship in familial terms. In Danticat's novel, Michel likens the vacuum of power and state of chaos initiated by Baby Doc's exile to that of a family abandoned by its patriarch. Michel explains that the dictator's departure "orphaned a large number of loyal militiamen" (140). As part of the authoritarian state, these men had "guarded the couple's command with all types of vicious acts," and in view of the unexpected absence of the First Family of the dictatorship, "the population was going after those militiamen, those macoutes, with the determination of an army in the middle of its biggest battle to date" (140). The political import of Baby Doc's exile to the Haitian nation is translated in terms of a broader history of familial abandonment and collective bereavement caused by the dictatorship. Michel understands himself to be part of "a generation of fatherless boys" and draws parallels between those orphaned by fathers who had "died in the dictatorship's prisons and fathers who had abandoned us altogether to serve the regime" (141). The oppressed population is determined to take vengeance, and a street mob in Michel's neighborhood wants to punish the militiaman Regulus, who Michel explains is the father of Romain, "my hero and the person who at the time I considered my best friend" (141).

Within this context of the nation as a patriarchal community of fathers and orphaned sons, Michel introduces his relationship with his best friend, Romain, the son of a macoute, as the model for a masculine mode of truth-telling, one that is opposed to the storytelling model offered by Michel's mother. Michel's belonging to the "we" of fatherless men is rooted in his mother's assertion that "three months before my birth I had lost my father to something my mother would only vaguely describe as 'political'" (141). His friendship with Romain is based in the shared experience of being fatherless boys, since Romain's father Regulus "abandoned Romain when Romain was a month old" (143). However, Romain challenges Michel's paternity when he confronts him with the knowledge that a local businessman, Christophe, is Michel's father, countering the mother's myth that his father fell victim to political violence. Michel describes this harsh truth, "that I had a father who lived and worked so close to me and still didn't call me his son, as the moment that everything changed" because "that day I became a man" (164). Michel's personal transformation mirrors that of the nation, so that Michel can describe his new self-definition similarly to how he describes the effects of the dictator's self-imposed exile: "Overnight, our country had completely changed" (140). The public and personal transformations produce analogous bonds of homosocial community. In gratitude for being ushered into masculinity by Romain, into true belonging via homosocial filiation, Michel explains to his diasporic unborn son that he will also be named Romain. This son-to-be will then embody the reconciliation between victims and perpetrators that Michel imagines through his storytelling. While the storytelling fashions a homosocial community, it is not homoerotic, as is the case with Yunior's narration of Oscar. Heterosexuality is also the norm for belonging in "Monkey Tails," since Michel's intimate audience of his unborn son is the product of his union with his nameless wife. Heteronormativity marks storytelling as another generative act.

In *Dew Breaker*, the homosocial line of inheritance remains shaped by the nation, since Michel's mode of storytelling, recording his nighttime message on cassette, is derived from a prior model set by the dictatorship.[32] Michel explains that the goal of the crowd hunting for Romain's father Regulus is retribution: "He'd beaten them up and stolen money and property from most of them and had put many of their relatives in jail or in the grave" (142–3). Though Romain does not even call "his father Papa," Michel hints that claiming Romain as a substitute father entails inheriting the dictatorship's legacy of dictation (143). As he describes Romain's assertion that his father Regulus will escape the wrath of his victims, that the "old man's probably far away from here now," Michel also aligns his friend's voice with the dictatorship's public announcements (150). Romain's "voice boomed" inside his servant's room, echoing the radio that was transmitting "a taped message from the exiled president" (150). Michel follows his ventriloquizing of Romain's voice with the first-person voice of Jean-Claude Duvalier, whose final message expresses a continued claim of power over the nation. The taped final message to the Haitian people explains, "I have decided to transfer the destiny of the nation into the hands of the military" (150). The chain of filiation continues in Michel's narration, since he notes that Baby Doc's "droning nasal voice [. . .] sounded almost the same as his father's" (150). Just as Romain's voice echoes that of Jean-Claude Duvalier, the tone and method of Baby Doc's speech carry the ghostly presence of his father, "whose daylong speeches were constantly rebroadcast on the radio each year on the anniversary of his death" (150). The Duvalier models for narration are prerecorded messages to the Haitian nation, with Baby Doc's 1986 radio announcement and Papa Doc's postdeath speeches giving form to Michel's recollection of the past for his son. Like Díaz's Yunior, Danticat depicts the diaspora that Michel is crafting as a homosocial community that is domesticated according to nationalist models of belonging. Michel's version of storytelling offers filiation to a closed community of orphaned men, while inheriting the same silences and exclusions that sustained the dictatorship's power. Michel's tape-recorded message to his unborn son enacts another layer of haunting, where the dictatorship's mode of policing the present via past utterances is inherited by a new generation of diasporic men.

The structure and form of Michel's storytelling characterize the dictatorship's gendered legacy. Michel's voice, for example, is unmediated. Following the radio mode of enunciation, Michel speaks directly of his experiences, using a first-person voice. The male narrative "I" positions Michel as an author-double akin to Díaz's Yunior. In his speech, Michel identifies with the community of fatherless boys. By citing a patriarchal lineage when speaking to his future son of these other relationships between father and son, between Papa Doc and Baby Doc, Regulus and Romain, Christophe and Michel, he also binds storytelling to (en)gendering a homosocial community. It is only through Michel's diasporic storytelling that these fatherless communities can be reconciled and reunified. By framing the nation as a patriarchal community of fathers and sons, Michel sees the new resurgence of political violence as blurring the roles of victim and victimizer, with "the blood of militiamen at the hands of former victims" mingling with "the blood of former victims at the hands of militiamen battling for their lives" (146–47).

Michel's template for a male voice dictating community bonds, like Yunior's in *Oscar Wao*, is undermined by its lines of inheritance. The tension embodied by this patriarchal storytelling model for processing violence is evident at the conclusion of the "Monkey Tails" chapter. Michel juxtaposes the paternity he chooses to claim when asked about his father with the alternative lineage he is narrating to his son. Michel explains in his taped narration that "to everyone who asks me about my father, I tell and retell the myth that my mother so carefully crafted and guarded for me, that my father perished before I was born, lost his life to something political" (164). The matrilineal fiction of el secreto abierto that falsely ushers Michel into the community of the dictatorship's victims remains Michel's public historical narrative for his origins. It is a falsehood that he will not even press his mother to admit: "'We were all trapped inside our houses, like in the old days before you were born, under the father.' 'The father?' I asked dumbly. I knew she meant the dictator father of the dictator son, but somehow I wanted to offer her an opening into a conversation that even I knew we'd never have. [. . .] I went to bed, trying to give the impression that it was the country's political problems that were disturbing me. I'd let my mother keep her secret; I didn't want her to feel like a liar" (162). Michel's mandate of discretion, allowing his mother to maintain her myth about his paternity, shows how he remains committed to maintaining certain silences, preferring to pretend that he is disturbed by the political chaos outside their home rather than by his mother's refusal to admit Christophe's paternity. Michel chooses another lineage for himself and his son, one that he freely admits is equally constructed by imagination. In his recorded message, Michel explains: "As for you, my son, your myth is this: it's now past midnight; if you're born today, on this, the anniversary of the day that everything changed for me, on the day that I became a man, your name will be Romain, after my first true friend" (164). The fabrication inherited from the maternal line will not be passed on to the next generation, to Michel's son, *nor* will Michel claim his biological paternity from Christophe. Instead, the purely homosocial and hypermasculine myth of Romain will be passed on to Michel's son, an acknowledged fiction that is about the origins of Michel's manhood in postcolonial violence. The tentative nature of this new fantasy of paternity is apparent when Michel notes that it is dependent on "if" the son is born on his due date, which is also the anniversary of Romain's revelation of paternity to Michel. The reader does not know the likelihood of whether the child will be born on his due date, but the real possibility that he will not means that Danticat's novel ascribes a short temporal window to Michel's alternative myth of origins. The Duvalier dictatorship's model of paternity is central to this personal inheritance, with the lineage of "the dictator father of the dictator son" haunting the diaspora's definition of kinship (162).

The context of the present, of Michel's 2004 nighttime narration, aligns storytelling with a homosocial filiation that is drawn from the Duvalier dictatorship. Women remain marginalized in this storytelling process, beginning with Michel's rejection of his mother's myth about his political prisoner father. Michel explains that the only company he had as a child consisted of women servants like "Rosie and Vaval, who were always too busy with my mother's chores to spend much time with me," leaving Romain to be "my only friend" (144). The diasporic present reiterates the narrator's isolation from and devaluation of female companionship in the way that Michel dismisses his wife from the message he is passing on to her son. Michel's wife, who is sleeping beside him as he records his story, vocally intrudes only at one point in the narrative and appears scripted by Michel: "Listen to your mother now as she says to me, 'Michel, are you still talking into that cassette? Go to sleep. If the baby comes tomorrow I'll need you rested.' And listen as I, your father reply, 'Just another minute.' And listen now as your mother says, half jokingly, I hope, 'I wish I was one of those women you *only* dreamed of sleeping with,' then goes back to sleep. Now we return to Romain" (151–52). The scripted dialogue of the woman who will actually give birth to his son is presented as an intrusion, a distraction from the story of the diasporic child's true paternity through Michel and Romain. The threat of her utterance is evident in the way that she critiques Michel's fantasy of female companionship—that as a young boy he dreamed of the servant women who surrounded him "fight[ing] one another for the honor of devirginizing me" (151). This confession prompts Michel's "wife to stir in the bed" and jokingly admit to her fantasy of being a woman who Michel only dreams of, rather than an uncomfortable pregnant wife who is "trying not to move from the one position she's able to sleep in these days" (151). Her incisive commentary speaks to another set of power relations between herself and Michel that belie his reduction of

her to a nameless woman in his bed, defined only by her relationship to
the men in the story as "my wife" or "your mother" (151). Nevertheless,
her potential as a more fully-fledged historical subject is closed down by
Michel's narration to their son. The homosocial line of inheritance from
Romain to Michel to the unborn son is bounded by the nation, since
Michel's mode of storytelling, recording his nighttime message on cassette, is derived from the dictatorship. The potential of Michel's wife as a
narrating subject of history is instead elaborated in the figures of Ka and
Freda, the female artists in *Dew Breaker*. These author-doubles are a
counterpoint to Michel, revealing how women engage patriarchal inheritances while encountering different challenges in claiming their narrative power to process the Haitian history of dictatorship.

Giving Voice in the Market, Voiceless in the Diaspora

Danticat's *Dew Breaker* addresses the challenges faced by women
attempting to find their place within the puzzle of diasporic community
and Haitian history. Several creative women appear in the novel, and
they all engage in public forms of artistic production: Ka is a sculptor,
Aline is a newspaper reporter, Beatrice sews wedding dresses, and Freda
is a funeral singer. The most developed female artists in the novel, Ka
and Freda, have much in common with Michel and his storytelling. Their
chapters are the only ones that share Michel's first-person narrative format, so that Ka and Freda are also author-doubles whose relationship
to their audience greatly influences how they process the history of dictatorship. Michel's story concentrates on the changing power dynamic
between the agents and the victims of the regime's oppressive control.
Ka and Freda represent opposing subject positions within the binary of
postcolonial violence and the struggle to negotiate their inheritance from
the father figure. Ka the sculptor discovers that she is a dew breaker's
daughter, while Freda the singer mourns the dictatorship's torture of her
father. The female artists inherit a patriarchal past of violent traumas;
Ka and Freda act as individual cultural representatives who give voice to
the collective suffering of a nation and its diaspora.

With Michel defining the Haitian diaspora in terms of homosocial filiation, the women artists in *Dew Breaker* navigate commercial venues in
order to circulate their art. This market places the highest value on narratives that mythologize the suffering of political victims. Because of the
constraints of market demands, the women experience greater difficulty
in passing on their versions of familial and national history. The market
value of the prisoner narrative means that Ka and Freda are limited to

that representation, and when it is no longer possible as a source of inspiration, the market avenues for their creativity also disappear. Ka and Freda find their voices silenced and/or mediated by others, resulting in a significant disconnection from community, a marginalization that the male storytellers do not experience. In fact, male characters are shown to successfully expand their communal bonds, while the restrictions on women's artistic creativity mean that they must find more *minor* modes of instantiating community.

The opening chapter, "The Book of the Dead," introduces the plot line about the dew breaker's family, including his daughter Ka. The novel progresses with the dewbreaker family chapters moving further into the past, each dedicated to a different family member's perspective (Anne's, Ka's, the dew breaker's). Many critics view the novel's form as fragmentary and "chronologically discontinuous" (Watts 95) or as following a "circular narrative movement" (Vega González 190), but I would argue that the dew breaker chapters operate upon a reverse chronology.[33] The novel structures these chapters as a part of a broader movement toward historically contextualizing the US diaspora within a Haitian past: "The Book of the Dead" contains Ka's father's revelation during a business trip to Florida that he worked as an assassin and a torturer for the regime (20); "The Book of Miracles" goes back to a time when Ka is unaware of her father's role within the Duvalier dictatorship and she attempts to confront a man during a New York City mass that she thinks is a former militiaman; and the final chapter in the novel, "The Dew Breaker," explains Ka's origin story, with her parents' encounter "circa 1967" during François "Papa Doc" Duvalier's dictatorship. The chapters in the contemporary setting of the United States contain vague historical references, while the final transition into the Haitian nation names a specific year and context of dictatorship. "The Book of the Dead" figures a successful Haitian-born performer, Gabrielle Fonteneau, who has purchased Ka's sculpture and who vaguely evokes the real-life celebrity of Garcelle Beauvais, who played major roles in television series like *The Jaime Foxx Show* (1996–2001) and *NYPD Blue* (2001–4). In "The Book of Miracles," the public figure in the chapter is political, with Emmanuel Constant as the militiaman who Ka thinks is attending the same church service as her family. The novel mentions that Constant was "tried in absentia in a Haitian court and sentenced to life in prison" (79), which means that the story is set sometime after 2001, the year when Constant is sentenced for his role in a 1994 massacre that occurred during the military dictatorship that followed the coup d'état of President Jean-Bertrand Aristide.[34] With these historical referents, the dew breaker family chapters evolve from a personal family story to public historical narrative, from the diaspora to the island, from popular culture to political violence, and from post-Duvalier politics to the Duvalier dictatorship. The historical novel as a whole mimics the structure of the dew breaker family chapters, moving from narratives of disconnected individuals to revealing the lines of relation linking these diasporic subjects. For instance, Michel's narrative becomes affiliated with that of Ka's family when the novel reveals that Michel is one of the three men living the family's basement.

The first-person author-doubles of Ka and Michel share the time-line progression from the contemporary diaspora to the national past of dictatorship. The market aesthetics of Ka's artistic experience flesh out the implications of Michel's narration, reflecting on the legacy of the Duvalier dictatorship for the abandoned militiamen versus their victims. Like Michel, Ka confronts a related myth about the politics of her parentage; she is told that her father was a target of the regime's authoritarian terror. Ka's art is a working-through of her father's fiction as a victim of political violence. The sculpture is "a three-foot mahogany figure of my father naked, kneeling on a half-foot-square base, his back arched like the curve of the crescent moon, his down cast eyes fixed on his very long fingers" (6). The moon's imagery evokes Michel's context of nightfall, recording his message to his son in the darkness—an image that foretells the revelation of Ka's father as a dew breaker. Ka's art processes the power relations of dictatorship from the perspective of the oppressed, since "it was the way I had imagined him in prison" (6). The market determines the value of Ka's diasporic artistic production, since Gabrielle Fonteneau, "a Haitian-born actress with her own American television show," is purchasing this *Father* piece (11). Fonteneau purchases the sculpture because it is an image of a "regal and humble" man who, she states, "reminds me of my own father" (11). The currency of this prisoner-subject is emphasized by Fonteneau's identification with the image as well as the myth's commodification. Ka's success as an artist is dependent upon the market appeal of such depictions of victimhood.

Ka's ability to build community bonds of filiation with someone like Fonteneau, a popular culture representative of the Haitian American diaspora, is foreclosed by her father's disclosure of his past. Ka's father contests his depiction by arguing that it is a fiction, that it is not a realistic portrayal of his relationship to the Duvalier dictatorship. He explains his motives for throwing the sculpture into a lake by stating that he was "the hunter, he was not the prey" (20). As Joan Conwell argues, by destroying the sculpture Ka's father "returns to the same censorship role that he relished more than thirty years ago" (228). I would add that the dew breaker father symbolizes the market readership that Danticat imagines above her shoulders as she writes, particularly the violent censorship that such an audience might wish to perform in response to art that threatens their conception of Haitian culture and identity. After labeling him "a harsh critic" (16), Ka realizes that her creativity may not recover from this revelation: "I don't know that I will be able to work on anything for some time. I have lost my subject, the prisoner father I loved as well as pitied" (31). Pity is both the inspiration for Ka's art and the emotional reaction that gives her sculpture currency in the market. Ka's position as author-double allows Danticat to explore the desires of her readerships to emotionally access and sympathize with her fictional characters while maintaining a judgmental distance regarding their tragic circumstances. Ka is an artist, but she is also the audience for her father's fiction as political prisoner. The loss of that fiction means that Ka will have to face a new history, that of her family's complicity with the Duvalier dictatorship. Ka is therefore both author-double and reader-double. She is an artist like Danticat, but Ka also stands in for the desires of the novel's audience, who want to pity the victims of state violence without facing the uncomfortable reality of their collusion.

The consequences of her father's censorship are twofold: first, silencing Ka's creativity and second, threatening her livelihood, the material success derived from her artistic career. The destruction of the sculpture and the mythic conception of Ka's father as a victim poses a serious threat to Ka's artistic identity. When her father disappears with the sculpture, Ka's insecurities regarding her career are evident when she tells the policeman writing the missing person's report that "I'm an artist, a sculptor," while confessing to the reader that "I'm really not an artist, not in the way I'd like to be. I'm more of an obsessive wood-carver with a single subject so far—my father" (4). Even before her idea of her father as a subject is challenged, Ka sees herself as being too specialized to be a genuine artist. Her narrative voice does not display the same confidence as Michel's, pointing to the gendered power dynamic of creative expression. Ka's lack of confidence as an artist finds its parallel in her description of herself as a teacher. Education is often depicted as an alternate means of processing a historical legacy, as I discussed with regard to the historical fiction of Julia Alvarez and Michelle Cliff in chapter 2. For Ka, however, the classroom is another space of disempowerment.

Ka explains that she works as "a substitute art teacher at a junior high school" and indicates that she lacks authority in her public role as an educator: "I overhear them referring to me as Teacher Kaka" (17). Her classroom audience challenges the author-double identity that she inherits from her father. Her father names her after the Egyptian concept of ka, "a double of the body" that is "the body's companion through life and death" (17). The students double Ka's name to ascribe a much less noble symbol for her pedagogical role as teacher.[35] Ka's insecurities are also displayed when she describes her relationship to creativity: she interprets the artistic process as an outside force dictating the will of her mind and body. When she is carving, Ka experiences a "sensation that my hands don't belong to me at all, that something else besides my brain and muscles is moving my fingers, something bigger and stronger than myself, an invisible puppetmaster over whom I have no control" (25). The puppetmaster description evokes the figure of the untouchable dictator whose power and control appears to infiltrate all aspects of life, even of the diasporic population outside the island, even into the contemporary present that lies beyond the formal political conclusion of the regime's reign.

Having "lost my subject, the prisoner father," Ka has difficulty imagining another horizon of inspiration (31). Ka's first-person narrative does not indicate what alternative subject or career she will pursue. Ka wants to "call Gabrielle Fonteneau back and promise her that I will make another sculpture" but is unable to do so because she does not "know that I will be able to work on anything for some time" (31). All she can do is mourn the loss of her creativity and regret the market interaction that unsuspectingly brought about this confrontation between her interpretation of her father as a victim of dictatorship and her father's memory of his violent past: "I wish I hadn't met Gabrielle Fonteneau, that I still had that to look forward to somewhere else, sometime in the future" (33). As Jo Collins points out, "Ka's aestheticization and apparent commercialization of what has seemingly been a damaging experience is problematic" (10). Her father's revelation of his dew breaker past leads Ka to fundamentally question the romantic narrative of diasporic exile that she previously ascribed to her father. The knowledge of her father as someone who actively supported the dictatorship's violent suppression of the Haitian population transforms Ka's interpretation of her father's immigrant identity. Ka always assumed that "my father's only ordeal was that he'd left his country and moved to [. . .] a place where he never quite seemed to fit in, never appeared to belong" (33). Ka reevaluates the meaning of her dew breaker father's migration so that "the only thing I grasp now [. . .] is why the unfamiliar might have been comforting, rather than distressing, to my father" (34). Her father is a victim neither of the dictatorship nor of exile—rather, Ka understands that immigration provided her father with the privilege of escape. Ka reinterprets her name and identity accordingly, within the diasporic context of her father's search for anonymity and invisibility: "He wanted no one to know him, no one except my mother and me, we, who are now his kas, his good angels, his masks against his own face" (34).

The penultimate chapter, "The Funeral Singer," introduces Freda as a model for who Ka will potentially become after this revelation bars her from established avenues of creativity. Freda is the only other first-person narrator in *Dew Breaker* aside from Michel and Ka. As with Ka, the marketplace values Freda's artistic sensibilities, but the dictatorship shuts down the spaces where she creatively expresses herself. The dictatorship's silencing of Freda's voice begins with her father's death: "I also left because long ago my father had disappeared. He'd had a fish stall at the market. One day, one macoute came to take it over and another one took my father away. When my father returned, he didn't have a tooth left in his mouth. [. . .] The next night he took his boat out to sea and, with a mouth full of blood, vanished forever" (172). The image of the father's bloody mouth evokes the dictatorship's history of violence as well as the problem of articulation within that political context of censorship. Structurally, "The Funeral Singer" forms part of the last third of the novel, which becomes more explicitly historical in setting, contextualizing the diaspora via the nation-past.

The pedagogical imperative of Danticat's writing is evident in the unique organization of Freda's narrative, which mimics an academic calendar, following the structure of a syllabus broken into weeks. This time-log structure speaks to the classroom context of Freda in the diaspora; she is enrolled in an adult education course. However, the form of this chapter also references the decontextualization that the Haitian diaspora faces in the United States, since the headings are dehistoricized and entitled merely "WEEK 1" or "WEEK 2." I discussed a comparable strategy of encoding the problem of decontextualization via form in novels by David Chariandy and Andrea Levy in chapter 2. Danticat translates this challenge to artistic voice into Freda's use of the first person: Freda never introduces herself; rather, her narrative is bookended by other characters naming her. The chapter opens with her mother naming Freda and citing her dead father as her audience: "Look, Freda,

Papa's listening to us up there" (168). Freda is not named again until the conclusion of the chapter, when Mariselle asks Freda to "sing your own funeral song" (181). This naming appears to give quite a pessimistic picture of the artist, opening with a dead father as the receptive audience to Freda's art and closing with the death of Freda's artistic self, narrated *via* her art. However, the death of a patriarchal model of enunciation does not entail the absolute demise of an artistic self—the voices of the women who name Freda, her mother and Mariselle, point to an alternative web of relation for the funeral singer.

"The Funeral Singer" introduces historical context in a similar manner to "Monkey Tails." Freda's remembrance of the past echoes that of Michel, since she speaks from the contemporary future of the diaspora about a history in Haiti. Michel narrates his childhood past from the perspective of the 2000s, while the 1970s are eventually revealed as Freda's present (180). The themes of paternal inheritance and mythic narration also connect the characters of Michel and Freda. Freda the singer mourns the dictatorship's torture of her father and finds her voice within the context of the market, an alternative public sphere to that of the nation-discourse that Michel engages. Like Ka's art, Freda's singing relies on market distribution, and its inspiration is drawn from the relationship between her paternal lineage and the Duvalier dictatorship: "The first time I ever sang in public was at my father's memorial Mass. I sang 'Brother Timonie,' a song whose cadence rises and falls like the waves of the ocean. I sang it through my tears, and later people would tell me that my sobs reminded them of the incoming tide. From that moment on I became a funeral singer. Every time there was a funeral in Léogâne, I was asked to sing" (175). Freda is chosen as the representative voice for loss, and her embodiment of the prisoner-father subject as an inheritance leads to the formation of a market for her singing. At the funerals, sites of mourning that are both personal and public, Freda sings "my father's fishing songs and sometimes [I would] improvise my own, right there, next to the coffin, in front of the family, at the funeral home or at the church" (175). The audience's recognition of a funeral song's emotional appeal translates into its artistic value within the market. Freda remarks that she is "always appreciated and well compensated for her artistic labor" (175). The financial value placed on that collective identification with her music allows her to embark on an artistic career. She acts as an author-double, an individual cultural representative who gives voice to the collective suffering of a nation and its diaspora.

Like Ka's art, Freda's singing is censored, and she questions the future of her creativity and employment. In the United States as a political refugee, Freda "wish[es] I could sing to introduce myself" (166). Her inability to sing is due to censorship by and her resistance to the Duvalier dictatorship: "I was asked to leave my country by my mother because I wouldn't accept an invitation to sing at the national palace" (172). Freda's exile begins with her decision to stop singing: "I made a choice that I'd rather stop singing altogether rather than sing for the type of people who'd killed my father" (179). The market's circulation of the mythic prisoner symbol is appropriated by the very power regime that violently produced that subject. Freda's refusal to engage this marketing of her music entails a forced exile from Freda's creative self and the means by which she made her living. When asked for her profession by the English-language teacher in the United States, Freda imagines the most honest response: "I do nothing, I want to say. Not yet. I have been expelled from my country. That's why I'm in this class at twenty-two years old" (167). Expulsion from Haiti equals the end of Freda's artistic career, and without her songs she has no narrative with market currency.

The phrase "not yet" indicates that the newly diasporic Freda may find a counternarrative by which to express herself. For Freda, unlike Ka, the search for a more minor mode of expression favors storytelling as an alternative means of instantiating a female diasporic community in the United States. While Michel's model of storytelling outlines the paternity of diasporic relation, Freda's move from singing to storytelling entails a shift from the paternal model of inheritance to a reassuring space of belonging within a female diasporic community. Her storytelling goal is to initiate a process of collective healing with the women in her class: "I thought that exposing a few details of my life would inspire them to do the same and slowly we'd parcel out our sorrows, each walking out with fewer than we'd carried in" (170). Freda's membership within this new community of Haitian women in the diaspora still necessitates the death of her role as cultural representative, as a singer. Mariselle asks her to "sing your own funeral song," and that leads Freda to "begin my final performance as a funeral singer, or any kind of singer at all" (181). The death of this artistic identity is intertwined with Freda's full incorporation into a close-knit community of diasporic women: "I sing 'Brother Timonie.' [. . .] Rezia and Mariselle catch on quickly and join in. We sing until our voices grow hoarse, sometimes making Brother Timonie a sister" (181). Freda's individual voice as a funeral singer becomes part of a chorus whose collective creativity empowers them to revise the homosocial funeral narrative of a fisherman into one that recognizes the losses of diasporic women. Singing in the market-place of funerals becomes replaced by this classroom community of women, whose collective art remains private and personal, outside the market but enabling closure: "And for the rest of the night we raise our glasses, broken and unbroken alike, to the terrible days behind us and the uncertain ones ahead" (181). The end of Freda's artistic career cor-responds with a transition into solidarity within a marginalized female community.[36]

Danticat frames the relationship between women and art differently than she does the relationship between men like Michel and their story-telling. Whereas the storytelling of men creates new bonds of commu-nity that allay or resolve the divisions inherited from the nation-state, women are instead forced to choose between their public modes of cre-ative expression and their desire to belong to a diasporic community. For the diasporic women of *Dew Breaker*, art and belonging are held in opposition to each other; they cannot have both. This opposition could be framed as individual voice versus communal identity, cultural repre-sentatives and public intellectuals articulating the nation versus minor collective voices of critique relegated to the margins. The artistic women in *Dew Breaker* must forsake their public careers and are left with no means of making a living from their art: along with Freda, Ka loses her artistic inspiration once her father confesses to his dew breaker past; Beatrice closes her bridal dress shop to escape a phantom torturer; and Aline must stop working as a newspaper writer to explore her queer sex-uality and pursue creative nonfiction. With nation and diaspora defined by homosocial kinship, the filiation of a female community appears to have no alternative lineage to root it, so that the women remain unmoored from the postcolonial nation and marginalized within the Haitian diaspora. Focusing on the "men and women whose tremendous agonies filled every blank space in their lives" (137), Danticat's novel makes clear that despite the shared context of postcolonial dictatorship, the possibilities for processing that history of violence are fractured by gendered modes of belonging.

By aligning dictation with dictatorship, Junot Díaz and Edwidge Dan-ticat complicate the concept of diaspora, contesting academic theoriza-tions that see diaspora as offering a utopic alternative to the nation-state. The power dynamics of dictation, inherited from authoritative regimes, shape diasporic subjectivity. *Oscar Wao* and *Dew Breaker* illustrate how the heterogeneity of diaspora might allow for the formation of new community bonds and solidarity, but at the same time competing notions of diasporic identity mean that the artistic processing of history will voice certain experiences while silencing others. Both Díaz and Danticat depict the gendered legacy of dictatorship, particularly its masculinist and homophobic discourses, as complicating any ethical imperative for the Caribbean diasporic writer. The gendering of postcolonial violence therefore finds its parallels in the gendering of artistic authority.

In describing their relationship to their art, Junot Díaz and Edwidge Danticat acknowledge the difficulties in maintaining a balance between their readerships' interests and the ethical imperatives informing their writing. Díaz explains that "an artist is always wrestling with this unique voice and with the unique vision they have" while also aware of certain "mainstream pressures," for example, "all they know about their convention, all the stories you know, all the things your friends like, and all the things you like" ("In Darkness" 15–16). The writer's context of literary history and popular culture translates into a burden of conformity: "Hey, this other way is easier, this other way's been done before, this way leads to acceptance" ("In Darkness" 15–16). Even as Díaz argues that "in my writing I have the courage that I didn't have" as a child to resist such conformity, he adds that "the struggle is there and it's almost never ending" ("In Darkness" 15–16). Of course, resisting mainstream pressures on artistic endeavors can, as Edwidge Danticat points out, lead to the charge of inauthenticity. In response to this criticism, Danticat responds, "Of course I'm inauthentic. Duh! It's the immigrant's reality and I am an immigrant. I am inauthentic here. And I'm inauthentic there. Let's put this all to rest now. Inauthenticity is my life and it's a perfect place for me to do the kind of writing I want to do. If you're inauthentic, you can make your own rules, which suits me just fine" ("Immigrant Artist" 48). While Danticat sees this criticism coming from the Haitian American and Haitian communities, she makes the case that such "people are responding, when they say these things, to another problematic reaction. When you belong to a minority group, even when you write fiction, people think it's sociology or anthropology" ("Immigrant Artist" 49). Caribbean diasporic writing, within the context of Global North ethnic writing, struggles with the expectations placed upon it by various consumers, from within and beyond their communities. The balance is not simply one of conformity versus resistance, but of desiring recognition from mainstream and minority communities that come with different definitions of authenticity for ethnic writers. The artistic project of speaking with authority to those communities, of depicting the Caribbean diaspora in an ethical manner to insiders and outsiders, is encoded in the market aesthetics of writers such as Díaz and Danticat.

Junot Díaz's and Edwidge Danticat's historical novels form part of the broader trend of market aesthetics in Caribbean diasporic writing, but these two writers have developed a uniquely different relationship to the market in comparison to the other authors I have thus far discussed. Namely, the awarding of the MacArthur "Genius" grant to Danticat in 2009 and Díaz in 2012 could be said to have shifted the weight of the market pressures on both authors. In their videos for the MacArthur website, the writers hint at the implications of receiving the five-year fellowship, which comes with a prize of $500,000. Danticat describes the fellowship as providing her with a room of her own, economically and artistically: "It means that in the business of [. . .] being a writer, of being a mother of two young children, it gives me a space, the opportunity to have a pause and really consider where I want to take my work next" (Danticat, "MacArthur Fellows"). Díaz also describes the grant as "transformational": "It allows you to focus on your art [. . .] with very little other concerns, [. . .] it's kinda like a big blast of privilege" (Díaz, "MacArthur Fellows"). The privilege of artistic self-reflection that Danticat and Díaz tie to the absence of financial burdens must also have some effect on the authors' perception of market pressures. Looking at the long-term trajectory of Díaz's and Danticat's writing can provide a glimpse into how market aesthetics of their historical fiction might be transformed by new directions in genre and writerly activism.

Danticat's and Díaz's post-MacArthur projects reveal how market aesthetics continue to be central to their writing, albeit refracted by the prize's "blast of privilege." Both writers continue to focus their work on Caribbean diasporic communities while doing so in different avenues or genres. Danticat has taken on editorial projects such as *Haiti Noir* (2011) and *Best American Essays* (2011) in addition to her collection of nonfiction essays *Create Dangerously* (2010). *Claire of the Sea Light* (2013), her first novel since *The Dew Breaker*, expands the expected geography of the Haitian diaspora in the United States by moving beyond New York and Miami to Boston, Los Angeles, Portland, San Francisco, Seattle, and Washington, D.C. Danticat's anthologizing of Haitian and Haitian American writing challenges her positioning as *the* voice of the Haitian diaspora. Additionally, Danticat's role as editor allows her to mentor emerging writers. Meanwhile, Díaz has followed *Oscar Wao* with the publication of *This Is How You Lose Her* (2012), a short story collection that returns to the sibling relationship of Yunior and Rafa from *Drown*. While exploring the familiar context of heterosexism through the figure of Yunior, Díaz has also expressed an interest in using his post-MacArthur privilege to publishing a science fiction novel, a goal that has previously eluded him. In a 2012 interview with the blog *Geek's Guide to the Galaxy*, Díaz explains that he abandoned his previous science fiction manuscripts because they could not compete for attention against the more immediate demands of his literary fiction: "I always had this dream that I was going to be this switch-hitter, that I was going to be one year writing a [literary] book like *Drown* and the next year writing *Shadow of the Adept*, and it never came to be, I moved so slow" (par. 3).

Market success allows Danticat and Díaz to move into other genres of writing and to reconceive their roles as cultural representatives. Alongside new avenues for creativity and activism, Danticat and Díaz remain committed to articulating a postcolonial imperative within the market aesthetics of their writing, identifying intimacy with the reader as the source of art's power. Intimacy is the ambivalent goal of such Caribbean diasporic writing, the means by which literature can aspire to transforming the social consciousness of the reader. In an interview, Díaz explains that "one principle that we have in literature and art is that the universal arises from the particular" ("Broken Hearts" 14–15). The specificity of experience, the cultural and ethnic particularities of a narrative, enable intimacy with the reader: "It's the actual thumbprint uniqueness, it's the granular idiosyncratic, one-of-a-kindness of a work of art that gives it power across time, across space, across language, that allows it to clear that most terrible of all barriers, the barrier that separates one soul from another" ("Broken Hearts" 14–15). Danticat likewise articulates her writerly goals in terms of trespassing across the barrier between reader and writer in order to make reading literature a transformative experience. In *Create Dangerously*, Danticat remarks, "I too sometimes wonder if in the intimate, both solitary and solidary, union between writers and readers a border can really exist" (16). Intimacy is a fraught space of cross-cultural encounter in historical fiction by Caribbean diasporic writers. Imagining the terms for a more ethical relationship between self and other inspires the market aesthetics of Caribbean diasporic writing.

Conclusion

Electronic Archives and the Digital Futures of Caribbean Diasporic Writing

CARIBBEAN DIASPORIC HISTORICAL FICTION offers a comparative vision of the past via narratives that are intimately wedded to the present, informed by the interrelated systems of globalization and multiculturalism. The postcolonial imperative of ethically depicting Caribbean history and subjectivities comes into conflict with the horizon of expectation created by reader reception, and this creative tension inspires the market aesthetics of Caribbean diasporic writing. The newest area where the shaping forces of market aesthetics can be seen is in the shift from print to digital. The paradox of globalization, with the mixed blessing of global access paired with commodification, of community with marginalization, finds its parallel in the digital world of the Internet. The Internet is neither here nor there, an abstraction that circulates material goods, a marketplace of ideas and products, and a space for public discourse that is not accessible to the entire public.[1]

This digital present already influences the market aesthetics of Caribbean diasporic historical fiction, with online readership communities producing expansive sets of paratexts. Such paratexts include book cover images uploaded by readers as well as annotations of literary texts. To think through how digital reception is influencing Caribbean diasporic writing, I analyze the annotated reference websites created for Junot Díaz's *Oscar Wao* and Díaz's subsequent contribution to another online annotation project for his novel. I also read Robert Antoni's historical novel *As Flies to Whatless Boys* (2013) as a model for how the form and content of Caribbean diasporic writing reference, feed into, and frustrate its readership's online searches to decipher references in the text. While my discussion of these digital encounters between text and audience hopefully gestures toward some new directions for the analysis of market aesthetics, I am equally invested in how Caribbean diasporic writing can speak back to the field of digital humanities. These creative experiments illuminate the potential and pitfalls heralded by the digital age of literature, revisiting the questions of intimacy, access, and literacy that animate my book.

Digital Horizons of Marginalia: Annotating *Oscar Wao*

The website *The Annotated Oscar Wao: Notes and Translations for The Brief Wondrous Life of Oscar Wao by Junot Díaz* was launched in December 2008 by Kim after her experience of reading the novel as part of a book club.[2] Kim began the annotation project when she had "read about 20 pages and found [her]self Googling every few words" (October 17, 2013). She distinctly remembers the passage in *Oscar Wao* that inspired her to annotate the novel. Kim recalls that she "was looking up 'Dale un galletazo'" online when she came across Erin Judge's "Open Letter to Junot Díaz." Judge's letter provided Kim with a sense of belonging, of being part of a broader community of readers that "were equally stymied" by the novel's Spanish words. In describing the challenge of Spanish in *Oscar Wao*, Kim recognized that this was not the only discourse in the novel that might require translation. Even though she did not "get *all* of the references," as "a science fiction and fantasy fan" she "definitely wasn't lost, and looking up obscure comic book references [was] fun" and "not a chore." The knowledge gaps regarding science fiction and comic books initiated an entertaining pursuit, whereas decoding the Spanish was less intellectually appealing and more strenuous investigative labor. Kim explains that her limited Spanish meant that she was "looking up even relatively basic words and phrases" and the "more complicated and vulgar words weren't in Google Translate of course, so those took more research." The annotation website collates this research so that the labor of translation is achieved with minimal exertion.[3] Kim's website invites a readership that is "having the same problems when they [are] reading" to enter a digital medium for instantiating community and creating an alternative text of meaning. At the same time, Junot Díaz gains a virtual space by which to envision his audience's responses to the rhetorical project of the novel's market aesthetics. Kim discloses that "Díaz actually sent me an email about 6 months after the site went live" that said: "Love what you've done and how many people you've helped with my crazy novel."

The Annotated Oscar Wao is a useful reference for readerships with access to the Internet, but its origins also point us to other forms of digital marginalia that flesh out the profile of these online researcher-readers and their horizons of experience. The open letter that confirmed Kim's desires for translation and inspired her to create the annotated website begins with Erin Judge explaining that because Judge's mother sent her to a "fancy college where I had the opportunity to study abroad," the mother often relied upon Judge for help with translating Spanish. What follows is a verbatim citation of a humorous instant messaging conversation between Judge and her mother, with her mother requesting that Judge translate several sexually explicit Spanish words. Once Judge finally asked where her mother had been hearing these shockingly improper terms, she realized that her mother was reading Díaz's novel *Oscar Wao*. The open letter ends with a plea that Díaz be more attentive to the needs of his reading audience: "Next time you write a book with widespread popularity that appeals to suburban women who aren't Eva Langoria [*sic*] Parker and don't know what the hell you're saying, please please PLEASE supply a glossary." The novel's untranslatability compels Judge to have an awkward exchange about sexual intimacy with her (explicitly non-Latino and therefore implicitly white) suburban mother. The conversation is so distressing that Judge is motivated to, albeit in an intentionally comical tone, author a public letter to Díaz. Contrasting her mother with Eva Longoria, a Mexican American actress who stands in for a suburban Latinidad, Judge makes an appeal for the consideration of different readership, one that is desperate for translation and, by implication, requires necessary distance from sexually scandalous material. Contrasting her mother with a symbol of Latinidad, Judge's allusion to the "forgotten" audience of white readers references the ways in which the novel others or alienates this readership.

Judge's open letter also aligns these readership demands with the profit logic of the marketplace. Judge takes Díaz to task for neglecting his duty as author-translator and tries to appeal to the market rationale that she thinks motivates Díaz's creativity, making the case that a translation glossary could be sold as "a companion guide," promising that such a product would be a "win-win-win" because "your publisher will love it" and "people would buy it." As I discuss in chapter 5, the translation choices in *Oscar Wao* reflect a writerly strategy that foregrounds el secreto abierto of queer sexuality as an allegory for the contradictions of the reader-text encounter. The market aesthetics of the novel appear mirrored by the anxiety of readers like Judge over the uncomfortable intimacy generated by the novel's linguistic politics. The labor involved in processing the indecent meaning of vulgar Spanish words appears to be of greater concern to Judge than the actual work of translating. In other words, the novel circulates terminology that, unbeknownst to the monolingual English reader, will create awkward occasions for translation. The conflict over intimacy in the historical fiction transforms into a struggle for the audience over how to negotiate the revelation of linguistic indecorum about sexuality.

The attention to vulgarity brings us back to a core element of the market aesthetics of Caribbean diasporic historical fiction and its imagining of an (im)possible intimacy with its audience. These examples of digital marginalia reveal that intimacy with the text produces a tense ethical negotiation for the reader. The problem of subjectivity and sexuality emerges in Kim's narrative of her annotation project, which speaks to how an online presence is a public identity that must be carefully managed. Kim explains that she maintains a first-name basis on *The Annotated Oscar Wao* to protect her privacy on such a public forum as well as to avoid the association of her identity with the problematic rhetoric that the website translates: "I didn't want search engine results for my name showing up with ethnic slurs and Spanish vulgarities" ("Re: Interview Request," 28 Aug. 2013). This strategy is completely understandable considering how little control an individual has over his or her cultural production once it circulates in the digital world. The anxiety over reception and access experienced by readers like Kim and Judge finds its parallel in the creative tension that informs Caribbean diasporic fiction, the competing demands of a writerly ethical imperative alongside market pressures of commodification and decontextualization. The task of managing a digital identity is a reminder that the Internet is not a system promoting egalitarian engagement but one that traffics data and products in streams or niches, classifying information by using networks of association that may differ from the original context producing that material.

The research process of annotation embodies the challenges of creating an online archive of meaning and context. The collective enterprise of *The Annotated Oscar Wao*, combined with the website's request for readers "to help improve this in any way," encourages the growth and input of a digital audience for the site and novel. Kim explains that from the initial formation of her online project she "collat[ed] the work of others" and "us[ed] information from other sources" to expand on her annotations ("Re: Interview Request," 17 Oct. 2013). As a result, Kim does not feel she can "claim any real ownership" of an online resource that continues to expand: "Even 4 years later, I'm still getting a few emails a month with updates, and several more emails thanking me for doing the project." At the same time, Kim had to make executive decisions about what meanings and translations to showcase in the annotations. While the website comes with a warning that it "give[s] absolutely zero warranties as to its accuracy or thoroughness," Kim found herself negotiating various demands from her readerships about the legitimacy of the annotations. Kim receives feedback on the content of certain annotations and has to settle disputes over meaning by prioritizing her definition of the website's readership. The arguments over translating "racial terminology and slurs" that had "very nuanced meanings" were particularly heated. Kim explains that some contributors "were *very* passionate about certain changes" and she had to come to the decision that "it's close enough and casual readers will get the idea." The ethical imperative of expanding access to these casual readers meant the necessary flattening out of (perhaps conflicting) layers of meaning, with the goal of streamlining the reading experience: "it's enough to know that a word means something like 'someone probably of mixed ancestry' so that you can just keep going with the story."

Kim's description of the intended audience for the annotations makes me reconsider the intersection of access and privilege on the World Wide Web. Taking into account the paratexts I have discussed thus far, which are created by college-educated white women, I want to explore further the idea that the production of online content tends to be the work of people who come from a specific ethnic, racial, and class background. The digital reception of *The Annotated Oscar Wao* indicates that the virtual audience originates from specific reception niches. Certain readers have the education and class status to find each other and create virtual communities online. Kim's ability to organize her research project as a digital reference for other readers is facilitated by her professional training and job experience: "I build websites for a living, so making this into an online resource wasn't difficult for me at all, and the hosting is essentially free on a server I already have" ("Re: Interview Request," 17 Oct. 2014). Digital literacy, class status, and professional networks shape the conception and construction of online communities. Certain forms of privilege enable readerships to virtually speak back to the historical novels of Caribbean diasporic writers, to create spaces of exchange that debate the interpretation of historical referents in the fiction.

The ability of these readerships to build virtual spaces for collaboration and interpretation on the Internet not only catches the attention of a writer like Díaz but also informs his decision to annotate a section of his novel online. The digital paratexts composed by readers and authors represent a vibrant and ephemeral electronic archive that informs the market aesthetics of Caribbean diasporic writing. Austin Allen, the editor of *Poetry Genius*, transcribed a section of *Oscar Wao* in 2013 for the site, which markets itself as "your guide to the global canon" with the mission to annotate "all literature." While most of the annotators for the novel's excerpt are anonymous, those contributed by "kidskeya" (an allusion to Quisqueya) were eventually "verified" as those of Junot Díaz. I asked Kim to comment on the annotations that Díaz offers on *Poetry Genius*, and she helpfully called my attention to the interface used by the site, explaining that she is "not a big fan of this style of pop-up annotation for longer prose, but any time you have a work with so many references and footnotes like this book, there just isn't going to be an elegant way to deal with it" ("Re: Interview Request," 17 Oct. 2013). The mode of embedding annotations via hyperlinks necessitates the short selection chosen from the novel for annotation, which is also in keeping with the site's primary focus on the genre of poetry. Kim notes how audience shapes the interfaces chosen to relay information. Distinguishing between her casual readers and those of *Poetry Genius*, Kim reads Díaz's annotations as a "good companion to my annotations (or vice-versa) but they're not serving the same audience." While Kim prioritizes clarity, intelligibility, and comprehension in the form and content of her online resource, Díaz's annotations are not motivated by similar goals of translation. The legibility of Díaz's annotations parallels the market aesthetics of his novel, since Kim found herself "looking up words used in his notes—I need an annotation for his annotation!" For instance, Díaz's annotation of the word *sertão* provides a narrative on "personal thoughts about seeing it in films, and has a few photos, but doesn't actually give you a definition for what the word means." This refusal on the part of Díaz to translate could be (and has been) interpreted in a variety of ways.[4] I want to emphasize that these annotation projects allow us to see how the digital medium, the method of communicating or embedding information online, is informed by a writerly imperative about readership and accessibility that is self-conscious about the way that online interactions are raced, classed, and gendered.

The market aesthetics of digital marginalia are shaped by the horizon of expectation for readership engagement. The broader context for the emerging engagement of Caribbean diasporic writers with their virtual audiences is the shift from print to digital publishing, which generates (or compounds) a crisis of imagination and income in the literary world. How can an author make a living in the digital age? In an interview with Jacob Sugarman ("Junot Díaz"), Díaz argues that "a lot of artists are figuring out how to make fucking money" and that this profit-logic is prompting the move of literary writers into genre fiction. Díaz says that "ultimately, I think it's a matter of privilege" because "literary writers can attack new markets [like science fiction] without ever losing their cachet as literary writers." The shift into specific genres could be in part attributed to the winnowing of a market for literary writing that is heightened by the often-heralded end to print culture and the paper economy. Díaz alludes to the ways in which class status within the field of literary writing can give certain writers the privilege of creative mobility. This privilege enables creative freedom, ensuring that authors' experiments with form and genre will not damage their literary cachet, their reputations as valuable cultural producers. Within this context, Díaz's digital annotations of his creative work signal an attempt to intervene in a medium that circulates his work, yet, as Kim's commentary suggests, also disengage from the standard mode of meaning production through the nontranslation of cultural referents that are deemed foreign or Other. Díaz self-consciously constructs the market aesthetic parameters of his online public persona. The annotations therefore mimic the (im)balance between intimacy and distance found in the market aesthetics of *Oscar Wao*.

Imagined Archives for the Digital Reader: Robert Antoni's *As Flies to Whatless Boys*

By examining the market aesthetics of Robert Antoni's *As Flies to Whatless Boys* (2013), I conclude this book about Caribbean diasporic historical fiction by offering some preliminary thoughts on how digital paratexts influence the genre. The online annotations and reception of Díaz's *Oscar Wao* suggest the rise of the researcher-reader persona, which is stratified by class and education (the suburban reader, the college-educated techie) but racialized and gendered in different ways, depending on the market imaginary. Robert Antoni's historical novel is attentive to the Internet as an alternative space for engaging readerships, with this encounter understood in terms of the ethical limits of intimacy. Miss Ramsol's e-mails and the appendix of an online archive are examples of how the novel references the mixed blessing of a global system of digital exchange.

The novel's historical narrative of the Tucker family's emigration from England to Trinidad is framed and interrupted by e-mails from the archival librarian, Miss Ramsol, to Antoni's author-double, Mr. Robot.

Miss Ramsol's electronic mail integrates into the novel a writing genre with Caribbean-inflected voice, humorous tone, and digital syntax and stylings. A print archive of documents accompanies the e-mails, each officially stamped "FROM THE DESK OF Miss Ramsol" (77). As the novel progresses, the e-mails detail how her archival research becomes a mode of seduction—culminating in an exchange of documents for sex with Mr. Robot, taking place in her office at the library. The intimate encounter between Miss Ramsol and the author-double allegorizes the problem of writerly access to the Caribbean archive and complicates a utopic vision of its digital future. Since Miss Ramsol's restrictive policing of the documents at the library is not loosened up by Mr. Robot's self-prostitution, he bypasses her authority by carrying in a personal photocopy machine during Miss Ramsol's "1/2 day off" (143). The fictionalized fight over archival access speaks to the challenges of Caribbean writers in researching material for the genre of historical fiction. The sexualized nature of the battle over this archive of knowledge, and Miss Ramsol's intransigence to the unrestricted photocopying of these documents, references the contemporary context of sex tourism at the same time that it speaks to the commodification of cultural production.

Consider the implications that the fictionalized intimate encounter between librarian and creative writer has for archives like the Digital Library of the Caribbean (dLOC). As the project's website explains, dLOC "provides access to digitized versions of Caribbean cultural, historical and research materials currently held in archives, libraries, and private collections." By allegorizing the encounter between a creative writer and the Caribbean archive in terms of sex tourism, Antoni's novel refers to the problematic imaginative and material costs implicated in the digital circulation of Caribbean print culture. The commodification of knowledge becomes identified as a (not so) new mode of exploiting the Caribbean. Because archival resources are difficult to access, these cultural and historical products are a draw for academics and writers alike. The finite resource of the archive rationalizes the profit logic of a gatekeeper like the archival librarian Miss Ramsol, who maintains the archive's inaccessibility in order to sustain the desire and need for academic tourists to travel and access localized knowledge. If digitization opens up these local archives to global readerships outside the Caribbean, how can the Caribbean imagine itself as anything other than an empty referent of a history that circulates beyond its borders? Caribbean diasporic historical fiction embodies the complex responses to this question, as a cultural product about context that enjoys global circulation because of the decontextualizing book market that commodifies history and ethnic others.

Antoni's novel reflects on the digital divide and the contextual silences generated by the Internet's archiving of metadata. The novel's archive of Miss Ramsol's e-mails is composed only of messages to the author-double Mr. Robot. The e-mails that Mr. Robot sends to Miss Ramsol are absent, accentuating the one-sided ephemerality of such digital exchanges. The reader does not know what prompts Miss Ramsol's sexual proposals and thus lacks an important context for her gatekeeping motivations in terms of Mr. Robot's contribution to the liaison. These archival silences decontextualize Miss Ramsol's narrative so that it veers into a parodic stereotype of hypersexual Caribbean subjectivity. The one-sided depiction of the e-mail exchange alludes to the inequalities that digital humanities approaches often take for granted. Miss Ramsol's messages provide the only glimpse the reader obtains into the contemporary context of the author-double, Mr. Robot. Her first-person narrative is a vital facet of the archival dialogue that the novel acknowledges as foundational to its imaginary. After all, without Miss Ramsol, there would be no documents verifying the Tucker family's historical context. The narrative mediator of these documents, Mr. Robot, remains an invisible and inaccessible figure in the novel. The reader accesses an archive of contemporary e-mails and historical documents that Mr. Robot accumulates via his interactions with Miss Ramsol and the Caribbean research library. Mr. Robot's flat, surface-level depiction through Miss Ramsol's e-mails makes him equally stereotyped as the parasitic creative writer, reiterating concerns about cultural betrayal that plague the Caribbean diasporic writer's market position as a native informant.

Antoni's *As Flies to Whatless Boys* acknowledges how digitalization can inspire Caribbean diasporic creativity while also exploring its limitations. The novel's appendix and online archive are indicative of Antoni's investment in a market aesthetic that is responsive to the print publishing crisis by stylistically "burst[ing] off the page."[5] During the Q&A following a reading in 2013, Robert Antoni announced that "the Internet will save writing."[6] Antoni was on his book tour for *As Flies to Whatless Boys*, and his comment was meant to reassure "all of you writers out there that think the Internet is the end of literature." By conceiving of digitalization as a tool rather than an obstacle, Antoni sees the Internet as providing the opportunity to invigorate the aesthetic project of Caribbean diasporic writing, enabling his fiction and its depiction of Caribbean history to circulate in different ways. The novel contains symbolic asterisks in the body of the narrative that direct the reader to an appendix of online references at the end of the novel. Like Díaz's online annotations, these imaginative hyperlinks connect the print and digital spheres. The Web links in Antoni's text guide the reader to digitally access two musical dream-video sequences that happen outside the narrative of the novel (so that they supplement rather than restate the plot). The appendix also contains links to an alternate archive of imagined and actual historical documents, only the first of which is stamped by Miss Ramsol.[7] The remaining materials are therefore positioned as an alternative to Miss Ramsol's photocopied archive. The online creative and historical sources can be understood as a raw digital archive, following Daniel J. Cohen's distinction of raw and cooked digital history:

> Raw digital history comprises documents, information and communications that are heterogeneous and that have little, if any, organization. Cooked digital history takes such historical materials and adds helpful markings and a measure of homogeneity. An offline cognate for this difference between raw and cooked digital history would be the distinction between various archives' unruly boxes of notes, manuscripts and letters by Benjamin Franklin and the carefully vetted, transcribed, formatted, annotated and indexed volumes of Yale University's *Papers of Benjamin Franklin*. (337–38)

We can draw parallels between the market aesthetics of Junot Díaz's and Robert Antoni's digital engagement with paratexts. Díaz engages and disrupts his readerships' digestion of his writing via the online annotations of his historical novel, while Antoni's novel introduces and withholds an alternate historical archive of raw materials from his audience. The digital archive rescues certain historical documents from obscurity, like Henry David Thoreau's 1843 defense of Etzler, "Paradise (to Be) Regained," while giving the illusion of accessing other materials. The online version of Etzler's play, "A Dialogue on Etzler's PARADISE Between the West-Indian Plantation Owner, 'Lord Louse' & His Former African Slave, 'Savvy'—or—'English vs. Nigrish,'" assumes the guise of a visually delicate and crumbling historical text. The historical persona of Etzler wrote a theatrical performance criticizing Caribbean plantation society, but the reader accesses a digital text that is instead a product of Antoni's imagination. The online archive feeds into and frustrates the reader's desire to access "real" documentation to contextualize the historical fiction.

Antoni's online reference website and its circulation of archival materials are mediated by privilege. In his discussion of digital archives,

Cohen explains that developing an interface for accessing online resources "comes with significant costs to both producers and consumers" (338). He notes that the organization and annotation of Web archives, "the construction of a database," and the "assistance of software tools and partial automation" are time-consuming and expensive (338). If the labor and costs involved in such a project are often prohibitive for institutions, imagine the challenges involved for an individual creative writer or reader. In the not-so-distant future, will Antoni's online archive be accessible, or will readers find broken links? Link rot occurs when the content of a hyperlink no longer exists—the referent is disconnected from its object of focus. The publisher for Antoni's historical novel, Akashic Books, is a small press that "can afford to be more eclectic" and "concentrate [. . .] marketing efforts on a smaller demographic of readers," but does it also have the funds to maintain online literary archives like Antoni's for all eternity (Edmondson 157)? The temporality and ephemerality of the digital archive are allegorized by the market aesthetics of Antoni's novel and its paratexts.

The market aesthetics of *As Flies to Whatless Boys* extend to the online interface of whatlessboys.com, the emphasis being on the term *whatless*, which the *Urban Dictionary* defines as "somebody who does not know what the hell is going on, but is curious to know what exactly is going on" (Anonymousssssssssssssssss [*sic*]). The inaccessibility of the online archive heightens the reader's self-consciousness as a subject who is not "in the know" despite the desire to become a "professional knower," recalling the phrase from David Chariandy's *Soucouyant*, which I discussed in chapter 2. The digital marginalia accessible via *CUNY Academic Commons* and produced within a classroom setting indicates the discomfort of readerships with the (im)possible intimacy of Antoni's online archive, as well as its appeal.[8] The post "As 'Links' to Whatless Boys" confirms the success of the novel's pedagogical imperative, that "a novel with so much detail could trick the reader into believing this [is] a new little nugget of Trinidadian history" (Martinez, par. 1). However, several commenters see the online archive undermining the literary project, mainly because the novel does not open with any indication that the readership should access it; the digital materials are only referenced in the appendix. As a result, "You must flip to the end of the book to realize those asterisks lead you to an online, multimedia space, that provides the visuals you wish were right in front of you the whole time" (Henriquez, par. 3). Potentially, a reader is entirely "oblivious to the fact while reading the book" (George, "Richest Literary Experience"). Even those readers who are aware of the digital archive might "ma[ke] it a good way through the book before remembering the accompanying website" (Martinez, par. 1). Two commenters interpret this delay as a failure of narration: "Why would he think, without any indication at all in the beginning of his novel, that ALL readers would know how to use the links while reading?" (George, "As 'Links'"). Negatively framing the disconnect between the novel and the digital repository of documents, this readership assumes that Antoni's horizon of expectation imagines a homogeneous audience savvy enough to find the novel's appendix at the beginning of the reading process.

The market aesthetics of Antoni's digital archive lead such readers to feel marginalized from the process of knowledge production, aware of missing the opportunity to contextualize scenes in the novel as they were reading. Maribi Henriquez interprets the inaccessibility of Antoni's archive as a writerly strategy: "I will tell you that when I googled the book this was NOT one of the first pages to come up on the search, I think that is intentional and somewhat genius" (par. 3). I concur with the assessment that "the site was [not] meant to be found easily" (par. 3). I would also add that the narrative delay calls attention to the digital divide in terms of both archives and readerships. Prioritizing the fictional encounter first, so that the reader engages the archive later, upsets the privilege that documentation holds within historiography. As one reader notes, the online archive holds no meaning or significance prior to one's reading of the novel: "I had visited the site before reading the book, and without the context, this site made no sense, which does work against it in many ways" (Martinez, par. 1). I propose that the work of Antoni's digital archive is not to contextualize the novel but rather to showcase the value of fictionality and opacity. The market aesthetics of Antoni's digital project emphasizes that the raw contents of historical archive alone cannot tell a story—narration is necessary, perhaps even a necessary evil, to imagine the past. As a companion to the novel, the online archive also undercuts the privilege of documentation as the sole means to affirm historical accuracy by emphasizing gaps in readerly access.

In addition to the frustration of discovering an archive that could have informed their first reading of the novel, readers translate the delayed or missed encounter with the audience in terms of a marketing failure. The fact that Antoni's archival website does not appear in "the top Google search results" is a problem "from a marketing standpoint," since "readers today are highly likely to Google their book interests before picking up the book to purchase it" (George, "Richest Literary Experience"). The digital archive is configured as a resource that should market the novel to readers, piquing their interest in the historical fiction. The contents of whatlessboys.com are deemed lacking in marketable information, missing contextual pages such as "one with marketing materials/Where-to-buy, another with the author's biography, and another being this page [from the novel], that includes information on what the page is for, and which link coincides with page/Chapter" (Martinez, par. 3). The digital reader reacts with similar priorities to those of the online audience responding to Díaz's novel; readerships articulate the value of accessibility, contextualization, and transparency using a market rationale of profit. The commenters on Antoni's digital archive also frame the project as undermining the historical fiction's ethical imperative of historical revision: "Context! Context! Context! It is missing totally from the website" (George, "Richest Literary Experience"). The market aesthetics of Caribbean diasporic historical fiction inhabit the tension between a desire to recover lost histories and a desire to maintain productive silences that thwart the colonizing gaze of the reader. Antoni's website frustrates the readership's desires for a seamless transition from print to digital and back, effectively frustrating the translation and contextualization of the novel's passages via the author-generated online resource of materials.

The contradiction between the decontextualized archive and the historical realism of the Tucker family's migration, between the shockingly sexual overtures of Miss Ramsol's e-mails and the dry, objective tone of the documents she provides Mr. Robot, is constitutive of Caribbean diasporic market aesthetics. The *CUNY Digital Commons* readership's concern regarding an obstructed intimacy with the archive mirrors the symbolic deployment of intimacy in Miss Ramsol's e-mails. As Henriquez points out, "The digital age is key in deciphering the written language of the emails, the forward tone, and mix of a growing personal touch and less formal/professional messages" (par. 2). The shift in intimacy alludes to intersecting power relations of the archives and the book market. Miss Ramsol's e-mails depict an inequitable and uneven access to the library archive, while the site whatlessboys.com forces the issue of access onto the reader through a delayed revelation of online resources and context. Miss Ramsol's gatekeeping, restricting the circulation of library materials, deploys opacity as a mode of resistance and marketability. Archival (in)accessibility entails a negotiation of privilege, the stakes of which are high for consumer and critic, artist and archivist, self and other.

I would temper the framing of digitalization as a tool easily accessible to all creative writers. The integration of digital elements, whether they require passive or interactive engagement from the reader, is dependent upon the publishing industry's conferral of literary privilege. The stratification of privilege shapes the experience and horizons of authors and audiences. My experience teaching Antoni's novel in 2013 to a group of upper-division English majors at a comprehensive public university also made me question the way we understand access to digital media. Even though I told students ahead of time about the appendix and e-mailed them the links to Antoni's open-source archive, I found that fewer than five out of thirty-three students would actually access the digital material. Perhaps this was because the majority of students owned the print rather than the electronic print version of the novel. Perhaps the novel could not compete with an infinite archive of media competing for student attention. Perhaps the students had divergent levels of digital literacy or access to the Internet that restricted their contact with the archive. Or perhaps, as I have argued here, the market aesthetics of the novel require that disengagement so that the reader becomes self-consciously aware of the archive's decontextualization. I want to offer an additional reason for the class disengagement from the online archive: the digital niches or networks of readerships.

To what extent is the interface of the whatlessboys.com site, or even the integration of the symbolic asterisks in the novel, aimed at different sets of readers? If, as David M. Berry mentions in his introduction to *Understanding Digital Humanities* (2012), the Internet "is becoming increasingly stream-like" (15), categorizing and sifting information in aggregate so that individuals do not have to perform the task of narrowing down the digital expanse of data, what content and subjectivities are being filtered out in the process? What if my students—a racially diverse and working-class population, often holding one or two jobs while attempting to attend school full time—are not market(able) readers for this text? Is there a growing divide between those works aimed at a classroom market reader and those aimed at an elite, tech-savvy market reader? As academic reading practices (including my own) shift toward Franco Moretti's "distant reading" model, I worry that there are Other readerships that will become invisible and/or potential readers who may be streamed out of the marketplace of ideas.[9] I raise the question of visibility in this conclusion to highlight a set of potentially marginalized readers as well as the preponderance on the Web of a particular classed, raced, and gendered viewpoint. In addition to privileging a researcher-reader in the literary and academic marketplace, some digital paratexts of Caribbean diasporic writing contribute to what Paul Gilroy terms "white-supremacist crowd-sourcing" ("'My Britain'" 381). Gilroy's 2012 essay on "zombie multiculturalism" remarks on the way that "technological innovations" rely on "anonymous Internet interaction" that facilitates "routine acts of racist commentary" (381). The problem of anonymity returns us to the tension within Caribbean diasporic historical fiction, the postcolonial ethical imperative and market aesthetics. How does the digital anonymity of readerships refuse intimacy in both productive and dangerous ways?

The demand for access, for intimate knowledge of Caribbean histories, will continue to shape the Caribbean diasporic imagination in the digital age. The digital paratexts of Junot Díaz and Robert Antoni's historical fiction voice dissatisfaction with the literature's contextualization. The online reception, whether popular or academic, rationalizes its demands for additional glossaries, appendixes, and other companion references with a market logic that privileges translation and accessibility. The market aesthetics of Caribbean diasporic fiction acknowledge these pressures in the form, style, and content of the novels as well as the authors' online archive and annotation projects. The digital presence of Caribbean diasporic writers is a writerly performance of (dis)engagement and (dis)articulation that references the profit logic that circulates knowledge, memory, and history as capital. The market aesthetics of Caribbean diasporic writing allegorize the mixed blessing of the Internet as another globalizing and decontextualizing venue, the opportunities and the drawbacks of digital publishing, via the queer metaphors of sexual intimacy. Caribbean diasporic historical fiction is as much ethically impelled to document silenced voices and histories as it is ambivalent about the historiographic ideology of documentation and the censorship it demands.

Notes

Introduction

1. The market popularity of Caribbean diasporic writing is often equated with cultural betrayal. Nesbitt remarks on the aesthetics of guilt in Danticat's texts, which "are already guilty before one even reads them, guilty of their own popularity" (202–3). Dalleo and I discuss the critical equation of market popularity with political accommodation in *The Latino/a Canon*.

2. Critics argue that decontextualization of canonical literature functions similarly, reappropriating its racial implications toward the ends of assimilation projects. Arac argues that *Huck Finn* is an icon of integration whose introduction to the canon in 1950s sought to domesticate newly desegregated African American readers.

3. See Brown's *Migrant Modernism* (2013) for how the locality of postwar London and the rhetorical purchase of modernism informed these anglophone Caribbean male writers. Also see T. Walters, who notes that even though she "grew up during the 1970s at the height of what is known as the Caribbean Artists Movement," she was not introduced as a child to Black British literature (170). The development of a public discourse of multiculturalism and of ethnic studies fields such as Black British literature forms a unique contemporary context for Caribbean diasporic writing.

4. For a historical overview of how presses and anthologies configured the US Latino/a literary canon from the 1960s onwards, see Dalleo and Machado Sáez, "Formation of a Latino/a Canon."

5. R. Walcott notes that "the idea of diaspora and the institution of black studies" have been used to "render the specific and localized concerns of black Canadians null and void" (26). Walcott calls for the reconceptualization of diaspora, suggesting that "black cultural studies, with its attention to locality in the context of globality, might be read as offering some space to explore the tensions of black studies" (30). I hope that my attention to Caribbean diasporic writing also acknowledges locality within globality via a discussion of "dialogues and differences" (32).

6. A comparative lens can place the US Civil Rights Acts of 1964 and 1968 alongside the British Race Relations Acts of 1965, 1968, and 1976. I discuss the reactionary policies that isolated diasporic communities as a threat to national identity later on in this chapter.

7. In *Triangular Road*, Marshall speaks to the transatlantic cross-pollination of ideas that took place as a result of the civil rights movement and describes how her European lecture tour with Langston Hughes led to encounters with Parisian leftist students seeking to learn more about the Movement as well as Black British activists who accused Hughes of being accommodationist (20–22).

8. Many influential Black Power activists and Black Arts movement artists have Caribbean cultural backgrounds, although the diasporic element of their identities is often subsumed in historical narratives about the Movement. The uncomplicated way in which figures like Stokely Carmichael are framed as African American is partly due to the primacy of black/white racial binaries in the United States. Dawson refers to the British definition of blackness as a pan-ethnic category that also subsumes cultural difference and ethnic diversity. Campbell's poem "Sidney Poitier Studies," from *Running the Dusk* (2010), is one example of how Caribbean diasporic writers in Canada employ a market aesthetics that reimagines the 1960s depiction of black masculinity. Campbell's poem "tests" the reader, asking him or her to evaluate various labels applied to Poitier, such as "Victorian rebel" or "Civil Rights cyborg" (27). The poem's form as an exam challenges the banking mode of multiple-choice testing pedagogy, emphasizing the impossible task of fitting such a nuanced historical figure into a single category of identity.

9. Arizona's passage of SB 1070 and HB 2281 in 2010 reveals that civil rights continue to be a struggle within the United States. One of the most controversial policies instituted by SB 1070 requires police to determine the immigration status of anyone whom they detain or arrest, a practice that many critics argue endorses the racial profiling of Latinos. Meanwhile, HB 2281 outlaws Chicano and ethnic studies courses in Arizona. It should also be noted that British legislation outlawing racial discrimination followed the 1962 Commonwealth Immigrants Act, which further limited immigration from the colonies, including the Caribbean, notwithstanding their status as British subjects.

10. Chancy cites Collier-Thomas and Franklin's *Sisters in the Struggle* (1991) to reference the example of "Rosemary Brown, who emigrated as a young woman in 1950 from Jamaica to Canada," and "her politicization in the context of the US civil rights movement" (92). Brown worked to "make the issue of black women's oppression central to Black Canadian organizations such as the National Black Coalition and the Negro Women's Organization of Ontario" (93).

11. Li discusses the 1971 announcement of the policy by the Canadian prime minister. The immigration waves of the 1970s from regions like the Caribbean eventually prompted the passage of civil rights laws such as the Canada Act of 1982 and the Canadian Multiculturalism Act of 1988.

12. See Murray's *Mixed Media*, which focuses on the "numerous feminist and/or womanist publishing imprints which emerged in Britain between 1972 and 1999" (2) as well as feminist presses in Canada and the United States during the same time period. Murray's research reveals how anglophone feminist presses of the 1980s provided a space for Caribbean diasporic fiction as well as dialogue between multicultural and postcolonial literatures. She foregrounds the Women's Press as "a key player in promoting culturally diverse women's writings during the 1980s" (73). The list of titles offered by the Women's Press were "constructed along the lines of racial and ethnic diversity" while also being "fused symbiotically with the growth of post-colonial theory among humanities academics during the 1980s and 1990s" (74).

13. Corrigan's review of US historical fiction resonates with the conservative response to the post-Sixties emergence of ethnic literature in the Global North.

14. For a more in-depth explanation of how the civil rights movement is discussed in US Latino studies, see Dalleo and Machado Sáez, *Latino/a Canon*, as well as my essay on Stavans ("Reconquista").

15. Mehta points out that "the Caribbean has been described as a diaspora space par excellence by writers and scholars such as Stuart Hall, Antonio Benítez-Rojo, Édouard Glissant, and Maryse Condé," who define the Caribbean "as a meta-archipelago with undetermined rhizomatic roots" (2).

16. When deployed as a hegemonic category, the concept of diaspora silences and excludes island-based literary production. Forbes remarks on how this process leads "'other' perspectives and 'other' identities articulated outside of the diasporic context (for instance, in fictions produced by writers at home) [to] often [be] ignored, unheard, or marginalized" (230).

17. A variety of critics have addressed the representation of slavery within the genre of historical fiction, primarily from the perspective of African American studies but also incorporating Caribbean literature: for example, Rushdy, Beaulieu, Handley, Mitchell, Sharpe, Keizer, Ryan, Halloran, and Plasa. From my own selection of authors, Cliff and James deal most explicitly with the historical legacy of slavery, but other noteworthy examples of Caribbean diasporic historical fiction include Phillips's *Cambridge*, Hopkinson's *The Salt Roads*, John's *Unburnable*, and Engle's *The Surrender Tree*.

1. Mixed Blessings

1. The 2010 earthquake in Haiti brought to light how contemporary representations of Haiti's poverty are disconnected from a history of US intervention. This type of decontextualization is challenged by films like *Poto Mitan*.

2. Walkowitz's "Location of Literature" contextualizes Phillips as a migrant writer by analyzing paratextual elements such as biographical descriptions accompanying Phillips's publications. She argues that *Dancing in the Dark* "display[s] the international history of African American and U.S. cultural

traditions" (541). For a comparative study of African American and Caribbean historical fiction, see Rody.

3. See Jay's *Global Matters* for a discussion of how Smith's novel depicts "the construction of new subjectivities in a postcolonial context in which the forces of globalization shape a bewilderingly complex form of 'Englishness' in multicultural London" (93).

4. Fischer's *Modernity Disavowed*, Paul Gilroy's *Black Atlantic*, and Trouillot's *Silencing the Past* are just a few of the critical works written about the marginalization of the Caribbean, and particularly Haiti, within histories of Western modernity.

5. See Dalleo's essay ("Independence") in *Cultural Critique* on how contemporary historical contexts like the US occupation of Haiti inform James's writing.

6. I'm thinking especially of abolitionist narratives like those of Mary Prince as well as of surrealist artists and writers like Wilfredo Lam and Aimé Césaire.

7. This contrasts with the aspirations of an earlier generation of Caribbean writers, including George Lamming and Derek Walcott, whose aim was to have their work placed with a "highbrow" publisher.

8. Self-consciousness emerges as a valuable form of positioning, even if or because it fails. Bongie asserts that his book "self-consciously fails" to resolve the "constitutive" tension between politics and memory (5). The "effort to work against the grain of [one's] inclinations" (16) is also popular among Caribbean diasporic writers, which speaks to the way such authors are intervening in the rhetorical debates within academia, particularly in postcolonial and multicultural studies.

9. I borrow this term from Keown, Murphy, and Proctor's introduction to *Comparing Postcolonial Diasporas*, which posits transcolonial comparativism as a mode of postcolonial analysis that focuses on "comparative links between empires" (1).

2. Kinship Routes

1. *Fruit of the Lemon* was published in 1999 by Headline Review, an imprint of Headline Book Publishing in Britain. Unlike this first edition, the 2007 US Picador version of the novel does not open with a family tree. The American reader instead encounters the first chart halfway through the novel, during "Coral's Story Told to Me by Coral." Although the nuclear family tree is absent, the American version reflects a journey of accumulated relations; the novel's Part II in Jamaica continues to build on the image presented by Coral's first oral history by expanding the tree chart, adding newly discovered family members.

2. Toplu interprets Faith's struggle in terms of a binary conflict: "the binary opposition of Faith's 'black' identity and her 'British' identity" (par. 7). Labeling this conflict as internal, Toplu sees it as expressing a "right to be treated like any other British-born citizen, irrespective of race or color" (par. 7). By contrast, I

argue that Faith's identity crisis is derived from precisely the color-blindness version of equality that veils the racist logic organizing British society.

3. I borrow hooks's term, which theorizes consumer culture and the exoticization of marginal cultures. I find particularly useful hooks's analysis of contemporary consumption practices within a context of imperialist desires.

4. Heterosexual intimacies remain on the margins of the novel since they go undepicted. Olivia's nakedness suggests a sexual encounter, while a squeezed knee references the implicit desire between Faith's brother Carl and his girlfriend (139). The "noises of sex coming from Marion's bedroom" (160) and Simon's absence from his room allude to an offstage sexual escapade that reinforces the violent trauma compelling Faith to isolate herself in her bedroom.

5. According to Glissant, errantry is "neither an arrowlike trajectory nor one that is circular or repetitive, nor is it mere wandering" (*Poetics of Relation* xvi). As a process of identity formation, errantry locates the subject "at every moment in relation to the other," in a web of community (xvi).

6. García's historical novel *Dreaming in Cuban* plots a similar trajectory for the protagonist and author-double, Pilar. See chap. 4 of Dalleo and Machado Sáez, *Latino/a Canon*, for an analysis of how consumer citizenship plays a role in this diasporic subject's return to the Caribbean island.

7. Carillo's *Loosing My Espanish* is another example of a novel that literalizes decontextualization by depicting a character with Alzheimer's.

8. Minto argues that Adele's "unraveling leads to [the narrator's] self-construction and his reconstruction of his family's history between Trinidad and Canada" (888), and Francis sees the novel "confront[ing] what Caribbean diasporic communities willfully forget in order to sustain themselves in metropolitan centers" (rev. of *Soucoyant* 76). See also Delisle, Coleman, Lee, and Roy.

9. Danticat's historical novel *The Farming of Bones* (1998) expresses a concern regarding reception and misinterpretation, particularly after Amabelle is beaten and unable to speak. The racist attack silences Amabelle, rendering her words "blurred and incomprehensible," and when her companions incorrectly interpret what Amabelle is trying to say, "they stopped listening" altogether, silencing her even further (199).

10. See Rinaldo Walcott for a discussion of Afro-Canadian writing and its (dis)engagement with African American popular culture.

11. Coleman argues that the narrator "tells the story of Adele's encounter with the soucouyant at the military base to his mother" in order to "assure her that he has long known the horrific story and that she need not carry its weight alone" (21–22). Delisle's interpretation of the narrator's relationship to Adele's memory is that, while burdensome, the son is a "suitable listener" who can successfully "restore [Adele's] self by reformulating that narrative" memory of the fire (3). I argue that the narrator tells the story *in order to* abandon his mother.

12. I disagree with Alonso Alonso's reading of the soucouyant folk tale as a "sign of repudiation" or a "process of familial and social ostracism through

which Adele and the whole society dehumanize this woman" (65). Adele's invocation of the soucouyant story does not fit in with the narrator's sense of how "professional knowers" objectify and dehumanize Others. Rather, Adele employs the soucouyant as a metaphor for the limits of her understanding, for the incomprehensibility of violence against her mother and herself, against Caribbean women and their bodies.

13. The narrator's relationship to tears, his inability to recognize his emotions to the extent that he abjects his own body, recalls the pattern of tears in Díaz's *Oscar Wao*. For both Chariandy's nameless narrator and Díaz's Oscar de León, tears are emasculating and mark these men as inauthentic within the dominant parameters of Caribbean diasporic masculinity.

3. Writing the Reader

1. J. M. Rodríguez's definition is useful for fleshing out the role that queerness plays in the market aesthetics of Caribbean diasporic historical fiction: "[Queerness] is a challenge to constructions of heteronormativity" and "creates an opportunity to call into question the systems of categorization that have served to define sexuality" (24).

2. In an interview, Danticat discusses one of Alvarez's rebuttals to this accusation of inauthenticity, "Doña Aida, with Your Permission," and affirms the hyphen as a space of belonging ("Immigrant Artist" 48).

3. The autobiographical novel *¡Yo!* was published in between *Butterflies* and *In the Name of Salomé*. Dalleo and I discuss how *¡Yo!* reflects on the creative struggles of a Latina writer in *Latino/a Canon*, chap. 5.

4. K. L. Johnson argues that the alternation between Camila's and Salomé's voices in the novel emphasizes their inability to connect as daughter and mother. She interprets the text's polyvocal structure as signaling a critique of hybridity as the foundation for Caribbean historiography and culture.

5. Camila's mother, Salomé, is also an author-double, a historical figure from the Caribbean nation-past who embodies the pressures and obstacles faced by contemporary Caribbean diasporic writers. The parallels between Salomé and Alvarez predict the turn Alvarez makes after writing this novel, moving from historical fiction into more supposedly "minor" genres, such as bilingual children's books and memoir. The public pressures on Salomé to be a public and political spokesperson for the nation stand in contrast to her uncomfortable encounter with a rag woman. This marginalized, homeless madwoman turns out to be an audience who can truly see Sálome's writerly desires but is an aspirational reader, someone that Salomé has no access to because of poverty, illiteracy, and even personal disgust. Salomé's training in the dominant conventions of society delimit her vision of her readership. A similar dynamic occurs in Cliff's novel between Clover and Scheherezade, but the lines between artist and audience are more blurred.

6. The student's family tree corroborates Marion's label as "best friend" (9).

7. Critics such as Rohrleitner, Socolovsky, and Erickson discuss Camila's romantic relationship with Marion but do not reference the classroom as a site where this romance originates.

8. E. Johnson argues that even as the novel's structural silences imply that the "whole tapestry [of history] can never be pieced together" (72), the "familial community Annie experiences amid the storytellers in the leper community" remains a positive model for how storytelling engenders belonging (71). Similarly, Issen contends that the leper colony storytelling symbolizes a "new kinship" that is "forged among people from different backgrounds who all try to end slavery" (185).

9. Lino Costa is the only critic who mentions Che Guevara as a contextual figure, although she does not draw any links between Guevara and the hologrammatical Malcolm X.

10. If the reader does not decode the hologrammatical man as Malcolm X, as often occurs when I teach the novel to undergraduates, then the reader is likely to categorize Pleasant as irrational and unstable—and not an authoritative historical subject.

11. W. Walters points out how the dialogue between Malcolm X and Pleasant forms part of the novel's "archive of conversations between historical figures" (520). By contrast, Dunick positions Malcolm X as "interruption" to the past encounter and present conversation between Pleasant and John Brown (47).

12. I wonder, for instance, if the Miss Carey of Pleasant's childhood is a historical figure, the same Mary Shadd Carey that Annie describes drafting forged papers (193).

13. Agosto argues that "Cliff uses Turner's painting to illustrate the commodification of the history of slavery" (31). The unveiling is concerned with the market for histories of slavery, perhaps speaking to the success of neo-slave narratives. I suggest that Cliff uses the painting to show how art's imperative to process violence is complicated by its audience, which is capable of nullifying or ignoring the artist's social critique. The audience's "ways of seeing" shape art's symbolic meaning as it circulates in the marketplace. W. Walters alludes to the effects that such reading lenses might have when she notes that "the (white) art historian attempts to put this 'thing' (the violent deeds of the Zong, its captain, owners, insurers) 'behind us' in an attempt to focus on form and color, indeed to aestheticize the painting and dehistoricize the parlor group's response to it" (518–19). Cliff uses the painting's unveiling to explore the critical silences and negative reception her novel will face in the market. W. Walters argues that "the white guests aestheticize the artwork in an attempt to ignore the bodies. [. . .] They are provided with a heroic, instead of a guilty, white identity" (520). I see the racialized reaction to the painting as a comment on the novel's reception as a text by a white Creole about slavery, expressing concern that it will simply reassure a white audience's privilege rather than indict their complicity with racist violence.

14. In *Create Dangerously*, Danticat discusses this "plea from the other side of the lens—a very rare moment when a poverty-stricken photography subject actually speaks—of the fear of being misread, mis-seen, and misunderstood" (145).

15. Elia states that "Cliff acknowledges [Annie] is her own fictional alter ego, and the two have many personal circumstances in common" (75), while Erica Johnson argues that "Annie is often read as a stand-in for Cliff herself" (62).

16. Homer invites Lilith a second time to attend the meetings and offers to continue her literacy lessons but is rejected. Lilith says that she does not need another mother, and when Homer indicates that it is not a maternal relationship that she seeks, Lilith reads Homer's invitation as a sexual proposition. Lilith shocks Homer by explicitly naming this queer desire: "You finger be the last thing me want in me pussy" (154). Female friendship is not an alternative imaginable to Lilith, as opposed to the only public dynamic available to Cliff's Clover and Alice.

17. See Fanon's essay "On National Culture," from *The Wretched of the Earth*.

18. See Gifford for a more in-depth analysis of how gender shapes the narrative project in James's novel.

4. Messy Intimacies

1. Clarke discusses the academic reception of Brand and criticizes literary critics for focusing on the politics espoused by the authors rather than the creative writing techniques. On the other hand, Dickinson analyzes the early reception of Brand in book reviews and its deployment of racist discourse.

2. The postcolonial period remains a setting distinct from the colonial or anticolonial periods, with the contemporary developments of globalization and decontextualization presenting different sets of problematics. See Flores's concept of the "lite-colonial" in *From Bomba*.

3. Francis's concept of antiromance expands the way critics conceive of how Caribbean women writers deploy romance. Francis is necessarily specific about the parameters of the antiromance genre, indicating that one of the themes that it rewrites is that of the bildungsroman, depicting "girlhood from an adult perspective without any hint of sentimentality" (*Fictions* 6). Although Menéndez, Brand, and Roffey are not revising the bildungsroman narrative, their work does share some elements with the antiromances that Francis describes, especially the attention to archival sources and the ambivalent representation of diasporic identity. The links between the postcolonial romances that I analyze and the antiromances that Francis describes point to some broader trends within Caribbean women's fiction.

4. Sims draws attention to the stylistic framing of Teresa's narrative, with each entry accompanied by the image of the "black, open fan whose shape usually associates it with imagination, change and femininity" (112).

5. I. Rodríguez highlights the tension between the individual and collective in androgynous descriptions of Guevara from anticolonial narratives. The utopic representation of Guevara rhetorically positions him as embodying "the convergence of the masculine, individual I with the collective subject representing the people" (50). A discursive ambivalence pervades this androgyny as a model subject for "the building of a new society" (61).

6. García's *Dreaming in Cuban* addresses matrilineal inheritance within the context of the Cuban Revolution. Pilar collects stories of her family from her grandmother Celia in what is depicted as an entirely positive, recuperative move that will allow Pilar to leave Cuba behind and become fully Cuban American. *Loving Che*, by contrast, depicts the intergenerational inheritance between a Cuban and a Cuban American in a much more ambiguous manner, highlighting the limits of intercultural communication. In chapter 4 of *The Latino/a Canon* (2007), Dalleo and I discuss how Pilar's decision to help Ivanito become a Marielito at the end of the novel fits into the politics of consumer citizenship in García's novel.

7. Alvarez Borland compares Menéndez's technique of integrating photographs into her novel with that of Cabrera Infante in *Vista al amanecer en el trópico* (1974).

8. At the beginning of the novel, the narrator of *Loving Che* defines relation or her community of belonging as entailing a totality of knowledge; by the end of the novel, the narrator defines relation by errantry.

9. For a discussion of how mainstream discourse defines US citizenship in terms of documentation and the implications of this for Latinidad, see Ontiveros.

10. As Delgadillo points out, the grandfather is the first to indicate that "there is more to be known, though it may not be known solely through an examination of documentary evidence" (607).

11. The narrator's personal history as a prior student of Dr. Caraballo and the awkward intimacy of their conversation recall my discussion of teacher-student encounters in chapter 3.

12. I disagree with Méndez Rodenas's interpretation that the "failure of the mother-daughter bond" translates into depicting "the revolution not as forward teleological progress, but as negation; the island as a place of imagination" (48). I argue that Cuba represents a real place for the narrator, since she travels there and encounters people like Judi, Caridad, and Manny. The teleology of revolution is also represented as progressive and forward moving because its anticolonial vocabulary continues to have more purchase than the dead end of the postcolonial present.

13. *Loving Che* supplements and complicates the "commodified nostalgia" that critics have analyzed in other works by Menéndez. Kadiyoti writes that nostalgia emerges in the short story collection *In Cuba I Was a German Shepherd* as a continuum that links exile and island Cubans: "Although in exile, the Cubans in Menéndez's story are in the same situation as the Cubans on the

island: on the wrong side of the fence, they and their well-known nostalgia for the past are on display for the 'foreign' (i.e. non-Cuban) tourists" (94). Nostalgia is assigned a negative value, since it upholds "the status quo" of the "pre-Castro island as paradise, without validating the real sense of loss that afflicts the displaced" (90–91).

14. Socolovsky makes an analogous case for the theme of longing in Menéndez's *In Cuba I Was a German Shepherd*, arguing that the "characters, in searching for their 'Cuban' voice, create one through longing for that voice and realizing that they may never attain it" ("Cuba Interrupted" 249). I supplement Socolovsky's point by contending that *Loving Che* identifies that longing with a nostalgia for anticolonialism and posits failure as a generative, creative force that defines the postcolonial Caribbean voice and diasporic identity.

15. I take issue with Quigley's interpretation of this scene as "Verlia's translation into territorial language [that] emphasizes cultural, embodied difference" (56). I find it particularly problematic that Quigley defines such difference in terms of ethnic stereotype, describing the curse by an anglophone Caribbean woman as "a voodoo-like marking of the face" (56). Brand's novel gives no indication that this curse has a religious valence, much less one associated with francophone Caribbean religious practices like vodoun. Also, Quigley's claim that Verlia is using "untranslatable sacred language" implies that her statements are somehow unintelligible. The conflict stems from Verlia's discomfort with her emotional reaction, as opposed to whether the policeman is able to translate her perfectly intelligible threat.

16. Manning's military spending is a relevant context for Roffey's visit to Trinidad in 2006, during which she interviewed her mother and began writing *The White Woman*. In 2011, Wikileaks published a 2006 US diplomatic cable that referred to the "much maligned" blimps of the People's National Movement (PNM) as "toys." For further information on this historical context, see Gibbings.

17. King notes that "portrayals of relationships between white women and Caribbean men of color represent the development of the Caribbean diaspora" in novels by Naipaul and Selvon (164). For the male characters, sexual intimacy with white women permits them to tentatively root themselves within Global North societies. By contrast, Roffey's novel depicts an interracial relationship within the Caribbean region but frames the relationship between Sabine and Eric Williams as imaginary and aspirational.

5. Dictating Diaspora

1. For critics who place Danticat and Díaz into conversation, see Irr and Mukherjee.

2. See González Echevarría's "The Dictatorship of Rhetoric/The Rhetoric of Dictatorship" from *Voices of the Masters* (1985), which discusses the figure of the author-dictator as a trend within postmodern Latin American literature.

3. Braziel and Mannur list scholars who see hybridity as "open[ing] diasporic subjectivity to a liminal, dialogic space wherein identity is negotiated" (5). Some of the critics they associate with this approach to hybridity are James Clifford, Paul Gilroy, and Kobena Mercer.

4. As Mahler points out, "Díaz promotes a writing that does not repress its own inherent violence but rather exposes it in order to disarm tyrannical power" (120). My aim is to show how Yunior embodies tyrannical power.

5. See Armendariz's article, whose title defines *Dew Breaker* as "A Case Study in Trauma Symptoms and the Recovery Process." See Collins for a critique of the trauma studies approach.

6. Walcott-Hackshaw argues that Danticat "establish[es] a parallel in the lives of Dany and Claude" because they both have "ambiguous feelings about their return," "are night talkers, people who speak their nightmares out loud," and return to "Haiti looking for answers about their families and themselves" (78). Despite these parallels, the novel does not elide the differences between these two men and the ways in which they recognize and do not recognize each other as part of the same diasporic community. See also Dash's essay on the intertextuality in "Night Talkers" as a dialogue with Dany Laferrière.

7. Patterson and Kelley offer a similar critique of celebratory definitions of diaspora by acknowledging how "one conception of diaspora renders the other invisible" (28). One case they give is how the US-centric lens of Paris as the locale of African American writers in exile renders invisible the presence of the intellectual community of black francophones in that same space, resulting in an "uncritical" and celebratory formulation of Harlem as the "black cultural capital" of the period (28). Patterson and Kelley argue that scholars should understand diaspora as both process and condition in order to develop an approach that analyzes overlapping diasporas that would otherwise be silenced.

8. In her response to Patterson and Kelley, Johnson-Odim notes, "Sometimes people share identity without sharing community" (52). I echo this understanding of conflicted community by arguing that even though Yunior and Oscar are both Dominican American men, the novel pits these US-born and immigrant characters against each other. Di Iorio Sandín, who focuses on the short story version of *Oscar Wao*, highlights the representation of "intra-Latino rivalry" in the homosocial tension between the Capitán and Oscar as they compete for Ybón's body ("Latino Scapegoat" 27). I expand upon her approach by discussing parallel tensions between Oscar and Yunior.

9. See Sommer's *Foundational Fictions* for a definition of this genre in relation to Latin American literature.

10. Reviewers and critics tend to see Yunior as just another character in the novel or cursorily mention Yunior's migration from *Drown*. Those who discuss Yunior as a character often limit themselves to his "tough-guy narration" (Hannan 66) or emphasize his relationships with other characters, for example, describing him as "Oscar's roommate" (Broun 21). Intertextuality is often a

parenthetical comment describing the narrator as a character "(who seems very much like the Yunior who appeared in some of Mr. Díaz's short stories)" (Kakutani, "Dominican Comedy") or as "(one of Díaz's narrators and a welcome holdover from *Drown*)" (Asim). Discussion of Yunior's intertextuality is limited to his name, which is taken as evidence that he is the brother of Rafa from *Drown*. While *Oscar Wao* does not explicitly identify its Yunior with those of *Drown*, Díaz's second short story collection, *This Is How You Lose Her*, returns to Rafa as the sibling context for the Dominican-born Yunior in *Drown*.

11. I am indebted to Flores for pointing out that the "most telling and severe divide among the Latino pan-ethnicity [is] the difference between immigrant and 'resident' minority Latinos" (*From Bomba* 197). Flores defines such difference in terms of "colonial status and class" (197).

12. A common trend in reviews of *Drown* is the affirmation of its presumed anthropological authenticity, enabling the reader to access the realities of downward mobility experienced in the murky depths of New Jersey. The 1997 paperback cover showcases blurbs that privilege the text's perceived realism, including its "searing snapshots" of poverty and its success in "captur[ing] the bleak peripheral existence of suburban people of color." The marketing of *Drown* figures poverty as the representative marker of Latinidad, with the collection providing presumably unmediated access to "real" Latinos.

13. The prevailing interpretation of Díaz's text is that the novel productively recenters marginalized subjectivities by privileging the diaspora over the nation. *Oscar Wao* is described as having a "Calibanian voice" (Perez 12) that "allows for an infinite exposure to difference" and "an ethics of love" (Perez 12, 99). The novel's representation of diasporic diversity is seen as challenging nation-state histories. The academic reception figures Díaz as undermining an isolationist and exceptionalist conception of US history by highlighting how it is intertwined with the fate of its Caribbean neighbors. The critical consensus also asserts that *Oscar Wao* counters the Dominican nation-state's influence on the diaspora by "reversing the power cliques" of Latin American and Caribbean dictatorship novels (Flores-Rodríguez 95) and introducing "Yunior [as] a narrative voice that diverges from that of the Trujillan model" (Hanna 504).

14. Yunior unveils himself as narrator on page 169 of the 335–page novel, at the halfway point of the text. Prior to this identification, the narrator employs twenty-one footnotes, whereas only eleven appear after Yunior is named.

15. Cox analyzes Díaz's use of "forensic," "epideictic," and "testimonial" modes in *Oscar Wao* as generating "coalition building" through "affective alliances" with the reading audience (110–11). I emphasize that such alliances also open up the possibility of the reader's complicity with Yunior's oppressive dictation.

16. Yunior reverses the equation from *The Matrix* (1999). In the film, Neo chooses the *red* pill to escape the Matrix; the blue pill reinstates the computer-generated reality.

17. Connor argues that Ysrael functions as Yunior's Other in *Drown*.

18. See King's discussion of Porfirio Rubirosa and the stereotype of the Latin Lover.

19. De Moya provides a relevant analysis of this Dominican model of sexuality as derived from a "totalitarian image of dominant masculinity" (73) that "produces intricate strategies (power games) for men to oppress other men" (98). The historical context for these power games is the Trujillo dictatorship, which "was shown as a theatre-state in which hegemonic masculinity (and its inversion) was the star" (98).

20. Yunior's dictation is motivated by homophobia, which Reddock identifies "as a policing force [. . .] monitoring and guiding boys and men's behavior that arises out of a male terror of being exposed as something other than heterosexual, as 'not a real man'" (xx).

21. Wood summarizes one of Sigmund Freud's stages of paranoia as "the Don Juan syndrome where homosexuality is denied by means of obsessive pursuit of women" (227). Yunior's "obsessive pursuit" is consistent in the novel, even humorous in its excesses, yet critical commentary has consistently rendered Yunior's sexuality as marginal to the story.

22. Prior critics have commented on the use of Spanish by Díaz as an oppositional or resistant writing technique. These passages from *Oscar Wao* illustrate that untranslated Spanish is not always-already a progressive strategy. The linguistic politics behind Spanish language use and translation in US Latino literature can be ambivalent or contradictory. For analyses of linguistic politics in Díaz's work, see Di Iorio Sandín, *Killing Spanish*; Arrieta; Schwartz; and Díaz, "Fiction."

23. Yunior's policing mirrors that of the state surveillance that Edelman describes as "reveal[ing] a scarcely suppressed desire to see, to recognize, and to expose the alterity of homosexuality and homosexual tendencies" (278). The policing of sexuality is tied to a desire to make the queer subject visible "and bespeaks a narcissistic anxiety about the definition of (sexual) identity that can only be stabilized and protected by a process of elimination or casting out" (278). Yunior's narrating of Oscar's honorable devirginization and death is an attempt to imagine closure to the sexual tension haunting Yunior.

24. López-Calvo states that the historical figures of dictatorship (Trujillo, Balaguer) are given nicknames by Díaz to ensure "that readers do not fall into the temptation of identifying with the tyrant" (80). I would add that the "alienation effect" produced by the depiction of political figures tempts the reader into an all-too-comfortable acceptance of Yunior's authority as dictator.

25. Flores's phrase "the diaspora strikes back" references the diaspora's claim to "full-scale membership in the national community" (*Diaspora Strikes Back* 4–5). Yunior articulates a diasporic response to the legacy of nationalism, while Oscar's migration from the United States to the Dominican Republic evokes the "unsettling and de-centering effect" that Flores identifies with the "remigrant" experience (5).

26. Danticat references Alvarez's *Something to Declare* in an interview as a model for how a writer wrestles with the accusation of cultural inauthenticity. Danticat adapts Alvarez's term of the hyphen to make the case that inauthenticity is "an immigrant's reality" ("Immigrant Artist" 48).

27. In an interview with Palmer Adisa, Danticat discusses how these stereotypes inflect the reading of her fiction: "A lot of readers facing my work have a load of stereotypes in mind. Some are willing to release them. Others are not. And I hate to say it, but some have them further reinforced by some of what I write. That's the complexity of the process" ("Up Close" 347).

28. The threat of intimacy depicted in terms of sharing personal stories with a public is a trope that repeats in many of the other historical novels I have discussed, for example, in *Fruit of the Lemon* with Faith's mother's warning not to "blab" about Faith's father's childhood and class upbringing.

29. Misrahi-Barak discusses the politics of orality and silence in Danticat's *Krik? Krak!* and *Dew Breaker*.

30. As Mullins points out, Danticat's novel not only depicts "specific historical instances of human rights violations, but also opens a metafictional reflection on the tasks charged to the literary imagination when fiction writers focus their attention on such violations" ("Labors" 8). My discussion of author-doubles consequently expands upon Mullins's argument about the metafictional elements of *Dew Breaker*.

31. Psychoanalytic approaches tend to focus on the depiction of fatherhood in *Dew Breaker*; for example, see Henton. Conwell also discusses how *Dew Breaker* develops "the father as metaphor for the historical relationship between the powerful and the powerless in Haiti" (221). She reviews the way that François Duvalier constructed himself as father of the Haitian nation. However, Conwell does not discuss the parallels between Michel's narration and the Duvaliers' speeches and as a result views him as an idealistic model for storytelling: "We understand that Michel possesses the strength of character to father justly and with self reflection" (235).

32. Irr notes that trauma in *Dew Breaker* is "always carefully filtered through the communications technologies of the modern state" (12). While she cites François Duvalier's speeches as an example of a "dictatorial use of the media" (13), Irr does not draw a parallel between Michel's use of a tape-recorded message for his son and the Duvalier media model.

33. Mukherjee defines *Dew Breaker* as a "collection of linked stories" (690), and Armendariz notes that most "critics have observed [that] what characterizes Danticat's collection most distinctly is the sense of disjunction and fragmentation" (34). The limitation of this perspective is that the focus on the novel's structural fragmentation often hinders the analysis of its chronological organization. The first chapter and final chapter are analyzed without a discussion of how the delay between the opening chapter of "The Book of the Dead" and the final chapter of "The Dew Breaker" entails a temporal shift from the present

into the past. Lawton de Torruella argues that the dew breaker renounces his anonymity and no longer hides behind his mask of victimization because Ka's sculpture has forced him out of his past and into the present. While the novel may open with the confrontation between the Ka's myth of her father and the dew breaker's revelation, the emplotment does not continue into the present to see the consequences of this confrontation for the dew breaker. Rather, the chronology leads us further into the past, into the secret's origins. The first chapter's revelation encourages readers to align themselves with Ka in terms of their ignorance of the father's past, so that the journey is more about traveling into the past than about confronting the consequences of that past in the present.

34. Braziel provides a detailed historical context for "The Book of Miracles," arguing that it "connects acts of terror [. . .] during the Duvalierist regime with similar acts of violence during the post-Duvalier period" (157).

35. The phonetic similarities between Danticat and "Kaka" allude to the MFA market context of the author's classroom experiences, which include teaching creative writing at New York University and the University of Miami.

36. The novel does not depict the final performance of the "Brother Timonie" song as "a clear sign that they have completed quite successfully the first part of the trauma process" (Armendariz 43). The foreclosure of Freda's artistic career is a form of trauma.

Conclusion

1. The invisible materiality of a physical infrastructure supports the Internet's vast communications network. Meanwhile, the complexities of net neutrality foreground another difficulty, with Internet service providers lobbying for the ability to create differentiated access to the Internet, charging more for faster access, which will obviously exacerbate the digital strata of privilege.

2. I refer to the website manager by her first name in order to respect the anonymity she maintains on the website. I first contacted Kim in August 2013, using the contact e-mail listed on *The Annotated Oscar Wao* site. Since the website did not explicitly list a set of contributors, I wanted to determine whether the digital project was the work of one individual or a group. As part of my e-mail exchange with Kim, I sent her a set of interview questions, and this chapter cites her responses.

3. For Kim, the work of researching and translating the references in *Oscar Wao* pales in comparison to the labor of creating the website for sharing these annotations. As a result, the individual labor of collating information from different sources rationalizes the work of creating an open-source site: "I figured I would put it up so everyone else could use it. If I was going to go through all the work of tracking down (most of) these references, writing them down and publishing them wasn't much extra work after that part" ("Re: Interview Request" [17 Oct. 2013]).

4. See Díaz, "Fiction," for an interview in which he articulates the linguistic politics of not translating Spanish into English for the reader.

5. The comments by Antoni that I cite in this section were given during the Q&A following his reading at Florida Atlantic University on September 13, 2013.

6. Thanks to Matthew Parker for his notes from Antoni's reading at Florida Atlantic University, which helped me verify my recollection of the writer's declarations on the promise of the Internet.

7. The historical persona of Etzler did write a play criticizing planter society, but Antoni provides us with only a fictionalized version online.

8. Kelly Josephs taught a Spring 2014 graduate course at the CUNY Graduate Center on the "Digital Caribbean," which produced the blog postings on *CUNY Academic Commons* ("Introduction"). Since I accessed the blog commentary via Google and the classroom context was not directly acknowledged by the posts, I contacted Josephs via e-mail on June 2, 2014, to see if she knew who had generated the posts. Josephs was kind enough to provide me with her course syllabus and a description of the blog post assignment, but she was unaware that the posts could be disconnected from the course content, or rather, read without accessing the relevant online course description and materials. As she noted, "The *CUNY Academic Commons* is a large conglomerate and this is just one site within it" ("Re: CUNY Academic Commons," 2 June 2014). Our academic exchange speaks to how classwork may circulate digitally in ways that we as teachers might not imagine, namely, decontextualized from the pedagogical frame that produced that work.

9. See Moretti's distinction of close versus distant reading from *Graphs, Maps, Trees* (2007). For an illustration of how this approach might be productively engaged, see Finn.

Bibliography

Acker, Jennifer. Rev. of *In the Name of Salomé*, by Julia Alvarez. *Hopscotch* 2.4 (2001): 168–69.

Agard-Jones, Vanessa. "What the Sands Remember." *GLQ* 18.2–3 (2012): 325–46.

Agosto, Noraida. *Michelle Cliff's Novels: Piecing the Tapestry of Memory and History*. New York: Peter Lang, 1999.

Allen, Austin. "Junot Díaz: *The Brief Wondrous Life of Oscar Wao* (Excerpt)." *Poetry Genius* Aug. 2013. Web. Accessed 1 Sept. 2013. http://poetry.rap-genius.com/Junot-diaz-the-brief-wondrous-life-of-oscar-wao-excerpt-lyrics.

Alonso Alonso, María. "Marvelous Realism and Female Representation from the Caribbean Diaspora." *Journal of Commonwealth Literature* 47.1 (2012): 59–71.

Alvarez, Julia. *In the Name of Salomé*. Chapel Hill, NC: Algonquin Books, 2000.

———. *In the Time of the Butterflies*. Chapel Hill, NC: Algonquin Books, 1994.

———. *Saving the World*. Chapel Hill, NC: Algonquin Books, 2006.

———. *¡Yo!* Chapel Hill, NC: Algonquin Books, 1997.

Alvarez Borland, Isabel. "Figures of Identity: Ana Menéndez's and Guillermo Cabrera Infante's Photographs." *Cuban-American Literature and Art: Negotiating Identities*. Ed. Isabel Alvarez Borland and Lynette M. F. Bosch. Albany: SUNY P, 2009. 31–45.

[Anonymoussssssssssssssss] [*sic*]. "Definition of Whatless." *Urban Dictionary*. Posted 19 Mar. 2008. Web. Accessed 2 June 2014. http://www.urbandiction-ary.com/define.php?term=whatless.

Antoni, Robert. *As Flies to Whatless Boys*. New York: Akashic Books, 2013.

———. *As Flies to Whatless Boys: Appendix*. Created Sept 2013. Web. Accessed 1 Sept. 2013. http://whatlessboys.com.

———. Q&A session after reading of *As Flies to Whatless Boys*. Florida Atlantic U. Boca Raton, FL. 13 Sept. 2013.

Aparicio, Frances. "Latino Cultural Studies." Interview by Juan Zevallos Aguilar. *Critical Latin American and Latino Studies*. Ed. Juan Poblete. Minneapolis: U of Minnesota P, 2003.

Appadurai, Arjun. *Modernity at Large: Cultural Dimensions of Globalization*. Minneapolis: U of Minnesota P, 1996.

Arac, Jonathan. "Huckleberry Finn as Idol and Target." 1997. *The Adventures of Huckleberry Finn*. 2nd ed. New York: Bedford/St. Martin's, 2003. 435–56. Case Study in Critical Controversy Series.

Arana, R. Victoria. "Sea Change: Historicizing the Scholarly Study of Black British Writing." *Black British Writing*. Ed. R. Victoria Arana and Lauri Ramey. New York: Palgrave-Macmillan, 2004. 19–45.

Armendariz, Aitor Ibarrola. "The Language of Wounds and Scars in Edwidge Danticat's *The Dew Breaker*, a Case Study in Trauma Symptoms and the Recovery Process." *Journal of English Studies* 8.3 (2010): 23–56.

Arrieta, Daniel. "El Spanglish en la obra de Junot Díaz: Instrucciones de uso." *Hispánica* 53 (2009): 105–26.

Asim, Jabari. "It's a Wonderful Life: An Overweight 'Ghetto Nerd' Struggles to Find Love and a Place to Call Home." Rev. of *The Brief Wondrous Life of Oscar Wao*, by Junot Díaz. *Washington Post* 30 Sept. 2007. WBK 3.

"August Frost. (Fiction)." Rev. of *August Frost*, by Monique Roffey. *Publishers Weekly* 3 Mar. 2003: 55.

Beaulieu, Elizabeth. *Black Women Writers and the American Neo-slave Narrative: Femininity Unfettered*. Westport, CT: Greenwood, 1999.

Berry, David M. "Introduction: Understanding the Digital Humanities." *Understanding Digital Humanities*. Ed. David M. Berry. New York: Palgrave-Macmillan, 2012. 1–20.

Bhabha, Homi K. "Global Minoritarian Culture." *Shades of the Planet: American Literature as World Literature*. Ed. Wai Chee Dimock and Lawrence Buell. Princeton, NJ: Princeton UP, 2007.

Birkett, Mary F. Rev. of *Earth Magic*, by Dionne Brand. *School Library Journal* 27.3 (1980): 83.

Bissoondath, Neil. *Selling Illusions: The Cult of Multiculturalism in Canada*. Toronto, ON: Penguin, 1994.

Blake, Robin. Rev. of *Every Light in the House Burnin'*, by Andrea Levy. *Independent* 19 Feb. 1995. 37.

Bolick, Kate. "Books in Brief: Fiction." Rev. of *August Frost*, by Monique Roffey. *New York Times Book Review* 6 Apr. 2003: 24.

Bongie, Chris. *Friends and Enemies: The Scribal Politics of Post/Colonial Literature*. Liverpool: Liverpool UP, 2008.

Bost, Suzanne. "Creoles and Color." *Mulattas and Mestizas: Representing Mixed Identities in the Americas 1850–2000*. Athens: U of Georgia P, 2003. 88–129.

Boyce Davies, Carole. *Black Women, Writing and Identity: Migrations of the Subject*. New York: Routledge, 1994.

Brand, Dionne. *In Another Place, Not Here.* New York: Grove, 1997.

Braziel, Jana Evans. "Diasporic Disciplining of Caliban? Haiti, the Dominican Republic, and Intra-Caribbean Politics." *Small Axe* 12.2 (2008): 149–59.

Braziel, Jana Evans, and Anita Mannur, eds. *Theorizing Diaspora: A Reader.* Malden, MA: Blackwell, 2003.

Brennan, Timothy. "The National Longing for Form." *Nation and Narration.* Ed. Homi K. Bhabha. London: Routledge, 1990. 44–70.

———. "Postcolonial Studies and Globalization Theory." *The Postcolonial and the Global.* Ed. Revathi Krishnaswamy and John C. Hawley. Minneapolis: U of Minnesota P, 2008. 37–53.

Brickhouse, Anna. *Transamerican Literary Relations and the Nineteenth-Century Public Sphere.* Cambridge, UK: Cambridge UP, 2004.

Brouillette, Sarah. *Postcolonial Writers in the Global Literary Marketplace.* New York: Palgrave-Macmillan, 2007.

Broun, Bill. "Romance Out of Reach." Rev. of *The Brief Wondrous Life of Oscar Wao,* by Junot Díaz. *Times Literary Supplement* 1 Feb. 2008: 21.

Brown, J. Dillon. *Migrant Modernism: Postwar London and the West Indian Novel.* Charlottesville: U of Virginia P, 2013.

Caminero-Santangelo, Marta, and Roy C. Boland Osegueda, eds. *Trujillo, Trauma, Testimony: Mario Vargas Llosa, Julia Alvarez, Edwidge Danticat, Junot Díaz and Other Writers in Hispaniola.* Spec. issue of *Antípodas* 20 (2009).

Campbell, Christian. "Sidney Poitier Studies." *Running the Dusk.* Leeds: Peepal Tree, 2010. 27.

Carillo, H. G. *Loosing My Espanish.* 2004. New York: Anchor Books, 2005.

Carter, Dawn. Rev. of *Another Place, Not Here,* by Dionne Brand. *Women and Environments* 41 (1997): 24.

Chancy, Myriam J. A. "Exile, Resistance, Home: Retelling History in the Writings of Michelle Cliff and Marie Chauvet." *Searching for Safe Spaces: Afro-Caribbean Women Writers in Exile.* Philadelphia: Temple UP, 1997. 166–212.

Chariandy, David. "'The Fiction of Belonging': On Second-Generation Black Writing in Canada." *Callaloo* 30.3 (2007): 818–29.

———. *Soucouyant: A Novel of Forgetting.* Vancouver, BC: Arsenal Pulp, 2007.

Clarke, George Elliott. "Harris, Philip, Brand: Three Authors in Search of Literate Criticism." *Journal of Canadian Studies* 35.1 (2000): 161–89.

Cliff, Michelle. *Abeng.* New York: Dutton, 1985.

———. *Free Enterprise.* 1993. San Francisco: City Lights Books, 2004.

———. *If I Could Write This in Fire.* Minneapolis: U of Minnesota P, 2008.

———. "An Interview with Michelle Cliff." Interview by Meryl F. Schwartz. *Contemporary Literature* 34.4 (Winter 1993): 595–619. Rpt. in *Contemporary Literary Criticism.* Eds. Jeffrey W. Hunter and Timothy J. White. Vol. 120. Detroit, MI: Gale Group, 1999. 595–619.

———. *No Telephone to Heaven*. New York: Dutton, 1987.

Cohen, Daniel J. "Digital History: The Raw and the Cooked." *Rethinking History* 8.2 (2004): 337–40.

Coleman, Daniel. "Epistemological Cross-Talk: Melancholia, Historical Trauma, and Spiritual Cosmology." Sept. 2008. U of Manitoba, Centre for Globalization and Cultural Studies. Web. Accessed 8 Feb. 2012. http://myuminfo.umanitoba.ca/Documents/i2092/ColemanEpistemologicalCrosstalkSept08.pdf.

Collins, Jo. "The Ethics and Aesthetics of Representing Trauma: The Textual Politics of Edwidge Danticat's *The Dew Breaker*." *Journal of Postcolonial Writing* 47.1 (2011): 5–17.

Connor, Anne. "Desenmascarando a Ysrael: The Disfigured Face as Symbol of Identity in Three Latino Texts." *Cincinnati Romance Review* 21 (2002): 148–62.

Conwell, Joan. "Papa's Masks: Roles of the Father in Danticat's *The Dew Breaker*." *Obsidian III: Literature in the African Diaspora* 6.2/7.1 (2005–6): 221–39.

Corrigan, Maureen. "A Quaint, Compelling 'Pilgrim' Tale in the New World." *Fresh Air*. National Public Radio. WLRN, n.p. 16 Nov. 2011. Radio. http://www.npr.org/2011/11/16/142348786/a-quaint-compelling-pilgrim-tale-in-the-new-world.

Cox, Sandra. "The Trujillato and Testimonial Fiction: Collective Memory, Cultural Trauma and National Identity in Edwidge Danticat's *The Farming of Bones* and Junot Díaz's *The Brief Wondrous Life of Oscar Wao*." Caminero-Santangelo and Osegueda 107–26.

Crampton, Robert. "England's White, Unpleasant Land." Rev. of *Never Far from Nowhere*, by Andrea Levy. *Times* 10 Feb. 1996. WE/13.

Cruz, Angie. *Let It Rain Coffee*. New York: Simon and Schuster, 2005.

Dalleo, Raphael. "'The Independence So Hardly Won Has Been Maintained': C. L. R. James and the U.S. Occupation of Haiti." *Cultural Critique* 87 (Spring 2014): 38–59.

———. "Post-Grenada, Post-Cuba, Postcolonial: Rethinking Revolutionary Discourse in Dionne Brand's *In Another Place, Not Here*." *Interventions: International Journal of Postcolonial Studies* 12.1 (2010): 64–73.

Dalleo, Raphael, and Elena Machado Sáez. "The Formation of a Latino/a Canon." *Routledge Companion to Latino/a Literature*. Ed. Frances Aparicio and Suzanne Bost. New York: Routledge, 2013.

———. *The Latino/a Canon and the Emergence of Post-Sixties Literature*. New York: Palgrave-Macmillan, 2007.

Danticat, Edwidge. *Breath, Eyes, Memory*. 1994. New York: Vintage, 1998.

———. *Create Dangerously: The Immigrant Artist at Work*. Princeton, NJ: Princeton UP, 2010.

———. *The Dew Breaker*. New York: Random House, 2004.

——. *The Farming of Bones.* 1998. New York: Penguin, 1999.

——. "An Immigrant Artist at Work: A Conversation with Edwidge Danticat." Interview by Elvira Pulitano. *Small Axe* 15.3 (2011): 39–61.

——. *Krik? Krak!* New York: Vintage, 1996.

——. "MacArthur Fellows, Meet the Class of 2009: Edwidge Danticat." Video. MacArthur Foundation. 26 Jan. 2009. Web. Accessed 20 Mar. 2013. http://www.macfound.org/fellows/49/.

——. "Up Close and Personal: Edwidge Danticat on Haitian Identity and the Writer's Life." Interview by Opal Palmer Adisa. *African American Review* 43.2–3 (2009): 345–55.

Dash, Michael J. "Fictions of Displacement: Locating Modern Haitian Narratives." *Small Axe* 12.3 (2008): 32–41.

Dávila, Arlene. *Latinos Inc. : The Marketing and Making of a People.* Berkeley: U of California P, 2001.

Dawson, Ashley. *Mongrel Nation: Diasporic Culture and the Making of Postcolonial Britain.* Ann Arbor: U of Michigan P, 2007.

Delgadillo, Theresa. "The Criticality of Latino/a Fiction in the Twenty-First Century." *American Literary History* 23.3 (2011): 600–624.

Delisle, Jennifer Bowering. "'A Bruise Still Tender': David Chariandy's *Soucouyant* and Cultural Memory." *Ariel* 41.2 (2010): 1–21.

De Moya, E. Antonio. "Power Games and Totalitarian Masculinity in the Dominican Republic." *Interrogating Caribbean Masculinities: Theoretical and Empirical Analyses.* Ed. Rhoda E. Reddock. Kingston: U of the West Indies P, 2004. 68–102.

Díaz, Junot. *The Brief Wondrous Life of Oscar Wao.* New York: Penguin, 2007.

——. "Broken Hearts That Span Time and Borders." Interview by Alden Mudge. *BookPage* Sept. 2012: 14–15.

——. "In Darkness We Meet: A Conversation with Junot Díaz." Interview by David Shook and Armando Celayo. *World Literature Today* 82.1 (2008): 12–17.

——. *Drown.* 1996. New York: Riverhead, 1997.

——. "Fiction Is the Poor Man's Cinema: An Interview with Junot Díaz." Interview by Diogenes Céspedes and Silvio Torres-Saillant. *Callaloo: A Journal of African-American and African Arts and Letters* 23.3 (2000): 892–907.

——. "Junot Díaz, Diaspora, and Redemption: Creating Progressive Imaginaries." Interview by Katherine Miranda. *Sargasso* 2 (2008–9): 23–40.

——. "Junot Díaz: 'Orson Scott Card Is a Cretinous Fool.'" Interview by Jacob Sugarman. *Salon.com.* 17 Sept. 2013. Web.

——. "Junot Díaz Aims to Fulfill His Dream of Publishing Sci-Fi Novel with Monstro." Interview by *Geek's Guide to the Galaxy. Wired* 3 Oct. 2012. Web. Accessed 20 Mar. 2013. http://www.wired.com/underwire/2012/10/geeks-guide-junot-diaz/.

————. "MacArthur Fellows, Meet the Class of 2012: Junot Díaz." Video. MacArthur Foundation. 2 Oct. 2012. Web. http://www.macfound.org/fellows/864/.

————. "Questions for Junot Díaz." Interview by Meghan O'Rourke. *Slate*. 8 Nov. 2007. Web. Accessed 8 Apr. 2008.

————. *This Is How You Lose Her*. New York: Riverhead, 2012.

Dickinson, Peter. "'In Another Place, Not Here': Dionne Brand's Politics of (Dis) Location." *Painting the Maple: Essays on Race, Gender, and the Construction of Canada*. Ed. Veronica Strong-Bong, Sherrill Grace, Avigail Eisenberg, and Joan Anderson. Vancouver, BC: U of British Columbia P, 1998. 113–29.

Digital Library of the Caribbean (dLOC). Web. Accessed 14 Dec. 2013. http://www.dloc.com.

Di Iorio Sandín, Lyn. *Killing Spanish: Literary Essays on Ambivalent U S. Latino/a Identity*. New York: Palgrave-Macmillan, 2004.

————. "The Latino Scapegoat: Knowledge through Death in Short Stories by Joyce Carol Oates and Junot Díaz." *Contemporary U.S. Latino/a Literary Criticism*. Ed. Lyn Di Iorio Sandín and Richard Perez. New York: Palgrave-Macmillan, 2007. 15–34.

Dobson, Kit. "Writing across the Borders." *Canadian Literature* 197 (2008): 164–66.

Dunick, Lisa. "The Dialogic of Diaspora: Michelle Cliff's *Free Enterprise*, Glissant, and the History of Slavery in the New World." *CEA Critic* 72.2 (2010): 37–51.

Dyson, Michael Eric. *April 4, 1968: Martin Luther King, Jr.'s Death and How It Changed America*. New York: Basic Civitas Books, 2008.

————. *Can You Hear Me Now? The Inspiration, Wisdom, and Insight of Michael Eric Dyson*. 2009. New York: Basic Civitas Books, 2011.

Edelman, Lee. "Tearooms and Sympathy, or The Epistemology of the Water Closet." *Nationalisms and Sexualities*. Ed. Andrew Parker, Mary Russo, Doris Sommer, and Patricia Yaeger. New York: Routledge, 1992. 263–84.

Eder, Richard. "Baying at a Havana Moon: Stories about Cuban Exiles 90 Miles Apart." Rev. of *In Cuba I Was a German Shepherd*, by Ana Menéndez. *New York Times Book Review* 24 June 2001: 14.

Edmondson, Belinda. *Caribbean Middlebrow: Leisure Culture and the Middle Class*. Ithaca, NY: Cornell UP, 2009.

Elia, Nada. "'The Memories of Old Women': Alternative History in Michelle Cliff's *No Telephone to Heaven* and *Free Enterprise*." *Trances, Dances, and Vociferations: Agency and Resistance in Africana Women's Narratives*. New York: Garland, 2001. 43–79.

Engle, Margarita. *The Surrender Tree*. New York: Henry Holt, 2008.

Erickson, Leslie Goss. "The Search for Self: Everyday Heroes and an Integral Re-visioning of the Heroic Journey in Postmodern Literature and Popular Culture." Diss. U of Nebraska, 2004. *Proquest Dissertations and Theses*. Web. Accessed 1 Apr. 2013.

Fanon, Frantz. "On National Culture." 1963. Trans. Richard Philcox. *The Wretched of the Earth*. New York: Grove, 2004.

Finn, Ed. "Revenge of the Nerd: Junot Díaz and the Networks of American Literary Imagination." *DHQ: Digital Humanities Quarterly* 7.1 (2013).

Fischer, Sibylle. *Modernity Disavowed: Haiti and the Cultures of Slavery in the Age of Revolution*. Durham, NC: Duke UP, 2004.

Flores, Juan. *The Diaspora Strikes Back: Caribeño Tales of Learning and Turning*. New York: Routledge, 2008.

———. *From Bomba to Hip-Hop: Puerto Rican Culture and Latino Identity*. New York: Columbia UP, 2000.

Flores-Rodríguez, Danalí. "Addressing Fukú in Us: Junot Díaz and the New Novel of Dictatorship." Caminero-Santangelo and Osegueda 91–106.

Forbes, Curdella. *From Nation to Diaspora: Samuel Selvon, George Lamming and the Cultural Performance of Gender*. Kingston: U of the West Indies P, 2005.

Foster, Aisling. "On Being British." Rev. of *Every Light in the House Burnin'*, by Andrea Levy. *Independent* 27 Nov. 1994: 38.

Francis, Donette. *Fictions of Feminine Citizenship: Sexuality and the Nation in Contemporary Caribbean Literature*. New York: Palgrave-Macmillan, 2010.

———. Review of *Soucouyant: A Novel of Forgetting*, by David Chariandy. *Journal of West Indian Literature* 17.1 (2008): 76–79.

Fraser, Kaya. "Language to Light On: Dionne Brand and the Rebellious Word." *Studies in Canadian Literature* 30.1 (2005): 291–308.

Fraser, Robert. *Book History through Postcolonial Eyes: Rewriting the Script*. New York: Routledge, 2008.

Freire, Paulo. "The 'Banking' Concept of Education." 1970. *Falling into Theory: Conflicting Views on Reading Literature*. Ed. David H. Richter and Gerald Graff. New York: Bedford/St. Martin's, 1999. 68–78.

García, Cristina. *Dreaming in Cuban*. New York: Random House, 1992.

———. *Monkey Hunting*. New York: Ballantine, 2003.

George, Jamal. "As 'Links' to Whatless Boys." Weblog Comment. Digital Caribbean Commons. *CUNY Academic Commons*. 29 Apr. 2014. Web. Accessed 25 May 2014. http://digitalcaribbean.commons.gc.cuny.edu/2014/04/29/as-links-to-whatless-boys/.

———. "The Richest Literary Experience for the iPad Friendly Reading Age." Weblog Comment. Digital Caribbean Commons. *CUNY Academic Commons*. 3 May 2014. Web. Accessed 25 May 2014. http://digitalcaribbean.commons.gc.cuny.edu/2014/04/30/therichest-literary-experience-for-the-ipad-friendly-reading-age/.

Gibbings, Wesley. "Blimp and Attack Helicopters 'Toys.'" *Trinidad Guardian* 4 Sept. 2011. Web. Accessed 28 Nov. 2011. http://www.guardian.co.tt/news/2011/09/04/blimp-and-attack-helicopters-toys.

Gifford, Sheryl. "(Re)Making Men, Representing the Caribbean Nation:

Individuation in the Works of Fred D'Aguiar, Robert Antoni, and Marlon James." Diss. Florida Atlantic U, 2013. Print.

Gikandi, Simon. "Postcolonialism's Ethical (Re)Turn: An Interview with Simon Gikandi." Interview by David Jefferess. *Postcolonial Text* 2.1 (2006). Web. Accessed 5 Mar. 2012. http://postcolonial.org/index.php/pct/article/view/464/845.

Gilroy, Beryl. *Inkle and Yarico.* Leeds: Peepal Tree, 1996.

Gilroy, Paul. *The Black Atlantic: Modernity and Double-Consciousness.* Cambridge, MA: Harvard UP, 1993.

———. "'My Britain Is Fuck All': Zombie Multiculturalism and the Race Politics of Citizenship." *Identities: Global Studies in Culture and Power* 19.4 (2012): 380–97.

Glissant, Édouard. *Caribbean Discourse.* 1981. Trans. J. Michael Dash. Charlottesville: UP of Virginia, 1989.

———. *Poetics of Relation.* Trans. Betsy Wing. Ann Arbor: U of Michigan P, 1997.

González Echevarría, Roberto. "Sisters in Death: A Novel about Three Women Whose Resistance to Trujillo Cost Them Their Lives." Rev. of *In the Time of the Butterflies,* by Julia Alvarez. *New York Times Book Review* 18 Dec. 1994: BR28.

———. *The Voice of the Masters: Writing and Authority in Modern Latin American Literature.* Austin: U of Texas P, 1985.

Gui, Weihsin. "Post-Heritage Narratives: Migrancy and Traveling Theory in V. S. Naipaul's *The Enigma of Arrival* and Andrea Levy's *Fruit of the Lemon.*" *Journal of Commonwealth Literature* 47.1 (2012): 73–89.

Hall, Stuart. "Cultural Identity and Diaspora." *Identity: Community, Culture, Difference.* Ed. Jonathan Rutherford. London: Lawrence and Wishart, 1990. 222–37.

Halloran, Vivian Nun. *Exhibiting Slavery: The Caribbean Postmodern Novel as Museum.* Charlottesville: U of Virginia P, 2009.

Hamill, María Cristina. "Exorcising Caribbean Ghosts: The Family, the Hero, and the Plantation in Julia Alvarez's *Saving the World, In the Name of Salomé* and Maryse Condé's *Tree of Life, I, Tituba, Black Witch of Salem.*" Diss. U of Michigan, 2007. *Proquest Dissertations and Theses.* Web. Accessed 1 April 2013.

Handley, George. *Postslavery Literature in the Americas: Family Portraits in Black and White.* Charlottesville: U of Virginia P, 2000.

Hanna, Monica. "'Reassembling the Fragments': Battling Historiographies, Caribbean Discourse, and Nerd Genres in Junot Díaz's *The Brief Wondrous Life of Oscar Wao.*" *Callaloo* 33.2 (2010): 498–520.

Hannan, Jim. Rev. of *The Brief Wondrous Life of Oscar Wao,* by Junot Díaz. *World Literature Today* 82.2 (2008): 65–66.

Henighan, Stephen. *When Words Deny the World: The Reshaping of Canadian Writing*. Erin, ON: Porcupine's Quill, 2002.

Henriquez, Maribi. "The Richest Literary Experience for the iPad Friendly Reading Age." Digital Caribbean Commons. *CUNY Academic Commons*. 30 Apr. 2014. Web. Accessed 25 May 2014. http://digitalcaribbean.commons.gc.cuny.edu/2014/04/30/therichest-literary-experience-for-the-ipad-friendly-reading-age/.

Henton, Jennifer. "Danticat's *The Dew Breaker*, Haiti, and Symbolic Migration." *CLC Web* 12.2 (2010). Web. Accessed 18 Apr. 2011. http://dx.doi.org/10.7771/1481–4374.1601.

Hickman, Trenton. "Hagiographic Commemorafiction in Julia Alvarez's *In the Time of the Butterflies* and *In the Name of Salome*." *MELUS* 31.1 (2006): 99–121.

Holloway, Karla F. C. *BookMarks: Reading in Black and White*. Piscataway, NJ: Rutgers UP, 2008.

hooks, bell. *Black Looks: Race and Representation*. Boston: South End, 1992.

Hopkinson, Nalo. *The Salt Roads*. New York: Warner Books, 2004.

Huggan, Graham. *The Postcolonial Exotic*. London: Routledge, 2001.

Hutcheon, Linda. *A Poetics of Postmodernism: History, Theory, Fiction*. London: Routledge, 1988.

Ilmonen, Kaisa. "Creolizing the Queer: Close Encounters of Race and Sexuality in the Novels of Michelle Cliff." Ed. Roy Goldblatt, Jopi Nyman, and John A. Stotesbury. *Close Encounters of an Other Kind: New Perspectives on Race, Ethnicity, and American Studies*. Joensuu, Finland: U of Joensuu P, 2005. 180–95.

Innes, C. L. *A History of Black and Asian Writing in Britain*. Cambridge, UK: Cambridge UP, 2003.

Irr, Caren. "Media and Migration: Danticat, Díaz, Eugenides, and Scibona." *Wretched Refuge: Immigrants and Itinerants in the Postmodern*. Ed. Jessica Datema and Diane Krumrey. Newcastle on Tyne: Cambridge Scholars, 2010. 9–26.

Issen, Laura Michelle. "Expressions of Socioeconomic and Cultural Complexities in Works by Derek Walcott, Jamaica Kincaid, and Michelle Cliff." Diss. U of Texas at Austin, 2000. *Proquest Dissertations and Theses*. Web. Accessed 1 April 2013.

James, C. L. R. *The Black Jacobins: Toussaint L'Ouverture and the San Domingo Revolution*. Rev. ed. New York: Vintage, 1989.

James, Marlon. *The Book of Night Women*. New York: Penguin, 2009.

———. "Is We Stoopid?" *Marlon James, Among Other Things*. 7 Aug. 2008. Web. Accessed 14 June 2012. http://marlon-james.blogspot.com/2008/08/is-we-stoopid.html/.

———. *John Crow's Devil*. New York: Akashic Books, 2005.

Jauss, Hans Robert. "The Identity of the Poetic Text in the Changing Horizon of

Understanding." *Reception Study: From Literary Theory to Cultural Studies.* Ed. James L. Machor and Philip Goldstein. New York: Routledge, 2001. 7–28.

Jay, Paul. *Global Matters: The Transnational Turn in Literary Studies.* Ithaca, NY: Cornell UP, 2010.

John, Marie-Elena. *Unburnable.* New York: Amistad, 2006.

Johnson, Erica L. "Memorializing the Ghost in *Free Enterprise.*" *Caribbean Ghostwriting.* Madison, NJ: Fairleigh Dickinson UP, 2009. 44–78.

Johnson, Kelli Lyon. "'The Terrible Moral Disinheritance of Exile': Asymptosy and Dis-integration in Julia Álvarez's *In the Name of Salomé.*" *Journal of Caribbean Literatures* 4.1 (2005): 149–62.

Johnson-Odim, Cheryl. "Unfinished Migrations: Commentary and Response." *African Studies Review* 43.1 (2000): 51–53.

Josephs, Kelly. *Introduction: The Digital Caribbean Course.* Digital Caribbean Commons. CUNY Academic Commons. Feb. 2014. Web. Accessed 2 June 2014. http://digitalcaribbean.commons.gc.cuny.edu/2014/02/02/introduction-the-digital-caribbean-course/.

———. "RE: CUNY Academic Commons: Robert Antoni." Message to the author. Sent 2 June 2014. E-mail.

Juan-Navarro, Santiago. *Archival Reflections: Postmodern Fiction of the Americas.* Lewisburg, PA: Bucknell UP, 2000.

Judge, Erin. "Open Letter to Junot Díaz." *So Make It Up.* Blogger.com. 4 Dec. 2007. Web. Accessed 14 Dec. 2013. http://somakeitup.blogspot.com/2007/12/open-letter-to-junot-diaz.html.

Kadiyoti, Dalia. "Consuming Nostalgia: Nostalgia and the Marketplace in Cristina García and Ana Menéndez." *MELUS* 31.1 (2006): 81–97.

Kakutani, Michiko. "As the Day Wanes, Missing the Cuban Sun." Rev. of *In Cuba I Was A German Shepherd*, by Ana Menéndez. *New York Times* 19 June 2001: E8.

———. "A Dominican Comedy: Travails of an Outcast." Rev. of *The Brief Wondrous Life of Oscar Wao*, by Junot Díaz. *New York Times* 4 Sept. 2007: E1.

Karem, Jeff. *The Romance of Authenticity: The Cultural Politics of Regional and Ethnic Literatures.* Charlottesville: U of Virginia P, 2004.

Keizer, Arlene R. *Black Subjects: Identity Formation in the Contemporary Narrative of Slavery.* Ithaca, NY: Cornell UP, 2004.

Keown, Michelle, David Murphy, and James Proctor. Introduction. *Comparing Postcolonial Diasporas.* London: Palgrave-Macmillan, 2009.

Kim. *The Annotated Oscar Wao: Notes and Translations for The Brief Wondrous Life of Oscar Wao by Junot Diaz.* Dec. 2008. Web. Accessed 24 July 2013. http://www.annotated-oscar-wao.com.

———. "Re: Interview Request." Message to the author. Sent 28 Aug. 2013. E-mail.

———. "Re: Interview Request." Message to the author. Sent 17 Oct. 2013. E-mail.

King, Rosamond. *Island Bodies: Transgressive Sexualities in the Caribbean Imagination*. Gainesville: UP of Florida, 2014.

Lawton de Torruella, Elena. "Diaspora, Self-Exile and Legacy: About Walcott's Shabine and Danticat's M. Bienamé." *Torre: Revista de la Universidad de Puerto Rico* 11.41–42 (2006): 509–18.

Lederman, Marsha. "Stunned by Success." *Globe and Mail* 19 Nov. 2007: R1.

Lee, Ruthann. "The Production of Racialized Masculinities in Contemporary North American Culture." Diss. York U, 2011. *Proquest Dissertations and Theses*. Web. Accessed 1 Apr. 2013.

Levy, Andrea. *Every Light in the House Burnin'*. London: Headline Review, 1994.

———. *Fruit of the Lemon*. London: Headline Review, 1999.

———. *The Long Song*. New York: Farrar, Straus and Giroux, 2010.

———. *Never Far from Nowhere*. London: Headline Review, 1996.

———. *Small Island*. 2004. New York: Picador, 2005.

———. "This Is My England." *Guardian* 19 Feb. 2000. Web. Accessed 2 Feb. 2013. http://www.guardian.co.uk/books/2000/feb/19/society1.

Li, Peter S. "The Multiculturalism Debate." *Race and Ethnic Relations in Canada*. Ed. Peter S. Li. Toronto, ON: Oxford UP, 1999. 148–77.

Lino Costa, Jeanine Luciana. "Remember Me: Identity Formation in Clarice Lispector, Isabel Allende, and Michelle Cliff." Diss. U of North Carolina at Chapel Hill, 2006. *Proquest Dissertations and Theses*. Web. Accessed 1 Apr. 2013.

Llanos-Figueroa, Dahlma. *Daughters of the Stone*. New York: St. Martin's, 2009.

López-Calvo, Ignacio. "A Postmodern Plátano's Trujillo: Junot Díaz's *The Brief Wondrous Life of Oscar Wao*, More Macondo Than McOndo." Caminero-Santangelo and Osegueda 75–90.

Machado Sáez, Elena. "Bittersweet (Be)Longing: Filling the Void of History in Andrea Levy's *Fruit of the Lemon*." *Anthurium: A Caribbean Studies Journal* 4.1 (2006). Web. Accessed 12 Sept. 2006. http://scholar.library.miami.edu/volume_4/issue_1/saez-bittersweet.html.

———. "Dictating Desire, Dictating Diaspora: Junot Díaz's *Oscar Wao* as Foundational Romance." *Contemporary Literature* 52.3 (2011): 522–55.

———. "Reconquista: Ilan Stavans and Multiculturalist Latino/a Discourse." *Latino Studies* 7.4 (2009): 410–34.

Magnani, Jessica. "Divided Loyalties: Latina Family Sagas and National Romances." Diss. U of Florida, 2007. *Proquest Dissertations and Theses*. Web. Accessed 1 April 2013.

Mahler, Anne Garland. "The Writer as Superhero: Fighting the Colonial Curse in Junot Díaz's *The Brief Wondrous Life of Oscar Wao.*" *Journal of Latin American Cultural Studies* 19.2 (2010): 119–40.

Mardorossian, Carine M. *Reclaiming Difference: Caribbean Women Rewrite Postcolonialism.* Charlottesville: U of Virginia P, 2005.

Marshall, Paule. *Triangular Road.* Philadelphia: BasicCivitas, 2009.

Martinez, Lusely. "As 'Links' to Whatless Boys." Digital Caribbean Commons. *CUNY Academic Commons.* 29 Apr. 2014. Web. Accessed 25 May 2014. http:// digitalcaribbean.commons.gc.cuny.edu/2014/04/29/as-links-to-whatless-boys/.

McCallum, Pamela, and Christian Olbey. "Written in the Scars: History, Genre and Materiality in Dionne Brand's *In Another Place, Not Here.*" *Essays on Caribbean Writing* 68 (1999): 159–83.

McGurl, Mark. *The Program Era: Postwar Fiction and the Rise of Creative Writing.* Cambridge, MA: Harvard UP, 2009.

Medovarski, Andrea. "'I Knew This Was England': Myths of Return in Andrea Levy's *Fruit of the Lemon.*" *MaComère* 8 (2006): 35–66.

Mehta, Brinda. *Notions of Identity, Diaspora, and Gender in Caribbean Women's Writing.* New York: Palgrave-Macmillan, 2009.

Méndez Rodenas, Adriana. "Engendering the Nation: The Mother/Daughter Plot in Cuban American Fiction." *Cuban-American Literature and Art: Negotiating Identities.* Ed. Isabel Alvarez Borland and Lynette M. F. Bosch. Albany: SUNY P, 2009. 47–60.

Menéndez, Ana. "Birnbaum v. Ana Menendez." Interview by Robert Birnbaum. *Morning News* 18 Feb. 2004. Web. Accessed 25 Nov. 2011. www.themorningnews.org/article/birnbaum-v.-ana-menendez.

———. *In Cuba I Was a German Shepherd.* New York: Grove, 2001.

———. *Loving Che.* New York: Atlantic Monthly P, 2003.

Minto, Deonne N. Review of *Soucouyant: A Novel of Forgetting,* by David Chariandy. *Callaloo* 33.3 (2010): 887–907.

Misrahi-Barak, Judith. "'My Mouth Is the Keeper of Both Speech and Silence . . . ,' or the Vocalisation of Silence in Caribbean Short Stories by Edwidge Danticat." *Journal of the Short Story in English* 47 (2006): 155–66.

Mitchell, Angelyn. *The Freedom to Remember: Narrative, Slavery, and Gender in Contemporary Black Women's Fiction.* New Brunswick, NJ: Rutgers UP, 2002.

Mordecai, Pamela, and Betty Wilson, eds. *Her True-True Name.* London: Heinemann, 1989.

Moretti, Franco. *Graphs, Maps, Trees: Abstract Models for a Literary History.* New York: Verso, 2007.

Mukherjee, Bharati. "Immigrant Writing: Changing the Contours of a National Literature." *American Literary History* 23.3 (2011): 680–96.

Mullins, Greg A. "Dionne Brand's Poetics of Recognition: Reframing Sexual Rights." *Callaloo* 30.4 (2008): 1100–1109.

———. "Labors of Literature and of Human Rights." *Peace Review: A Journal of Social Justice* 20.1 (2008): 4–12.

Murray, Simone. *Mixed Media: Feminist Presses and Publishing Politics*. London: Pluto, 2004.

Nesbitt, Nick. *Voicing History: History and Subjectivity in French Caribbean Literature*. Charlottesville: U of Virginia P, 2003.

Newman, Judie. *Fictions of America: Narratives of Global Empire*. New York: Routledge, 2007.

Ontiveros, Randy J. "Immigrant *Actos*: Citizenship and Performance in El Teatro Campesino." *In the Spirit of a New People*. New York: New York UP, 2014. 131–69.

Owen, Katie. "A Man for All Seasons; New Fiction." Rev. of *Sun Dog*, by Monique Roffey. *Times* 15 June 2002: 14.

Palumbo-Liu, David. Introduction. *The Ethnic Canon: Histories, Institutions, and Interventions*. Ed. David Palumbo-Liu. Minneapolis: U of Minnesota P, 1995. 1–27.

Parikh, Crystal. *An Ethics of Betrayal: The Politics of Otherness in Emerging U.S. Literatures and Culture*. New York: Fordham UP, 2009.

Patterson, Tiffany Ruby, and Robin D. G. Kelley. "Unfinished Migrations: Reflections on the African Diaspora and the Making of the Modern World." *African Studies Review* 43.1 (2000): 11–45.

Perez, Richard. "Transamerican Ghosts: The Face, the Abyss, and the Dead of New World Post-coloniality." Diss. City U of New York, 2008. *Proquest Dissertations and Theses*. Web. Accessed 14 May 2010.

Perfect, Michael. "'Fold the Paper and Pass It On': Historical Silences and the Contrapuntal in Andrea Levy's Fiction." *Journal of Postcolonial Writing* 46.1 (2010): 31–41.

Phillips, Caryl. *Cambridge*. New York: Alfred A. Knopf, 1992.

———. *Dancing in the Dark*. New York: Vintage, 2005.

Plasa, Carl. *Slaves to Sweetness: British and Caribbean Literatures of Sugar*. Liverpool: Liverpool UP, 2009.

Polk, James. "Spiritual Combat." Rev. of *John Crow's Devil*, by Marlon James. *New York Times* 13 Nov. 2005: 54.

Poto Mitan: Haitian Women, Pillars of the Global Economy. Dirs. Renée Bergan and Mark Schuller. Writer/Narrator Edwidge Danticat. Tèt Ansanm Productions, 2009. Film.

Prasad, Raekha. "Two Sides to Every Story (Novelist Andrea Levy)." *Guardian* 4 Mar. 1999: T4–6.

Puri, Shalini. "Beyond Resistance: Notes toward a New Caribbean Cultural Studies." *Small Axe* 7.2 (2003): 23–38.

Quigley, Ellen. "Picking the Deadlock of Legitimacy: Dionne Brand's 'Noise Like the World Cracking.'" *Canadian Literature* 186 (2005): 48–67.

Reddock, Rhoda E. Introduction. *Interrogating Caribbean Masculinities: Theoretical and Empirical Analyses*. Ed. Rhoda E. Reddock. Kingston: U of the West Indies P, 2004. xiii–xxxiv.

Reid, Julia. "Sisters' Strife of Life." Rev. of *Never Far from Nowhere*, by Andrea Levy. *Scotsman* 27 Jan. 1996: 17.

Rev. of *August Frost*, by Monique Roffey. *Kirkus Reviews* 1 Dec. 2002: 1727.

Rev. of *In Cuba I Was A German Shepherd*, by Ana Menéndez. *Library Journal* 15 Apr. 2001: 135.

Rich, Charlotte. "Talking Back to El Jefe: Genre, Polyphony, and Dialogic Resistance in Julia Alvarez's *In the Time of Butterflies.*" *MELUS* 27.4 (2002): 165–82.

Robinson-Walcott, Kim. "Claiming an Identity We Thought They Despised: Contemporary White West Indian Writers and Their Negotiations of Race." *Small Axe* 14.2 (2003): 93–110.

Rodríguez, Ileana. *Women, Guerillas, and Love: Understanding War in Central America*. Minneapolis: U of Minnesota P, 1996.

Rodríguez, Juana María. *Queer Latinidad: Identity Practices, Discursive Spaces*. New York: New York UP, 2003.

Rodriguez, Richard. *Hunger of Memory*. 1982. New York: Bantam, 1983.

Rody, Caroline. *A Daughter's Return: African American and Caribbean Women's Fictions of History*. New York: Oxford UP, 2001

Roffey, Monique. "For Books' Sake Talks To: Monique Roffey." Interview. *For Books Sake* 5 Oct. 2012. Web. Accessed 10 Feb. 2013. http://forbookssake. net/2012/10/05/for-books-sake-talks-to-monique-roffey.

———. *The White Woman on the Green Bicycle*. 2009. New York: Penguin, 2011.

Rohrleitner, Marion. "Intimate Geographies: Romance and the Rhetoric of Female Desire in Contemporary Historical Fiction by Caribbean American Women Writers." Diss. U of Notre Dame, 2007. *Proquest Dissertations and Theses*. Web. Accessed 1 April 2013.

Roy, Wendy. "The Word Is Colander: Language Loss and Narrative Voice in Fictional Canadian Alzheimer's Narratives." *Canadian Literature* 203 (2009): 41–61.

Rushdy, Ashraf H. A. *Neo-slave Narratives: Studies in the Social Logic of a Literary Form*. New York: Oxford UP, 1999.

Russell, Catherine. Rev. of *Primitive Offensive*, by Dionne Brand. *Quill and Quire* 49.9 (1983): 76.

Ryan, Tim A. *Calls and Responses: The American Novel of Slavery since* Gone with the Wind. Baton Rouge: Louisiana State UP, 2008.

Saldaña-Portillo, María Josefina. *The Revolutionary Imagination in the Americas and the Age of Development*. Durham, NC: Duke UP, 2003.

Santiago, Esmeralda. *Conquistadora*. New York: Knopf, 2011.

Saul, Joanne. "'In the Middle of Becoming': Dionne Brand's Historical Vision." *Canadian Woman Studies* 23.2 (2004): 59–63.

Schwartz, Marcy. "Language, Violence, and Resistance." *Voice-Overs: Translation and Latin American Literature*. Ed. Daniel Balderston and Marcy Schwartz. Albany: State U of New York P, 2002. 42–44.

Scott, David. *Conscripts of Modernity: The Tragedy of Colonial Enlightenment.* Durham, NC: Duke UP, 2004.

Sharpe, Jenny. *Ghosts of Slavery: A Literary Archaeology of Black Women's Lives.* Minneapolis: U of Minnesota P, 2003.

Simon, Sherry. "Introduction: Land to Light On?" *Adjacencies: Minority Writing in Canada.* Ed. Domenic A. Beventi, Licia Canton, and Lianne Moyes. Toronto, ON: Guernica, 2004. 9–20.

Sims, Robert L. "Che Guevara, Nostalgia, Photography, Felt History and Narrative Discourse in Ana Menéndez's *Loving Che.*" *Hipertexto* 11 (2010): 103–16.

Smith, Dorsía. "A Violent Homeland: Recalling Haiti in Edwidge Danticat's Novels." *Narrating the Past: (Re)Constructing Memory, (Re)Negotiating History.* Ed. Nandita Batra and Vartan Messier. Newcastle upon Tyne: Cambridge Scholars, 2007. 133–40.

Smith, Zadie. *White Teeth.* New York: Random House, 2000.

Socolovsky, Maya. "Cuba Interrupted: The Loss of Center and Story in Ana Menéndez's *In Cuba I Was a German Shepherd.*" *Critique* 46.3 (2005): 235–51.

———. "Patriotism, Nationalism, and the Fiction of History in Julia Álvarez's *In the Time of the Butterflies* and *In the Name of Salomé. Latin American Literary Review* 34.68 (2006): 5–24.

Sommer, Doris. *Foundational Fictions: The National Romances of Latin America.* Berkeley: U of California P, 1991.

———. *Proceed with Caution, when Engaged by Minority Writing in the Americas.* Cambridge, MA: Harvard UP, 1999.

Spivak, Gayatri Chakravorty. *A Critique of Postcolonial Reason: Toward a History of the Vanishing Present.* Cambridge, MA: Harvard UP, 1999.

———. *Outside the Teaching Machine.* New York: Routledge, 1993.

Stephens, Michelle. *Black Empire: The Masculine Global Imaginary of Caribbean Intellectuals in the United States.* Durham, NC: Duke UP, 2005.

Sutherland, Julia. "Cuban Missives: Ana Menéndez's Plot Is Layered with Passions Both Sexual and Political." Rev. of *Loving Che,* by Ana Menéndez. *Financial Times* 31 Jan. 2004: 31.

Thomson, Ian. "God 'and Rum' on the Rocks." Rev. of *John Crow's Devil,* by Marlon James. *Independent* 28 Oct. 2005: 21.

Thorpe, Michael. Rev. of *In Another Place, Not Here,* by Dionne Brand. *World Literature Today* 22 Mar. 1997. http://www.thefreelibrary.com/In+Another+Place,+Not+Here.-a019918604.

Toplu, Şebnem. "Home(land) or 'Motherland': Transnational Identities in Andrea Levy's *Fruit of the Lemon.*" *Anthurium: A Caribbean Studies Journal* 3.1 (2005). Web. Accessed 6 Nov. 2005. http://scholar.library.miami.edu/anthurium/volume_3/issue_1/toplu-homeland.htm.

Torres-Saillant, Silvio. *An Intellectual History of the Caribbean.* New York: Palgrave-Macmillan, 2006.

Trouillot, Michel-Rolph. *Silencing the Past: Power and Production of History*. Boston: Beacon, 1997.

Vásquez, Sam. "Violent Liaisons: Historical Crossings and the Negotiation of Sex, Sexuality, and Race in *The Book of Night Women* and *The True History of Paradise*." *Small Axe* 16.2 (2012): 43–59.

Vega González, Susana. "Exiled Subjectivities: The Politics of Fragmentation in *The Dew Breaker*." *Revista Canaria de Estudios Ingleses* 54 (2007): 181–93.

Vincent, Isabel. "The Color of Change." *Globe and Mail* 23 Aug. 1990.

Walcott, Rinaldo. *Black Like Who?* Toronto, ON: Insomniac, 1997.

Walcott-Hackshaw, Elizabeth. "Home Is Where the Heart Is: Danticat's Landscapes of Return." *Small Axe* 12.3 (2008): 71–82.

Walkowitz, Rebecca L. "The Location of Literature: The Transnational Book and the Migrant Writer." *Contemporary Literature* 47 (2006): 527–45.

Walters, Tracey. "A Black Briton's View of Black Literature and Scholarship." *Black British Writing*. New York: Palgrave-Macmillan, 2004. 169–76.

Walters, Wendy W. "'Object into Subject': Michelle Cliff, John Ruskin, and the Terrors of Visual Art." *American Literature* 80.3 (2008): 502–26.

Watts, Richard. "Contested Sources: Water as Commodity/Sign in French Caribbean Literature." *Atlantic Studies: Literary, Cultural, and Historical Perspectives* 4.1 (2007): 87–101.

"The White Woman on the Green Bicycle." Rev. of *The White Woman on the Green Bicycle*, by Monique Roffey. *Publishers Weekly* 28 Mar. 2011: 35.

Whitfield, Esther. "Umbilical Chords." Rev. of *In Cuba I Was a German Shepherd*, by Ana Menéndez. *Women's Review of Books* 18 (2001): 31.

Wood, Robin. *Hollywood from Vietnam to Reagan . . . and Beyond*. New York: Columbia UP, 1986. 2003.

Woodhead, Cameron. Rev. of *The White Woman on the Green Bicycle*, by Monique Roffey. *Age* 27 June 2009: 26.

Young, Kerry. "An Interview with Kerry Young." Video. *Book Diva*. Created by Bloomsbury. 23 May 2011. Web. Accessed 10 Feb. 2013. http://www.bookdiva.co.uk/2011/05/an-interview-with-kerry-young/.

———. "Interview with Kerry Young." *Words of Colour* [n.b.]. 21 May 2012. Web. Accessed 10 Feb. 2013. http://wordsofcolour.co.uk/interview-with-kerry-young/.

———. "Kerry Young." Radio interview by Harriet Gilbert. *Strand*, BBC. 14 June 2011. Web. Accessed 10 Feb. 2013. http://www.bbc.co.uk/programmes/p00hk0w4.

———. *Pao*. New York: Bloomsbury, 2011.

Yúdice, George. "Rethinking Area and Ethnic Studies in the Context of Economic and Political Restructuring." *Critical Latin American and Latino Studies*. Ed. Juan Poblete. Minneapolis: U of Minnesota P, 2003. 76–102.

Zaleski, Jeff. Rev. of *In Cuba I Was A German Shepherd*, by Ana Menéndez. *Publishers Weekly* 7 May 2001: 221.

Index

consumerism (*continued*)
151, 155, 161, 193, 209; academic
discourse about, 23, 26, 29, 31, 207,
217n3; citizenship and, 16, 47, 50, 65,
66, 74–75, 217n6, 221n6; students and,
4–5, 111. *See also* commodification;
neoliberalism
Cruz, Angie, 24
Cuban Revolution, 39, 90, 91, 92, 93, 96,
130–131, 133, 136, 145, 221n6. *See also*
Castro, Fidel; Guevara, Ernesto "Che";
Menéndez, Ana: *Loving Che*
cultural insiderism, 22, 58, 161, 194
CUNY Academic Commons, 209, 228n8

Dalleo, Raphael, 84, 89, 140, 142, 213n1,
213n5, 215n14, 216n5, 217n6, 218n3,
221n6
Danticat, Edwidge, 3, 24, 31, 37, 45,
119, 148, 153, 193–195, 213n1,
218n2, 220n14, 222n1, 226n26–27;
Breath, Eyes, Memory, 176–177; *The
Dewbreaker*, 17, 154–159, 176–193,
223n5–6, 226n29–33, 227n35; *The
Farming of Bones*, 21, 217n9
de Moya, E. Antonio, 172, 225n19
Dessalines, Jean-Jacques, 137
Díaz, Junot, 3, 31, 37, 45, 119, 148, 153,
192–195, 206, 222n1, 228n4; *The
Brief Wondrous Life of Oscar Wao*,
ix, x, 17, 38, 40, 42, 46, 72, 82, 94,
154–175, 176, 178, 180, 181, 182, 193,
197–203, 209, 211, 218n13, 223n4,
223n8, 224n13–16, 225n20, 225n22–
25, 227n2–3; *Drown*, 159–163, 195,
223n10, 224n12, 225n17
Digital Library of the Caribbean, 204
Duvalier, François, 185, 226n31–32
Duvalier, Jean-Claude, 155, 156, 157,
159, 177, 178, 179, 181, 183, 185, 186,
187, 190, 191, 227n34
Dyson, Michael Eric, 124–127

Edmondson, Belinda, 24–25, 28, 207
emplotment, 36, 38, 48, 69, 73, 87, 95,
117, 123, 129, 138, 146, 156–157,
227n33. *See also* romance; tragedy
Engle, Margarita, 215n17
ethics; intimacy and, 20, 45, 83, 203,
224n1; market popularity and, 123,
200; of historical revision, 1–3, 6,

32, 41–44, 66, 81, 97, 99, 103–106,
111, 197, 209; of intercultural
understanding, 24, 28, 33, 38, 40, 47,
100, 201, 224n13; postcolonialism and,
2, 15–16, 19, 21, 25–26, 27–28, 31–44,
46, 74, 80, 82, 103, 108, 137, 154–155,
197, 211; relationship with reader and,
7, 25, 27, 40, 44, 46, 50, 58, 67, 82,
90–91, 93, 96, 101, 109, 119, 123, 155,
193–195, 201; teaching and, 21, 94, 96,
101, 104–105, 113, 114

Fanon, Frantz, 116, 121, 138, 220n17
feminism, 9, 98, 104, 111, 126, 127–129,
146–147, 215n12. *See also* masculinity;
patriarchy; sexuality
Flores, Juan, 124–127, 220n2, 224n11,
225n25
Francis, Donette, 36, 217n8, 220n3
Freire, Paulo, 87–88, 119

Garcia, Cristina, 24, 129, 217n6, 221n6
Gikandi, Simon, 5–7, 92
Gilroy, Beryl, 147
Gilroy, Paul, 58, 211, 216n4, 223n3
Glissant, Edouard, 13, 26, 87–88, 112,
119, 215n15, 217n5
globalization, 2, 13–15, 48, 53, 63, 65,
66, 67, 74, 75, 197; academic discourse
about, 3–7, 9–10, 15, 19, 29–30, 92,
216n3; decontextualization and, 12, 28,
32, 211, 220n2; market and, 23, 28, 30,
40–41, 47, 76–77; postcolonialism and,
5, 32, 216n3. *See also* neoliberalism
González Echevarría, Roberto, 84, 222n2
Google, 198, 208, 228n8
Grenada Revolution, 121, 137, 140–1,
142, 144, 145. *See also* Brand, Dionne:
In Another Place, Not Here
Guevara, Ernesto "Che," 100, 120–122,
124, 131–132, 135–136, 137–142, 144,
146, 219n9, 221n5. *See also* Menéndez,
Ana: *Loving Che*

Haitian Revolution, 32. *See also* James,
C. L. R.; L'Ouverture, Toussaint; Scott,
David
Hall, Stuart, 37, 157–158, 215n15
Halloran, Vivian Nun, 26, 104, 215n17
haunting, 16, 73, 107–108, 155, 157,
163, 167–168, 170, 181, 183; specter

Nick Nesbitt, *Universal Emancipation: The Haitian Revolution and the Radical Enlightenment*

Doris L. Garraway, editor, *Tree of Liberty: Cultural Legacies of the Haitian Revolution in the Atlantic World*

Dawn Fulton, *Signs of Dissent: Maryse Condé and Postcolonial Criticism*

Michael G. Malouf, *Transatlantic Solidarities: Irish Nationalism and Caribbean Poetics*

Maria Cristina Fumagalli, *Caribbean Perspectives on Modernity: Returning the Gaze*

Vivian Nun Halloran, *Exhibiting Slavery: The Caribbean Postmodern Novel as Museum*

Paul B. Miller, *Elusive Origins: The Enlightenment in the Modern Caribbean Historical Imagination*

Eduardo González, *Cuba and the Fall: Christian Text and Queer Narrative in the Fiction of José Lezama Lima and Reinaldo Arenas*

Jeff Karem, *The Purloined Islands: Caribbean-U.S. Crosscurrents in Literature and Culture, 1880–1959*

Faith Smith, editor, *Sex and the Citizen: Interrogating the Caribbean*

Mark D. Anderson, *Disaster Writing: The Cultural Politics of Catastrophe in Latin America*

Raphael Dalleo, *Caribbean Literature and the Public Sphere: From the Plantation to the Postcolonial*

Maite Conde, *Consuming Visions: Cinema, Writing, and Modernity in Rio de Janeiro*

Monika Kaup, *Neobaroque in the Americas: Alternative Modernities in Literature, Visual Art, and Film*

Marisel C. Moreno, *Family Matters: Puerto Rican Women Authors on the Island and the Mainland*

Supriya M. Nair, *Pathologies of Paradise: Caribbean Detours*

Colleen C. O'Brien, *Race, Romance, and Rebellion: Literatures of the Americas in the Nineteenth Century*

Kelly Baker Josephs, *Disturbers of the Peace: Representations of Madness in Anglophone Caribbean Literature*

Christina Kullberg, *The Poetics of Ethnography in Martinican Narratives: Exploring the Self and the Environment*

Maria Cristina Fumagalli, Bénédicte Ledent, and Roberto del Valle Alcalá, editors, *The Cross-Dressed Caribbean: Writing, Politics, Sexualities*

Philip Kaisary, *The Haitian Revolution in the Literary Imagination: Radical Horizons, Conservative Constraints*

Jason Frydman, *Sounding the Break: African American and Caribbean Routes of World Literature*

Tanya L. Shields, *Bodies and Bones: Feminist Rehearsal and Imagining Caribbean Belonging*

Stanka Radović, *Locating the Destitute: Space and Identity in Caribbean Fiction*

Nicole N. Aljoe and Ian Finseth, editors, *Journeys of the Slave Narrative in the Early Americas*

Stephen M. Park, *The Pan American Imagination: Contested Visions of the Hemisphere in Twentieth-Century Literature*

Maurice St. Pierre, *Eric Williams and the Anticolonial Tradition: The Making of a Diasporan Intellectual*

Elena Machado Sáez, *Market Aesthetics: The Purchase of the Past in Caribbean Diasporic Fiction*